SOVIET POLICY TOWARDS SOUTH AFRICA

SOVIET POLICY TOWARDS SOUTH AFRICA

Kurt M. Campbell

Fellow, Center for Science and International Affairs
John F. Kennedy School of Government
Harvard University

St. Martin's Press   New York

First published in the United States of America in 1986

Printed in Hong Kong

ISBN 0-312-74853-1

Library of Congress Cataloging-in-Publication Data
Campbell, Kurt M., 1957–
Soviet policy towards South Africa.
Bibliography: p.
Includes index.
1. Soviet Union–Relations–South Africa. 2. South
Africa–Relations–Soviet Union. 3. Soviet Union–
Foreign relations–1975– . I. Title.
DK69.4.S6C36 1986 327.47068 86-10092
ISBN 0-312-74853-1

For my family

Contents

Contents

Preface

My interest in Soviet policy towards South Africa began during an undergraduate year spent at the University of Erevan in Soviet Socialist Armenia in 1978–9. The State University of Erevan, like Patrice Lumumba University in Moscow, offers places to students from the Third World, and I attended lectures with several students from the newly-independent countries in southern Africa. Research on the topic began at Brasenose College, Oxford, in 1981, where I was the holder of a Marshall Scholarship from the British government. This book has been adapted from my D.Phil. thesis which was accepted by Oxford University in October 1984. The final reworking and revision of the study was undertaken while I served as a Research Associate at the International Institute for Strategic Studies in London and during a post-doctoral year with the Russian Research Center at Harvard University from 1983 to 1985.

My work has benefited immeasurably from two journeys to southern Africa, from several extended visits to the Hoover Institution Library at Stanford University, and from one trip to the Soviet Union. In South Africa, I was fortunate to gain access to the official files containing the diplomatic correspondence between the Soviet Union and South Africa housed at the Ministry of External Affairs Archives in the Union Buildings in Pretoria. I also visited the Africa Institute in Moscow as a guest of the USSR Academy of Sciences. Whilst in Moscow, I served as the Rapporteur for a discussion between American and Soviet specialists concerning the contemporary situation in southern Africa which was sponsored by the Rockefeller Foundation.

I am grateful to a variety of organisations and institutions for providing financial assistance in the course of researching and writing this book. First and foremost, a scholarship from the Marshall Aid Commemoration Commission enabled me to attend Oxford University. A Graduate Award Fellowship from St Cross College helped meet maintenance expenses during 1983–4. The International Institute for Strategic Studies provided funding for an extended journey to southern Africa in the spring of 1984. Further, the Rockefeller Foundation of New York covered my transportation costs to the Soviet Union. Miscellaneous grants from the Cyril Foster Fund, Brasenose College, and the South African Institute for International Affairs were also useful. Finally, a fellowship from the Russian Research Center at Harvard, which was funded by the Olin Foundation, gave me the opportunity to transform my dissertation into a book.

This study, in addition, owes a considerable debt to several colleagues, friends and relations. I should like to thank especially my thesis supervisor, the late Professor Hedley Bull, for his encouragement, guidance and patience. Professor William Gutteridge was also instrumental in the preparation of the book. My friends, Mathew Guerreiro, Robb London, John Chipman, Mitch Reiss, James Clifford and Eric Greer, all read and commented on the text during various stages of its preparation. I am particularly grateful to Neil MacFarlane, Christopher Coker and Tom Lodge for their efforts on my behalf. Two librarians, Hilja Kukk at the Hoover Institution and Jacqueline Kalley at Jan Smuts House, gave me every assistance in tracking down obscure publications and documents, for which I am appreciative. My thanks go also to Hilary Parker and Alma Gibbons at the London School of Economics for their typing skills, displayed admirably in the preparation of this manuscript. Finally, my family has been an endless source of inspiration during these past five years, and it is to them this book is dedicated.

K.M.C.
Harvard University

Abbreviations

ANC	African National Congress
BOSS	Bureau of State Security
CI	Communist International (Comintern)
CIA	Central Intelligence Agency
CMEA	Council for Mutual Economic Assistance (Comecon)
COD	Congress of Democrats
CPC	Communist Party of China
CPSA	Communist Party of South Africa (before 1950)
CPSU	Communist Party of the Soviet Union
ECAFE	Economic Commission for Asia and the Far East
ECCI	Executive Committee of the Communist International
EPTA	Expanded Programme for Technical Assistance
FNLA	Front for the National Liberation of Angola
FRELIMO	Front for the Liberation of Mozambique
ICU	Industrial and Commercial Workers' Union
ILO	International Labour Organisation
ITUC–NW	International Trade Committee of Negro Workers
KGB	Soviet Committee for State Security
KPD	German Communist Party
KUTV	Communist University of the Toilers of the East
LAI	League Against Imperialism
MPLA	Popular Movement for the Liberation of Angola
NIS	National Intelligence Service
OAU	Organisation of African Unity
ONUC	United Nations Peace-keeping Operation for the Congo
OPEC	Organisation of Petroleum Exporting Countries
PAC	Pan-African Congress
PAIGC	African Party for the Independence of Guinea and Cape Verde
RILU	Red International of Labour Unions (Profintern)

RSA	Republic of South Africa
SACP	South African Communist Party (since 1950)
SACPO	South African Coloured People's Organisation
SACTU	South African Congress of Trade Unions
SADCC	South African Development Coordinating Conference
SAFSU	South African Friends of the Soviet Union
SUNFED	Special United Nations Fund for Economic Development
SWAPO	South West Africa People's Organisation
UDF	United Democratic Front
UN	United Nations
UNCTAD	United Nations Conference on Trade and Development
UNESCO	United Nations Economic Scientific and Cultural Organisation
UNITA	Union for the Total Independence of Angola
USSR	Union of Soviet Socialist Republics
YCL	Young Communist League
ZANU	Zimbabwe African National Union
ZAPU	Zimbabwe African People's Union

Introduction

Our assistance is provided to the national liberation movement in order to free the oppressed peoples of South Africa. (Anatoly A. Gromyko, Director of the Institute of African Studies, USSR Academy of Sciences, 21 April 1984)

The Soviet Union is preparing its total onslaught in order to enslave us here in South Africa. (P. W. Botha, South African Prime Minister, 5 January 1983)

South Africa may, and I believe will, become as great a threat to the peace of the world in the 1990s as the Middle East is today . . . conflict there will fragment world opinion, and it is entirely possible – if not probable – that much of Southern Africa will fall within the Soviet sphere of influence. (Robert S. McNamara, former President of the World Bank, 21 October 1982)

This study is an attempt to discover the nature of Soviet policy towards South Africa. The objectives of the Soviet Union in the region are a subject of much interest and concern both to South Africa and the West. With the coming of black majority rule in Angola, Mozambique and Zimbabwe, and the political future of Namibia hanging in the balance, the situation in southern Africa has shifted dramatically during the past decade. The white buffer states that once separated the Republic from Black Africa have all collapsed, and South Africa now stands alone as the last bastion of white minority rule on the continent. The USSR, by virtue of its prominent role in the long-standing struggle for national liberation in southern Africa, has gained considerable influence in the region. As a consequence of Soviet aid to insurgent groups and outspoken Russian support of the anti-apartheid movement in international forums, many in the West fear that the USSR will continue to garner handsome political dividends in the continuing struggle over the future of

1

South Africa. Indeed, the Soviet presence in Angola and Mozambique poses a worry to some Western observers for, as they interpret it, a fundamental shift in the global balance of power is at stake.

The existence of a Soviet threat is indeed a common denominator in much of the discussion concerning the political future of South Africa. Liberals and conservatives alike invoke the spectre of the USSR when making their respective arguments for a particular Western course of action towards South Africa. Liberals claim that if the Atlantic Community refuses to acknowledge the just plight of the politically disenfranchised black population, nor supports them in their endeavour to achieve majority rule, the Soviet Union, because of its support of the national liberation movement, will be the sole beneficiary of African goodwill. Conservatives, on the other hand, argue that unless the Alliance is prepared to back the Republic in this struggle between East and West, the entire southern African continent will be lost to Soviet control. Yet, while there is almost universal agreement about the desire to restrict Soviet influence in South Africa, there is less understanding about the actual nature of Soviet activities in the region.

The interest of the USSR in southern African politics and its demonstrated willingness to assist the national liberation movement raises some important questions about the formulation and execution of Soviet policy towards South Africa. Is there any continuity exhibited between Imperial Russian and later Soviet policies towards the region? What factors help or hinder Soviet policy in South Africa? How have strategic, ideological and commercial factors influenced Soviet activities? How does the Soviet Union perceive the development of the national liberation struggle in South Africa? What priority does South Africa hold in the hierarchy of Soviet foreign policy? What, ultimately, are Soviet interests in Southern Africa?

The belief in a Soviet threat to South Africa rests on various assumptions concerning the motivations, goals and effectiveness of Soviet foreign policy. The increased Soviet involvement in southern Africa has led some commentators to conclude that the Soviet Union plans to gain control of South Africa's minerals, on which Western powers depend, and of the sea lanes around the Cape of Good Hope, by which oil is transported to Europe from the Middle East. This conclusion is endorsed enthusiastically by South African politicians and military strategists who use it to solicit American support against their black rivals in southern Africa. South African Prime Minister P. W. Botha's conception of Soviet intentions are representative. He has argued that South Africa is 'witnessing an encircling strategy which is being deployed step by step across the globe', and 'the main onslaught on the Republic of South Africa, under the guidance of the planners in the Kremlin, is to overthrow this state and to create chaos in its stead, so that the Kremlin can establish its hegemony here'.[1] Indeed, there is evidence to suggest that 80 per cent of whites in South Africa currently believe their country is beset by a Soviet directed 'total onslaught'.[2]

A major concern surrounding Soviet activity in the region centres on the vulnerability of the Cape route. It is alleged that if the USSR establishes naval bases in Mozambique, Angola, and other African littoral states, Soviet forces could conceivably threaten Western shipping and disrupt oil and raw material supplies that emanate from or pass around South Africa. Ian Greig has written that 'the steady increase of Soviet naval strength in the Indian Ocean area during 1975 and 1976, caused increasing concern to a number of governments highly dependent on vital lines of communications in those waters'.[3] Also typical of this viewpoint are the observations of General George S. Brown, formerly of the United States Joint Chiefs of Staff, who contends that 'the threat to the Atlantic area is primarily from the Soviet Union's maritime forces. Increasing Soviet naval capabilities to operate along the littoral of Africa has put increasing pressure on our capability to protect important South Atlantic trade routes which provide materials essential to the United States and Western Europe'.[4] Still more alarming appraisals can be found in the literature concerning South African security. Robert J. Hanks stated that the 'entire Southern Atlantic coast of Africa is not only barred to the West, but is actually a region of Soviet naval and air domination', and he warns that 'it is evident that Western forces operate at a significant, if not fatal, disadvantage along almost 7,000 miles of the Cape Route'.[5] It is clear that for many, the Soviet naval presence in the Indian Ocean is threatening to the West.

Another familiar feature of the debate concerning Soviet policy towards the region is the alleged Russian challenge to South Africa's strategic minerals. That the Soviet Union is identified as the other major supplier of several of these strategic minerals, has led numerous commentators to suggest that the USSR has embarked upon a policy of denial of resources to the West by fomenting revolution and civil strife in southern Africa (this policy is often referred to as 'the strategy of denial'). Advancing this argument, van Rensburg asserts that 'a major Soviet objective in Southern Africa is to obtain access to its enormous reserves of raw materials, or preferably control over these resources'.[6]

Equally apparent in the literature dealing with Soviet policy in South Africa are dire warnings of Soviet influence and control over the African National Congress (ANC) and the South African Communist Party (SACP). It is sometimes suggested that the former group has been infiltrated and subverted by the latter and that both are mere instruments of the Kremlin. After lengthy and often controversial proceedings, the Senate Sub-Committee on Security and Terrorism offered these recommendations about the relationship between Moscow and the ANC:

> We may well sympathize with the original goal of the ANC to achieve democratic political rights and expanded freedoms for the black peoples of . . . South Africa. We cannot, however, delude ourselves that their purpose now is the achievement of those praiseworthy objectives. They have, from the testimony the sub-committee has received and from the statements and actions of its leaders, been deeply infiltrated by those who seek to advance the imperialistic ambitions of the Soviet Union.[7]

Jan du Plessis, a South African publicist, states simply that 'at present, Soviet strategy against South Africa is carried out by the SACP and the ANC'.[8]

The Soviet Union threat to the Cape route and to South Africa's strategic minerals, as evidenced by the growth of the Soviet Indian Ocean Squadron and Moscow's purported control over the ANC and the SACP, has led South African leaders to proclaim that the Soviet Union has launched a 'total onslaught' against the Republic. Western observers, while generally hesitant to embrace these expansive South African claims, often write about Soviet policy in southern Africa as being either opportunistic, adventurist or coercive.[9] The conventional wisdom among Western conservatives is that 'the cornerstone of Soviet policy in Southern Africa is supplying arms, advisors and training to its clients – whether they be nations or insurgents – in order to destabilize the area',[10] until the region is 'from a *strategic* point of view, under its control'.[11]

Above are listed many of the tenets associated with the perceived or presumed Soviet threat to South Africa, and the purpose of this book is to re-examine afresh the nature of Soviet policy towards South Africa. Many contemporary Western observers pursuing the motivations of Soviet involvement in Southern Africa have focused mainly on the strategic implications of the USSR's activities in the region while dismissing or overlooking the historical experience of Russia, and later the Soviet Union, in South Africa. In particular, scant attention has been directed to the ideological dimension of Soviet policy. This study will provide a history of Soviet relations with South Africa covering state, party and commercial contacts. In addition, this enquiry will include an analysis of the Soviet role in the United Nations debate over apartheid. A section will also be devoted to recent Soviet activities in the southern African region, with particular reference to the USSR's relationship with Angola and Mozambique. Beyond this, the strategic issues raised by the Soviet naval presence in the Indian Ocean will be reviewed where these relate to South Africa. Furthermore, this study will trace the evolution of Soviet thinking on South Africa as reflected in Soviet theoretical journals, political tracts and in official statements.

The study is organised as follows. This introduction sets out the main issues and questions which will be discussed in the book. Chapter 1 concerns the Anglo–Boer War, the occasion of the first Russian foray into South Africa. This survey is meant principally to illustrate the Russian legacy of Soviet policy in South Africa. Chapter 2 begins with the Bolsheviks' rise to power and the founding of the Soviet state in 1917. This section will examine the Soviet role in the growth of resistance politics in South Africa and the USSR's relationship with the SACP and later with the ANC. The chapter will review the affairs of the Communist International from the second congress of the Comintern in 1920, when the question of colonial revolution was first dealt with in any detail, through the dissolution of the world communist organisation in 1943. The growing militancy of the national liberation movement after 1960, as exhibited by the actions of the military wing of the ANC, *Umkonto We Sizwe* (the Spear of the Nation), will also be discussed.

Chapter 3, 'Soviet Diplomatic Relations with South Africa', traces the course of official contacts between South Africa and the USSR from 1942 to 1956. This examination is essentially a diplomatic history beginning with the initial discreet advances of Soviet diplomats in 1941 for the purpose of establishing an official legation in Pretoria and concluding with the closure of the Soviet Embassy in 1956. Chapter 4 considers the USSR's role in the United Nations debate concerning the question of apartheid in South Africa. The Soviet Union has consistently supported the anti-apartheid movement in the UN from the earliest meetings of the international forum in 1946. This survey will give particular attention to the evolution of

Soviet perceptions of the role of the Third World in the world body, because Soviet policy on the issue of apartheid is greatly influenced, if not dictated, by Russian policy towards Black Africa in general.

The dilemma posed by the Soviet–South African minerals nexus is perhaps the most interesting and certainly the most controversial area of relations. Chapter 5 looks in depth at the clandestine contacts between the two countries for the marketing of diamonds, gold and platinum. Together, the Soviet Union and South Africa provide a large percentage of the world's supply of these and other strategic minerals, and this section will consider the competition and collaboration which has resulted from this unique situation. There will also be a related discussion about the potential international consequences, in the world mineral markets, should a militant black government assume power in South Africa – and the possible Soviet reaction to this development. Chapter 6 addresses the issue of Soviet espionage in South Africa. This section will begin with a brief overview of the purported espionage activities of Soviet diplomats in Pretoria. It will, in addition, cover the circumstances surrounding the apprehension of Soviet agents in South Africa on spying missions, culminating with the capture and conviction of Commodore Dieter Gerhardt.

Chapter 7, concerning the contemporary political situation in southern Africa, considers the recent history of Soviet policy towards the region. Particular attention is devoted to the increase of Soviet influence in Mozambique and Angola since the collapse of the Portuguese African Empire during the 1974–6 period. The USSR's relations with its allies, Cuba and East Germany, and its competitors, the United States and China, in southern Africa will also receive serious consideration. The rise of the Soviet naval operations in the Indian Ocean will receive scrutiny in relation to the Soviet activity in southern Africa. This chapter seeks to present an overview of the political, strategic and ideological motivations which together comprise the primary thrust of Soviet foreign policy. Finally, the concluding chapter will be devoted to answering questions advanced at the beginning of the introduction.

It is appropriate here to mention a few words about sources. This study covers nearly ninety years of diverse contacts between the RSA and the USSR. I have adopted a fairly eclectic approach to obtaining information, and consequently this study has been drawn from a wide range of both published and unpublished sources. Some of the interviews conducted during the preparation of the book were given on a confidential basis, and I have taken great care to respect the privacy of those who requested anonymity. However, I have sought to provide corroborating evidence wherever possible in making my arguments. It is hoped that the bibliography will provide a useful guide to material available on Soviet–South African relations and spur further attention to a field which is generally under-researched and little understood.

The purpose of this book is to provide a history of the USSR's involvement with South Africa and an understanding about the formulation and execution of Soviet foreign policy in the region. The study covers state, party and commerical contacts between the Soviet Union and South Africa. Furthermore, attention is given to the complex motivations driving Soviet actions. In so doing, this enquiry will challenge the conventional wisdom in the West concerning Soviet aspirations and advance an alternative appraisal about the USSR's activities on the southern African continent. Particularly, it will be argued that in its conception and practice there is no 'grand strategy' for waging a 'total onslaught' against South Africa in Soviet policy. It will be shown that Soviet foreign policy is revolutionary, in its support for national liberation; cautious, in its desire to avoid a major commitment in the region; and realistic, in the knowledge that developments in southern Africa are peripheral to Soviet national interests.

1 The Heritage of Russian Involvement in South Africa: The Anglo–Boer War

It is pleasing for me to know that the ultimate means of deciding the course of the war in South Africa lies entirely in my hands.(Czar Nicholas II, 1899)

The war in South Africa is a proof of the insignificance of the power of money when pitted against moral force. (Leo Tolstoy, 1900)

The Russian people have had an historic interest in South Africa . . . from the time of the Anglo–Boer War. (Pavel S. Atroshenko, Soviet Consul-General in Pretoria, 1948)

I

Soviet foreign policy has historical roots in southern Africa dating back to the initial Russian involvement in the Anglo–Boer War (1889–1902). In several respects Soviet activities in this part of the continent represent a continuation of those undertaken during the Czarist period. In order better to understand the nature of Soviet involvement in South Africa it is worth examining the heritage of Russian activity in the region. Although Russia before the Revolution did not have much interest or influence in South Africa, nevertheless, Russian statesmen sought to exploit the Transvaal war to their advantage. As Russia had no colonies of her own in Africa, the primary objective of her diplomacy in South Africa was the prevention of British colonial expansion, or what Wilson has termed 'the contest of preventive imperialism'.[1] Russian leaders endeavoured to subvert British supremacy by providing moral and military assistance to the Boers, challenging British positions in India, and by pursuing diplomatically a European coalition to confront British aggression in South Africa.

It is important to note, however, that the Anglo–Boer War was not the occasion of the first Russian foray into Africa. Indeed, Czarist interest in sub-Saharan Africa was not confined to South Africa. Early Russian activity on the continent has been traced from the initial religious mission to Ethiopia in the 1700s, through attempts made by Czar Alexander III to establish colonies on the Red Sea.[2] The Czarist concern for north-eastern Africa at the end of the nineteenth century was motivated by Russia's desire to disseminate Orthodox Christianity, challenge the British, and to secure, through Egypt, access to the Red Sea. Although Russia had no lasting presence on the African continent, it did play a modest role in the imperial struggle for African territory spanning the turn of the century. Having failed to establish colonies of her own, Russia sought to deny others what she herself could not have.

Most of Europe, including Russia, was united against Great Britain on the issue of the South African war. Britain's European rivals, while careful not openly to oppose British imperial policies, attempted to exploit the conflict with varying degrees of commitment. Germany, France, Russia and the Netherlands all provided aid and comfort to the Boers. Germany was the chief benefactor of military equipment and personnel while the Netherlands provided the majority of medical relief and ambulance units to South Africa. France, which had recently reached an agreement with Britain concerning their respective spheres of influence in Africa, was unwilling to interfere overtly in a region claimed by the British. French assistance was thus limited to sending a few military specialists to fight with the Boer commandos. Imperial Russia dispatched military and medical personnel along with supplies to South Africa. In addition, Russian statesmen advocated the formation of a diplomatic coalition of European states to protest against British imperial policies in South Africa. The Germans, French and Dutch, due either to vital interests in Africa or historical ties to the Boers, were all cautious adversaries of Britain in the South African conflict. The reasons for Russian involvement are more difficult to cite. As previously mentioned, Russia had no colonial presence in Africa and could not claim any particular cultural or historical affinity with the Boers. Hence, the primary motivation for Russian activity in the Transvaal war can best be described as a desire to disrupt British influence in Asia and Africa. A brief review of Russian involvement in the Anglo–Boer war renders this intention clear.

II

The early Boer victories against the British on the borders of the Cape Colony and Natal were greeted with surprise and satisfaction in Russia. The implications of these initial British defeats at the hands of 'Boer farmers' were acknowledged by statesmen throughout Europe. It was apparent that the stability of Britain's imperial position and the strength of her military had been overestimated. Lord Kitchener, fresh from his victorious conquest of the Sudan in 1899, was transferred to the Cape in an attempt to stem the torrent of fighting. Russian statesmen watched these developments carefully for an opportunity to exploit the conflict to Russia's advantage.

British setbacks in South Africa offered Russia the occasion to challenge Britain's colonial position in India, but Anglo–Russian intrigue in the region was not new or unusual. In 1895 Russia annexed the Pamir region in what is today the Soviet Republic of Tadzhikistan, and only a narrow strip of Afghan territory separated the Czar's domains from the northern most outposts of British India. This annexation exemplified the protracted rivalry in Central Asia between Imperial Russia and the British Empire that existed before the successful conclusion of the Anglo–Russian Entente in 1907. By the time war engulfed South Africa in 1899, Russia and Britain had been at odds in Asia for generations. It was not surprising, therefore, that Russian statesmen saw an alliance with the struggling, distant Boers as a means of taking advantage of Britain's uncertain imperial posture.

Czar Nicholas II recognised that this serious test of British authority in South Africa might have a distinct bearing on Britain's imperial posture in India. The British position in India during 1899 was precarious. The region was experiencing a severe famine and, to compound British worries, Indian troops were required for the fighting in South Africa.[3] The Czar perceived these developments as an opportunity to further Russian interests in South Asia and strengthen Russia's position in relation to Britain. He elaborated on his scheme in a letter to his sister in October 1899:

It is pleasant for me to know that the ultimate means of deciding the course of the war in South Africa lies entirely in my hands. It is very simple – just a telegraphic order to all troops in Turkestan to mobilize and to advance towards the frontier [of India]. Not even the most powerful fleet in the world can keep us from striking England in that her most vulnerable point. But the time is not ripe for this yet; we are not sufficiently well prepared for serious action mainly because Turkestan is not as yet connected by continuous railway with the hinterland of Russia.[4]

The Russian failure to complete the railway system in Central Asia precluded the possibility of implementing the Czar's plan. Nevertheless, Russia did take advantage of the outbreak of hostilities in South Africa by undertaking military manoeuvres in the area of Turkestan.[5]

Although Russian military intervention in India was never pursued, there was hope among Boer leaders that Russia would challenge the British in Asia. Dr W. S. Leyds, the South African Republic Envoy in Europe reported to F. Reitz, the Secretary of State for the Transvaal that 'from very good authority I gather that the Russians will be in Herat in May [1900]. I send this news for what it is . . . a probability, but not a certainty'.[6] However, even if the story were true – and it rapidly proved to be false – Herat was close to the Russian border in the extreme north-west of Afghanistan. It was a long step from being a serious threat to the British position in India and, as the tide of the war turned against the Boers, hope faded for a possible military challenge in India.[7]

In addition to the proposed moves against India, the Russian government considered other methods of opposing Great Britain. Primary among these was the Russian attempt to elicit support from France and Germany for the purpose of 'taking common action against the ever increasing aggressions and expansions of England'.[8] The beginning of the Anglo–Boer War coincided with Russian Foreign Minister Muravieff's trip to France and his unofficial visit was transformed into a diplomatic mission. His task was to enquire about the official attitude of France and Germany in connection with the struggle in the Transvaal. A possible alliance between Russia and these European states was envisaged to confront British aggression in South Africa.

Despite Russian efforts, open collaboration between the European powers proved impossible. This was due mainly to those existing difficulties between France and Germany which arose from the German annexation of Alsace–Lorraine, and to Germany's rapprochement with Britain since their treaty in 1898. These continental powers, in the character of the times, encouraged Russia to act unilaterally against Britain. But both carefully abstained from a commitment to acting in concert. Kaiser William II urged the Russian Ambassador in Berlin, Count Osten-Sacken, that 'only Russia can counter-attack the pressure of the perfidious Albion without compromising her interests, that only she is in the position to threaten England's Achilles heel . . . in India'.[9] He concluded by assuring Osten-Sacken that 'everything you undertake in that direction will have all my sympathy and I guarantee you the absolute neutrality of Europe'.[10] Such intrigues were at a zenith during this period and the issue of the Anglo–Boer War was thus drawn into the fray of European power politics. Yet Russia's ambition to thwart British imperial growth is of primary importance when considering Russian involvement in the Transvaal war. This desire is exemplified by the Russian search for a European coalition to stand against Great Britain on the South African issue.

When the British forces in South Africa began to regain the upper hand by the end of February 1900, Russian leaders shifted the emphasis of their diplomacy in an attempt to salvage something from the deteriorating Boer position. By March the British had amassed 120 000 troops in South Africa, and were moving swiftly on to the offensive. On 5 March President Kruger of the Transvaal and President Steyn of the Orange Free State sent a joint communiqué with a peace offer to Prime Minister Salisbury. The singular condition mentioned in the communication called for Great Britain to recognise the independence of both republics as sovereign states. Concurrently, Boer statesmen attempted to enlist support for their cause from various European states. The possibility of diplomatic intervention between the antagonists received the active support of the Russian government and the Foreign Ministry approached Germany with the suggestion that a European coalition might act jointly to petition Britain to end the war 'in the interests of humanity'.[11]

The formal Russian proposal from the Czar was presented to the Kaiser on 2 March. It read: 'In the opinion of the Imperial Cabinet and in view of the latest events[12] and successes of the English armies, it appears that the moment has arrived for the Continental states, particularly those interested in African affairs, to endeavour to prevent the serious consequences which might be the result of the complete annihilation of the South African Republics.' With this aim in view the Russian government suggested applying a 'joint friendly pressure [*pression amicale*] of European governments on the English government' in an attempt to 'put an end to the bloody slaughter in South Africa'.[13] German statesmen expressed reservations about acting in concert and stressed that Russia must act as the official initiator of intervention. Responses from the other European countries were ambiguous, and on 20 March the Russian government notified the various capitals that efforts to form an alliance for the purpose of securing an early end to the South African war had been suspended. Great Britain also rejected categorically Russian attempts to mediate in the conflict in the Transvaal.

By the end of the summer of 1900, the military situation had changed dramatically in South Africa. Officially, the Orange Free State and the Transvaal had been annexed by Great Britain, but guerrilla warfare raged on in the South African countryside. However, Russian statesmen were more concerned by events unfolding not far from Russia's borders. Attention was primarily focused on the Boxer Rebellion in China and other developments in the Far East. Although these more immediate concerns required consideration from Russian leaders, the Imperial government did maintain its interest in the South African conflict. Even after the Boer position appeared hopeless, Colonel E. J. Maximov, a Russian officer serving with the 'Foreign Legion' in the Transvaal, encouraged President Steyn of the Orange Free State to continue his struggle against the British forces. Maximov sought to assure the Boer president that peace initiatives to Britain were not the only hope. He advised Steyn to send a Boer delegation overseas to visit the various European capitals (St Petersburg, Berlin, Paris and the Hague) in an attempt to enlist support for the struggling Boers.[14] The Boers did send a delegation to Europe in September 1900 and it was headed by Leyds, the South African Envoy in Europe. Although he was greeted with notable displays of public enthusiasm, nothing tangible was achieved by Leyds' visit. Russian statesmen, acting alone, were unwilling to exacerbate relations with Great Britain by forming an alliance with the South Africans. Hence, Russia made no offer of assistance to Leyds.

III

However, the most interesting thing about Leyds' trip to Russia was not his private audience with the Czar, but the public interest his visit generated. A proud, religious people fighting against the full force of the British Empire, the Boers were excellent candidates for Russian sympathy and support. The Boer struggle struck a responsive chord in the minds of many Russians, and when the South Africans successfully routed the British forces during the early part of the war, this Russian sympathy for their cause matured into earnest respect. The Anglo–Boer War provoked the interest of Russian society as a whole, and the Boer cause received active support in liberal and conservative circles alike. Indeed, developments in far away South Africa were followed with curiosity throughout Russia. Rarely had an issue captured the imagination of the Russian populace and generated such an extensive body of literature.[15]

Russian conservatives, who were well represented in the military elite and among the aristocracy, tended to view the South African conflict within the context of Russo–British rivalry. Specifically, the conservatives saw Britain as a hostile enemy and adversary of Imperial Russia. The Russian conservative press, which included such publications as the *Pravitelstvenii Vestnik* (*Government Gazette*), were very supportive of the Boer cause. Many conservative publications advertised the Russian 'volunteer' movement: a scheme designed to enlist army reservists willing to fight with the Boers in South Africa. The conservatives were highly critical of Britain's colonial heritage and tended to accentuate the exploitive aspects of British imperialist policies. These sentiments are aptly expressed in a pamphlet on the South African war in which the author states: 'The shocking war between England and the Transvaal is a sad example of an imperial power boldfacedly trampling upon everything that is believed to be true and good.' Britain's aims were to 'enslave the Dutch settlers, the independent Boer republics, only because they happen to have diamonds and gold'.[16] The conservatives also advocated that their government take advantage of British misfortunes in South Africa to strengthen Russia's position in Central Asia and north-eastern Africa.[17] The conservatives, with their clear interest in foreign issues, represented the dominant foreign policy influence in turn of the century Russia and the primary impetus behind Russian involvement in South Africa.

The Russian liberals, while admiring of Britain's system of parliamentary democracy, were also not supportive of the British war with the Boers. These liberals, like the conservatives, interpreted the Boer War as a genuine movement for, and expression of, national independence. They tended to view British imperialism as primarily beneficent, inculcating British culture and traditions in the inferior peoples of backward lands. This was clearly not the case with regard to the Boers. The Boers were perceived by liberals to be an autonomous people with a strong Dutch cultural tradition and their struggle with the British characterised a sense of national identity. However, since many prominent Russian liberals envisaged a future alliance with Britain, the liberal press were not inclined to be too critical of British activities in South Africa, nor too supportive of Russian involvement in the conflict.

The Russian Marxists interpreted the South African conflict not as a justifiable expression of Boer self-determination, but rather as exemplifying an imperial rivalry for colonial territory. Lenin was the most prolific of the Russian Marxists, and his writings would later serve as the foundation for Soviet theoretical work on South Africa. After returning from his Siberian exile in 1900, Lenin left Russia and lived successively in Brussels, Paris, London and Geneva. Through his pamphlets, with their penetrating analysis of post-Marxian socialism, and through his newspapers *Iskra* (*The Spark*) and *Vperyod* (*Forward*), Lenin gained acceptance as leader of the Militant Russian Social Democrats, who later were to assume the name 'Bolsheviks' in 1903. *Iskra*, which Lenin managed to have smuggled into Russia, enjoyed a wide readership in Moscow and Petrograd.

In the first issue of *Iskra*, Lenin made a fleeting reference to the South African struggle: 'For the sake of gain of a band of capitalists, bourgeois governments waged endless wars, caused the deaths of many regiments of soldiers in unhealthy tropical countries . . . take the rebellion in India . . . or the present day war of the English against the Boers.'[18] While observing the phenomenon of the Anglo–Boer War and other imperial struggles at the turn of the century, Lenin also developed the thesis for his systematic critique of modern imperialism presented in *Imperialism as the Highest Stage of Capitalism*.[19] Lenin contended that monopoly capitalists in Europe were driven to search for profits through investments abroad, employing the control which they had acquired over government to direct foreign policy towards the acquisition of empire with a view to securing markets, raw materials, and above all, opportunities for investing their surplus capital. However, the competition for colonial acquisition among imperial powers would eventually lead to war. Lenin asserted that imperialism took its final shape in the period between 1898 and 1917, and the Anglo–Boer War and other such conflicts stood as landmarks in the new era of world history.[20]

Lenin saw South Africa's mineral wealth as the primary target of British imperialists whose aim was to appropriate it. The Russian Marxists condemned any such imperial wars of annexation and strongly criticised British imperialists like Cecil Rhodes for their conduct.[21] While critical of British imperial policy in South Africa, the Marxists emphatically withheld support from Russian groups seeking to aid the Boers. Lenin denounced Russian 'imperialists and capitalists' who expressed interest in siding with the Boers. He believed their concern was motivated not by a progressive proletarian doctrine, but by a quest for empire. Any 'internationalist' support would have to address the issue of the oppressed nature of South Africa's non-white population, the legitimate owners of the country. However, the Marxists characterised the situation in South Africa primarily in terms of class rather than race. For example, Lenin did differentiate between 'white workers' and 'capitalists' in South Africa, the former receiving his full support during the white miners' strike of 1913.

A clear expression of Lenin's perception of the Anglo–Boer War and its relevance to Russia appeared in *Svobodnoye Slovo (Free Word)* in 1900. The article was written in connection with a proposal to boycott British shipping in support of the Boers:

> The majority of people in most countries are on the side of the Boers, fighting for their independence the hirelings of a band of capitalists who have managed to create a 'public opinion' in England, which approves of this truly abject war. This sympathy is of a 'platonic' nature and manifests itself mainly in applause at the sound of the Boer National Anthem, which is constantly being played in most of the restaurants of European cities.
>
> Certain more dynamic personalities look for a more active manner of expressing their feelings. It is well known that quite a few 'volunteers' have gone to the Transvaal. In the streets of St Petersburg, one could a few months ago, meet simple country lads who were looking for the railway station to catch a train to Pretoria or Johannesburg.

The sentiments inspiring these Russian lads are very touching but also very naive and do not stand up to the light of reasoning. They saw the evil done by the English in faraway South Africa, and do not see the evil, no less terrible, committed close at hand whose victims they are themselves.

One can say the same thing about the feelings guiding the Dutch workers proposing to boycott, i.e. refuse to load or unload all English ships until such time as the British government ceases the bloodshed in South Africa.[22]

Lenin sought to redirect the energies of the Russian populace away from active involvement in foreign intrigues towards participation in their own struggle with Russian autocracy. Mention of South Africa and the Anglo–Boer War in Marxist journals tapered off significantly after the suspension of hostilities in 1902, at a time when the attention of Russian Marxists was focused on events transpiring within Russia. (Greater consideration will be given to Marxist theories of imperialism and self-determination in the following chapter.)

Quite apart from the political interest which the Anglo–Boer War generated in Russia at the turn of the century, the Russian people were impressed by a religious empathy for the Boers. The struggle between the Boers and Great Britain was referred to in the Russian press as a 'struggle between spirit and flesh'. As one commentator noted: 'The Boer is our own Russian peasant, Hollander though he might be. He prizes his land and his labour, defending the farm and his freedom; he reminds us of our own Russian peasant who has had to fight for his freedom on many occasions.'[23] Another observer saw Biblical significance in the Boer plight:

A mere handful of Boers stand facing the biggest empire of the world, and not only make a stand but they gain victories against the forces of its usually victorious enemy . . . There is something Biblical in their struggle like the fight of young David against the Philistine Goliath.[24]

Popular Russian support for the Boer cause cannot be solely attributed to imperial rivalry with Great Britain, or to effective government propaganda designed to interest the populace in a distant South African war. The allegiance many Russians felt for the Boer farmers of the Transvaal and the Orange Free State was certainly influenced by strong moral and religious convictions. The

Russian literature of the late nineteenth century was given to philoso-
phical reflection on the constant, inexorable struggle between the
forces of good and evil and was imbued with a deep sense of moral
and religious responsibility for the fate of its own nation and mankind
as a whole.[25] Quite possibly it was this worldview, so apparent in
literature and religious discourse of the period, which attracted the
Russians to the Boer cause. As Leo Tolstoy once commented, 'the
war in South Africa is a proof of the insignificance of the power of
money when pitted against moral force'.[26] It was natural that Russians would want to support directly the efforts of the Boers and not
surprising that an initial effort to organise medical and military
assistance for the Boers came from St Petersburg's religious community.

IV

Shortly after the outbreak of hostilities the Russian Red Cross Society,
at the urging of a number of St Petersburg's religious leaders, sent
an offer of medical assistance to both the involved parties. This
proposal was sent through the office of the Russian Foreign Ministry.
In an attempt to allay British suspicions concerning Russia's all too
apparent sympathy for the Boers, an offer of medical assistance was
sent to Great Britain in compliance with the European code of
neutrality. The British politely declined Russian assistance, but the
Transvaal government accepted it with deep gratitude. (A number of
European countries, as discussed previously, provided medical supplies and Red Cross ambulance units to South Africa in support of
the Boers.) An official ambulance was equipped and staffed by the
Russian Red Cross and subsequently provided invaluable service in
western Natal (the ambulance was manned by approximately forty
medical personnel). A second ambulance, the Russo–Dutch unit,
was staffed by volunteers, half of whom were Russian and the other
half Dutch. The facility was equipped and dispatched to South Africa
by Pastor H. A. Gillot of the Dutch colony in St Petersburg who,
through public subscriptions, had acquired the necessary capital. This
ambulance unit was divided into groups, which served in hospital
trains and medical aid stations, both in the towns and in the field
(there was a contingent of ten Russian doctors and nurses in this
unit).[27] Most of the personnel of both ambulances retreated with the
Boer commandos along the railway to Delgoa Bay after the fall of

Pretoria in July 1900, and returned to Russia shortly thereafter.[28] However, one section of the Russo–Dutch ambulance was captured by the British at the battle of Kroonstad; one of its doctors served until the end of the war, eventually as the personal physician to General de la Rey of the Boer army.

At the onset of the struggle, the Russian government was not prepared to intervene officially on any level in the South African war, and these efforts to organise medical units to assist the Boers were considered a potential threat to Russia's stated neutrality in the conflict. Nevertheless, after considerable pro-Boer lobbying conducted by Pastor Gillot and others, coupled with the increasing support for the Boers in other European capitals, the Russian leadership cautiously allowed such activities to continue. Indeed, although this operation appears to have been undertaken without the direct support of the government, official cooperation was in all probability requisite to facilitate the unit's departure to South Africa. Russian statesmen, intrigued by the potential opportunities which the South African war might offer, resolved to watch carefully for an occasion to exploit the conflict to Russia's advantage. In the meantime, the provision of medical personnel and supplies to the Boers was deemed to be an appropriately supportive, yet discreet activity.

In addition to medical assistance supplied to the Boers, the Russian government tacitly consented to, and participated in, the recruiting of military personnel to fight with the Boers. Indeed, a number of Russian soldiers found active service with the Boer commandos. The Russian 'volunteer' movement (a campaign heartily publicised by the conservative press) sought to enlist volunteers wishing to travel to South Africa and fight alongside the Boers in their struggle against Britain. The exact number of Russian volunteers to journey to South Africa has never been accurately determined, but most estimates range between 150 and 220 men.[29] A large number of these volunteers were officers of Russian guard regiments who were granted reserve status by the government to free them from their duties. The majority of these recruits arrived in South Africa early in 1900.

There were three main squads in which the Russian soldiers served during the war. The 'international legion', certainly the most illustrious unit of fighting men, was formed by a decree of the Council of War in March 1900. There were approximately three hundred troops in the regiment from around the world serving under the French Colonel De Villebois Mareuil. The Russian Colonel E. J. Maximov served as his second-in-command, and after Mareuil's death, he assumed the duties of command for a time.[30]. The number of Russian volunteers in this unit is estimated to have vacillated between forty and eighty men. After the international legion was disbanded, a group of about forty soldiers formed the 'Russo–Hollander Corps' under the command of Colonel Maximov (this legion was subsequently nicknamed the 'Maximov Corps'). A third detachment of commandos termed 'the Russian Corps' served with the Russian Red Cross ambulance in an area east of Bloemfontein.[31] The Russian troops in their various regiments fought with the Boer army in the battles of Glencoe, Balmoral, Colenso, Kroonstad, and Vaal Krantz from the beginning of the war until the official cessation of hostilities in May 1902, when most of the soldiers returned to Russia. Many of the Russian volunteers who served with the Boer commandos were decorated for their gallantry, and the Russian fighting man was generally well-respected by his fellow Boer comrade-in-arms. However, there is no evidence to suggest that these few Russian soldiers in any way altered the inevitable outcome of the conflict.

The military attachés attached to the Boer and British forces each furnished the Russian authorities with detailed information regarding the capabilities of the respective antagonists. The Czar's inordinate interest in the war prompted the Russian General Staff to assign a military agent to the Boer army. The man chosen was Lieutenant V. I. Romeiko-Gurko, the son of a famous Russian general. On arrival in South Africa late in February 1900, he presented himself to President Steyn and soon thereafter joined the Boer forces in the eastern Transvaal.[32] The services of Romeiko-Gurko were invaluable to the Czarist government. His astute descriptions of the military campaign enabled the Russian leadership to evaluate the effectiveness of the Boer tactics and methods. Lieutenant Colonel M. A. Stakhovich, the Russian military attaché with the British army, also provided useful observations of Britain's strategy in the conflict. Colonel Stakhovich relayed several reports concerning the logistics and deployment of the British forces which would have proven of considerable value in the event of direct Anglo–Russian hostilities.[33]

Both officers discussed the military and political blunders committed by the British in their dispatches, together with suggestions concerning the most effective means of exploiting these miscalculations. The military attachés were impressed by the depth of the indigenous nationalist feeling in South Africa and were quick to recognise the tenacity of the Boer struggle for independence as a potential threat to Britain's colonial position in southern Africa. The Russian government, partly because of excellent reporting from the scene, perceived correctly the intensity of the Boer independence movement as an anti-British force.[34]

V

The Anglo–Boer War impressed the Russian leadership both with the value of Boer nationalism as a potential threat to Britain's regional hegemony and with the strength of British resolve to resist any such threat. Russian statesmen actively considered exploiting the situation in South Africa at the time of the Russo-Japanese War, when tension between Great Britain and Russia was again running high. Indeed, the possibility of utilising Boer activism to divert British attention away from events transpiring in the Far East received serious discussion. The Director of the Asian Department at the Foreign Ministry reported to Foreign Minister Lamsdorff on 28 February 1904:

> The possibility of a new, ever-persistent war in South Africa constitutes a factor of first-rank importance in international politics. This factor ultimately would make it possible to exclude England from those powers whose interference in the present war we fear, and thus almost entirely free our hands for energetic activity in the Far East.[35]

South Africa, the site of a moribund conflict, appeared a logical place to incite trouble for Great Britain. Although several prospective schemes designed to accomplish this task were considered, one plan in particular captured the imagination of the Russian leaders. The former Boer General Pinaart-Joubert advanced a proposal in which the South African natives would be used to cause disturbances. This activity would occupy the British forces until the Boers themselves were able to reorganise and take the offensive. Joubert's comments concerning the revolutionary potential of South Africa's native population are explicative: 'I found that all of Africa resembles a huge field covered with dry grass which needs only a match held up to it in order to catch fire, and I intend to be that match.'[36] Joubert's presumption that Boer agitators could provoke an anti-British uprising among South Africa's blacks perhaps skirted over the fact that the sympathies of non-white people of South Africa, in so far as they existed or were important, were with the British not the Boers.

In an effort to entice the Russian leadership into providing military equipment and financial assistance for his plan, Joubert made the extraordinary offer that Russia should serve as suzerain over the eventual Boer state which would emerge from the conflict. What is possibly more astonishing than the proposal of General Joubert was the positive reaction of the Imperial Russian government to the scheme. Several Russian statesmen, including Lamsdorff, expressed a belief that the Joubert scheme would be an appropriate course of action. However, after serious consideration the Russian govenment yielded to the measured, reasonable arguments offered by Ambassador Nelidov in Paris. Nelidov asserted that Russia should be thinking 'not about new additions to the imperial title', but rather about ways to 'retain in its entirety the old one'.[37] With international troubles in the Far East and intensifying domestic strife, it seemed inopportune for the Russian government to be debating the merits of reckless commitments to new intrigues in Africa. Russian statesmen resigned themselves to the political realities of the situation and abandoned all attempts to renew the South African war.

Undeniable political considerations and a shortage of financial resources influenced the decline of active Russian interest in South Africa during the period following the Russo–Japanese War. Indeed, events transpiring close to Russian borders in East Asia and the Revolution of 1905 fully absorbed the attention of Russian leaders. In addition, the successful conclusion of the Anglo–Russian agreement in 1907 codified a more cooperative relationship between the two states. As Britain had served as a vital catalyst in stimulating Russian interest in South Africa initially, the relaxation of tensions between the two countries removed a primary impetus for continued involvement in South Africa. It was only after the Bolsheviks had successfully achieved power in 1917, that Russian statesmen would turn their attention once again to Africa in general and South Africa in particular.

2 The Soviet Union and the Growth of Resistance Politics in South Africa

> If we propound the solution of the right of self-determination for the colonies . . . we lose nothing by it. The most outright national movement is only water for our mill, since it contributes to the destruction of imperialism. (Nikolai Bukharin, member of the Executive Committee of the Comintern, 1919)

> The ANC has . . . been deeply infiltrated by those who seek to advance the imperialistic ambitions of the Soviet Union. (Senator Jeremiah Denton, Hearings before the United States Senate, 1982)

> Our support of the ANC is longstanding. The revolutionary alliance of the SACP and the ANC will continue to receive Soviet assistance in the struggle for national liberation. (Boris R. Asoyan, Deputy Director, Institute for African Studies, USSR Academy of Sciences, 1984)

I

From the very inception of Soviet power, the new regime displayed an interest in the colonial regions of Asia and Africa. The Bolsheviks accorded due attention to national and colonial questions and reinstituted the Communist International (Comintern), in part, to formulate and implement Soviet policy towards the underdeveloped areas. Although the problems posed by revolution, civil war and invasion required the near full attention of the Bolsheviks in the first years of their rule, the fledgling Soviet state adopted an internationalist foreign policy which addressed not only Europe, but Africa as well. Imbued with a sense of mission to fulfil Marxist–Leninist prophecy in

23

the awakening colonial world, the Soviet leadership was determined to play a role in political developments on the African continent. South Africa was the cornerstone of early Soviet policy in sub-Saharan Africa, and Moscow regarded the Communist Party of South Africa as the 'ideological and organizational leader of the revolutionary communist movement in other parts of Black Africa'.[1]

This chapter will trace the Soviet involvement with South African resistance politics from the earliest resolutions of the Comintern on the colonial question to the contemporary period of assistance to the national liberation movement. The ideological and practical considerations which serve as a motivation for Soviet policy will be examined. In addition, the evolution of the relationship between the Soviet Union and several South African organisations, in particular the Communist Party of South Africa (CPSA) and the African National Congress (ANC), will also receive scrutiny. It will be argued that the USSR's support of political resistance, while long-standing, is not without its frustrations and failures, and indeed the vagaries of Soviet foreign policy have on several occasions served to impede rather than promote the national liberation struggle. This chapter will focus on developments in South African society only as these relate to Soviet policy, but mention will be made, where appropriate, to relevant and related literature. By highlighting the primary characteristics and impact on Soviet policy towards South African resistance movements over nearly seventy years, a greater appreciation can be gained of the USSR's ideological and political objectives in southern Africa.

In the wake of the political upheaval brought about by the Bolshevik revolution, with Russia's external political efforts concentrated in Europe, it is perhaps surprising that the new leadership looked beyond the confines of the former Russian state to the colonial regions of Africa in the derivation of Soviet foreign policy. What factors first attracted Soviet interest in a region so far removed from Soviet territory? One answer can be found in the experience of the First World War. European powers, particularly France, resorted to raising troops from colonial areas and sent subject armies to serve on the Eastern Front during the war.[2] Trotsky observed in 1919 that, 'the colonial peoples were drawn into the European war on an unprecedented scale: Indians, Negroes, Arabs, and Madagascans . . .'[3] (The terms non-European, Bantu, native and African are used interchangeably in this chapter to refer to South Africa's black population.) There are indications that the Bolsheviks feared that

these same powers would use Africa as a reservoir for the recruitment of colonial troops to assist in the Allied intervention in the
Russian civil war.[4] Thus, the very security of the Soviet revolution
was, in a small way, connected to African colonialism.

However, the principal motivation behind the early Soviet interest
in Africa was ideological and the theoretical approach of the new
regime to the underdeveloped areas represented a dramatic departure from classical Marxist theory. Both Marx and Engels restricted
their field of observation to Europe and North America and did not
conceive that the colonial regions of Asia and Africa could play a
potentially revolutionary role in the same sense as the advanced
European nations. Marx regarded the colonial territories as playing a
very minor role in the development of world affairs and actually
considered imperialism to be a historical necessity, drawing the
down-trodden peoples of the overseas areas into the dynamic realm
of European politics.[5]

When Lenin developed his own thinking on imperialism he empha-
sised the significance of colonial revolution for the collapse of capitalism. In describing the origins of the First World War, Lenin argued
that European territorial rivalry in Africa resulted in conflict between the capitalist powers.[6] Lenin's conception of imperialism led
him to the conclusion that imperialist war was inevitable and to the
belief that European capitalism was sustained by African raw materials and 'super profits' generated from the nefarious exploitation of
colonial labour. The prominence of the underdeveloped world was
evident in early Soviet theory,[7] and in the last article written before
his death, Lenin proclaimed that 'the outcome of the struggle will be
determined by the fact that Russia, India and China, and so forth,
account for the overwhelming majority of the population of the
globe'.[8] Indeed, Lenin's own interest in the 'colonial question' was
reflected during the early years of Comintern activity. In a speech in
the Comintern in 1921, Lenin declared 'it is evident that in the
decisive battles of the world revolution, the movements of the colonial peoples will play a greater revolutionary role than we dare
hope'.[9]

The Soviet propensity to encourage revolution in Africa can also
be attributed to Russian sympathy for the plight of indigenous
peoples living under colonial rule. Wilson has noted that: 'This
feeling of empathy, which was apparent in the Czarist attitude toward
Africans, accorded remarkably well with the spirit of exuberance
prevalent among Russian communists during the first years of the

Comintern's career.'[10] However, the Russian tendency to identify with the oppressed populations of underdeveloped regions, as reflected in the Soviet advocacy of colonial independence, was more a costless gesture than a serious foreign policy platform. As Bukharin aptly surmised: 'If we propound the solution of the right of self-determination for the colonies . . . we lose nothing by it. The most outright national movement is only water for our mill, since it contributes to the destruction of . . . imperialism.'[11] Thus, for a combination of practical and theoretical motivations the USSR, through the forum of the Comintern, championed the rights of the politically dispossessed colonial peoples in the early period of Soviet rule.

The Communist International was inaugurated in Moscow on 4 March 1919 through the efforts of the Russian Communist Party with the intention of furthering proletarian revolution in other countries. At the Second Congress of the Comintern in July 1920, Lenin laid the theoretical basis for communist activity in the colonial world with his 'Theses on the National and Colonial Questions'.[12] While this statement made no specific reference to South Africa, the 'Negro Question' did receive consideration at the Second Congress. The American delegate, John Reed, argued that communist organisers should look to various negro movements in the United States and Africa as potential vehicles for spreading communist influence.[13] The Comintern viewed South Africa within the context of the colonial and national issue and more specifically in terms of its concern for blacks in Africa. Yet, South Africa received only scant attention during the initial proceedings.

The Communist International was affiliated in South Africa to the Communist Party of South Africa which had come into existence on 30 July 1921 with a nearly exclusively white membership of several hundred.[14] The CPSA was the first Communist Party in Africa. Its core members came largely from the International Socialist League in Johannesburg, a militant left-wing group which supported working-class solidarity across racial lines. With the establishment of the Comintern, the League reorganised into the CPSA under the leadership of William H. Andrews. Many of the original members were Eastern European Jewish immigrants who came to South Africa after the turn of the century.[15] This was South Africa's first proclaimed Marxist political party and the only multiracial political organisation of the period.[16] The relationship between the Comintern and the CPSA was a complex one, complicated by geographical and ideological distance, but the loyalty of the CPSA to the Comintern deepened in the early 1920s with several prominent South African communists visiting Moscow for Comintern meetings.

While the CPSA became increasingly sustained and guided by overseas developments in the international socialist movement, the Comintern itself began to move away from its original ecumenical responsibilities and became further ensconced within the Soviet bureaucracy. An examination of the proceedings of the Fourth Comintern Congress held in 1922 reveals that the Comintern no longer existed to further the cause of world revolution, but rather acted to enlist the support of foreign communists in the task of defending and promoting the interests of the Soviet state.[17] In the alliance between the Soviet Union and the world revolutionary movement there had developed, in the opinion of E. H. Carr, 'a reversal in the balance of obligation, from which there would henceforth be no turning back'.[18] As this relationship crystallised, it became impossible to distinguish between the foreign policy of the Soviet Union and the Comintern approach to world affairs. It is this development, perhaps more than others, which serves to illuminate the twists and turns in Comintern policy towards South Africa.

II

The most striking aspect of Comintern policy towards South Africa between 1921–7 is the degree to which the ideology of the Comintern diverged from the ideology espoused by the CPSA. Looking outward from South Africa, the CPSA identified with the Comintern's anti-imperialist platform yet perceived South Africa not as a colonial country but rather as a rapidly industrialising capitalist society.[19] The first Comintern programme for South Africa called upon the CPSA to integrate blacks into the white labour movement. In 1924, the Red International of Labour Unions (Profintern), a department of the Comintern, directed the CPSA to 'commence work among the negro working masses, endeavoring to secure the fusion of parallel organizations of whites and negroes . . .'[20] However, as Sidney Bunting, a prominent South African communist well understood, the white labour movement was 'backward and lacking in solidarity'[21] and this posed serious difficulties for the CPSA. While many communists supported multiracial political organisation, the vast majority of the white working class did not, and on one occasion this dilemma forced the CPSA to side with white workers in favour of the colour bar. In 1922 the CPSA supported the Rand miners' strike under the banner 'For a White South Africa', and although the Comintern played no role in this decision, it was tainted by association in the eyes of many black South Africans.[22]

The Comintern's call for multiracial organisation and 'united-front' tactics in South Africa was met with some dissatisfaction by CPSA members. Bunting, speaking before the Fourth Comintern Congress in 1922, argued that to persuade white workers 'to abandon their prejudice against native labour organization was nearly an impossible task'. Furthermore, Bunting was sceptical whether Communist organisers would agree to carry on 'propaganda directly among the native workers', because this work aroused 'fierce resentment among the Europeans'.[23] There was some consternation among Comintern participants, too, that a white South African was speaking on the negro question. A Soviet publicist writing in 1922 indicated that the American negroes rather than the white South Africans would be regarded as spokesmen for negroes throughout the world.[24] The final 'Theses on the Negro Question' from the Fourth Congress placed the negro question squarely within the context of the national and colonial question. The 'Theses' noted the success of Marcus Garvey's black movement in the United States and W. E. B. Du Bois' Pan-African Congress, and Comintern spokesmen urged that efforts to organise negroes be increased everywhere. Furthermore, the Comintern reaffirmed the primacy of the American negro in communist strategy.[25]

With some misgivings, the SACP supported the position accorded South Africa in the context of the world negro problem, the revolutionary centre of which the Comintern perceived to be in America. However, as Sheridan Johns observed, 'a precedent had been established for the Comintern to consider the problem of South African blacks in the possibly irrelevant context of the American Negro problem or the world Negro problem'.[26]

The Fourth Congress also placed the CPSA under the jurisdiction of the Anglo–American Colonial Group of the Comintern, along with member parties from Canada, Britain, the United States, India and Australia. The matching of South Africa with Great Britain and the United States set a further precedent by raising the possibility that South Africa would be viewed in the context of American or British affairs wholly unrelated to the particulars of the South African situation.

The CPSA laboured from 1924 to build an effective multiracial political party with some success. South African communists, under directives issued from the Fourth Comintern Congress, began infiltrating Clements Kadalie's Industrial and Commercial Union (ICU), which in 1927 counted almost 250 000 black workers.[27] The CPSA managed to place three of its members on the Executive Committee of the ICU before Kadalie broke with the communists for 'interfering more and more in the general affairs of the union'.[28] The CPSA then assisted in the establishment of a new black organisation called the League of African Rights under the leadership of James T. Gumeda. South African communists also moved to infiltrate the African National Congress (ANC) – an organisation that many of them regarded as hopelessly unrevolutionary – in order to transform it into a 'fighting nationalist revolutionary organization . . .'[29] Thus, the CPSA began in earnest to organise African labour unions and to participate in a variety of indigenous South African groups.[30]

Although the CPSA was able to attract some black converts, the Party remained predominantly European. The negro membership of the Party in 1927 numbered probably somewhere between fifty and a hundred, but Edward Roux, a founder of the Young Communist League, held that the CPSA was making progress in winning African support.[31] Whether the CPSA could have, in the words of George Padmore, developed a 'black colouration',[32] it is impossible to know, because with the Comintern's 'Black Republic' resolution in 1928, the Party lost the foothold it had achieved among South Africa's black population.

Before turning to a discussion of the climactic Sixth Comintern Congress, it will be helpful to review Soviet policy towards South Africa in the previous 1920–7 period, when the CPSA enjoyed relative independence from Comintern directives. It is clear that South Africa was very much on the periphery of the world revolutionary movement. The CPSA followed Comintern guidance when it was applicable to South Africa, even invoking the ultimate authority of the Comintern to settle disputes within the Party, but disregarded decisions taken in Moscow when these were inappropriate to local situations. This relative independence demonstrated by the CPSA was possible because of the lack of direct contacts between South Africa and the Soviet Union. During this initial period of Comintern activity, Russian communists displayed a lack of knowledge of local conditions in South Africa and made little distinction between blacks in South Africa and in the United States. Although the Comintern's proclaimed objective was to further the cause of colonial revolution, it did not fully appreciate the complexity of South African society, nor did it heed the advice of local communists in the formulation of ECCI directives. These tendencies would all become clear during the deliberations on the adoption of the 'Black Republic' scheme for South Africa.

III

The pronouncements emanating from the Sixth Comintern Congress held in Moscow during 1928 represented a dramatic departure from previous Comintern policy towards the colonial world. Stalin was in the final stages of consolidating his rise to ultimate power in the Kremlin, and Comintern developments must be viewed within the context of Stalin's rivalry with the left wing of the Party, and his personal rivalry with Trotsky.[33] Furthermore, the Comintern's policy of comparatively indiscriminate cooperation with nationalist movements culminated in the betrayal of the Communist Party of China (CPC) at the hands of the Kuomintang in 1927.[34] Thus, Stalin's embarrassment about his support for the ill-fated CPC–Kuomintang alliance, and strong left-wing opposition to his bid for unquestioned power, provided a strong incentive to promote the decisive return to orthodoxy in the 'United Front from Below' policy. Indeed, internal threats to Stalin's pre-eminent position, and the failure of the 'United Front from Above' strategy in China, encouraged a conservative shift in tactics and a tightening of discipline in communist organisation. This strategy involved a move away from cooperation between bourgeois nationalists and local communists for a joint revolutionary leadership, in favour of a proletariat-led 'fighting front' with the Communist Party in the vanguard. Of particular significance for South Africa, Stalin also instructed the Comintern's leadership to adopt a new programme on the negro question which called for the right of self-determination for negroes in the American South as well as for black Africans in South Africa.[35]

It was in late 1927 that the CPSA learned of the radical new Comintern policy for the black population of South Africa. The new platform, under the banner of 'an independent native South African republic, as a stage towards a workers' and peasants' government with full, equal rights for all races, black, coloured and white', was a departure from previous Comintern policy towards South Africa and was met with disbelief and disagreement from many CPSA members.[36] The news of this dramatic reorientation came from James La Guma, the first black member of the CPSA to reach Moscow. In an interview with Nikolai Bukharin, the Comintern's leader, La Guma received an analysis and prescription for South Africa which has been summarised by Sheridan Johns:

> Defining South Africa as a colony or semicolony of British imperialism, Bukharin postulated that the immediate struggle in South Africa was primarily an anti-imperialist nationalist struggle, rather than a direct anticapitalist proletarian struggle. According to Bukharin's analysis the Africans of South Africa were being kept in subjugation by British finance capital and its local ally, Afrikaner imperialism, in order to provide superprofits, most of which were exported to Britain, but some of which were distributed among resident South African capitalists and landowners to maintain their acquiescence in the dominance of overseas capital. To end the rule of British finance capital, it was the task of the communists, according to Bukharin, to join with African nationalists in the national struggle to oust British and Afrikaner imperialism. The immediate goal was not a socialist state, but an independent democratic 'Native' republic as a stage towards the final overthrow of capitalism in South Africa. Within the new bourgeois–democratic republic in which Africans would predominate there would be full 'minority' rights for coloreds and Indians and all nonexploiting whites.[37]

The purpose of the new Comintern strategy was, in the view of George Padmore, 'to satisfy the nationalist aspirations of those Negroes who still hankered after "Black Zionism" and turn them away from Garveyism to Communism'.[38] Furthermore, applying the Leninist–Stalinist doctrine of self-determination, which had been developed in response to the minority nationalities of the Russian empire,[39] the 'Theses on the Revolutionary Movement in Colonial and Semi-Colonial Countries' adopted by the Sixth Congress stated that colonial peoples should be granted 'unconditionally and without reservation, complete state independence and sovereignty'.[40] The Comintern Executive Committee also gave notice that the SACP should 'reorganize itself on the shop and street nuclei basis' which would further the Bolshevisation of the party.[41]

The full details of the new programme outlined by Bukharin to La

Guma reached the CPSA in early 1928 in the form of a 'Draft Resolution on South Africa'. To most of the white members of the Party, the 'Native Republic' slogan contradicted the policy of non-racial, proletarian solidarity the CPSA had pursued since its inception. Instead of struggling for the equality of all workers, the CPSA was being called upon to further African nationalism at the expense of a multiracial approach to South Africa's situation. Most of the white membership of the CPSA opposed the new line from Moscow, and the majority of the party instructed Bunting and his wife to proceed to Moscow for the Sixth Congress to voice their objections to the Comintern authorities.[42]

On arrival in Moscow, the South African representatives found a climate of hostility and tension. Apparently, before the Buntings' arrival, word had reached Moscow from South African communists supportive of the 'Black Republic' scheme. Sydney Bunting rose to address the Sixth Congress on a number of occasions to voice his opposition to the new Comintern programme and to offer his views of South African conditions. The Buntings were accused of white chauvinism, were avoided by some Comintern delegates and ignored by others.[43]

Bunting stated that a recent article in *Inprecorr* about South Africa contained information 'which could only be called a fairy tale. It was full of the most crass misstatements about the conditions there.'[44] Bunting argued for a recognition of the uniqueness of the South African situation on the continent owing to 'a whole nation of [white] classes, established there for centuries, of Dutch and English composition'.[45] In this context, Bunting stated that the Comintern strategy should be directed towards accentuating the class struggle, rather than narrow nationalist forces. Turning to the slogan of the 'independent native South African republic', Bunting stated that the new programme would arouse intense opposition among the white workers and make multiracial organisation virtually impossible. He pointed out that the new slogan would suggest to whites an African dictatorship and drive white workers to side with the exploiting class against the black population. In addition, there was concern that the new communist scheme, with its support of separate development for blacks, bore a striking similarity to the government-sponsored programme of apartheid. Bunting declared that the key to revolution was in South Africa's rapidly expanding black proletariat, rather than the peasantry in which the Comintern held such high hopes. Bunting specifically rejected Comintern instructions that the CPSA work to strengthen the ANC, arguing that it was a 'moribund body' which 'has had its day'.[46] In closing, Bunting warned that the racialism embodied in the Comintern's new directives would give the government a pretext to move against the CPSA and create violent racial hostilities in South Africa.[47]

Despite the strong opposition from the CPSA representatives, the final thesis on 'The South African Question' and the revolutionary movement in the colonies ignored their recommendations. The Comintern determined that South Africa was ruled by the white Afrikaner bourgeoisie in alliance with British imperialists against the native population. The Comintern instructed the CPSA to increase its organisation among workers and peasants and adopt a Bolshevik organisational structure to build up a mass party. The CPSA was to use the already controversial 'Native Republic' slogan to attract the black peasantry, which was the 'basic moving force of the revolution'.[48] Cooperation with 'embryonic national organizations among the natives, such as the African National Congress' was also demanded. Furthermore, greater trade-union organisation was encouraged among black and white workers. However, in an implicit criticism of the CPSA, the resolution stated that 'the white toiling masses must realize that in South Africa they constitute national minorities . . .'[49]

The Buntings were warned in Moscow on several occasions that 'the majority of the leadership of the South African Party must unconditionally correct their attitude, their opposition in the question of the slogan of the Native Republic must be given up'.[50] However, the party leaders thought the programme unsuitable and continued in their opposition. In the early 1930s, backed by the full authority of the Comintern, Sydney Bunting, Bill Andrews, Solly Sachs and other prominent leaders were purged from the party by the new stalwarts of the CPSA who sought to follow slavishly Moscow's decrees. The party did increase its efforts to mobilise the African labour unions in the 1930s, yet the Native Republic scheme did not attract supporters and disappeared from the CPSA platform by 1936. At that point, the demands of the 'Popular Front' in Europe brought a new turn in Comintern policy.

To recount, the Sixth Congress of the Comintern in 1928 marked the end of the CPSA's autonomy from Moscow and the beginning of absolute discipline to central authority which was demanded by Stalin. The programme for a Native Republic was essentially a unilateral decision taken in Moscow and, quite apart from its theoretical peculiarities, represented a test of loyalty for party members.[51] The extensive resolution on 'The South African Question' was notable in the sense that Moscow accorded considerable attention to developments in South Africa. However, the Comintern still had not come to terms with the class and race complexities of the South African situation.[52] The Comintern's policy of applying Leninist–Stalinist theories of self-determination to South Africa failed because the vast majority of blacks did not want a separate state, but rather full citizenship rights.[53] Comintern authorities ignored completely warnings that a policy aimed at the formation of independent black republics would create a host of problems for the CPSA. Nevertheless, party members who 'refused to carry out slavishly the instruction of Moscow' were purged.[54]

IV

The rise of Nazi Germany coupled with Japan's invasion of Manchuria led the Comintern to change its general programme of 'world proletarian revolution' to a 'united front against reaction' in 1935. As Germany and Japan moved toward entente in 1934, the Soviet Union turned to Britain and France, the major colonial powers, in pursuit of a defensive alliance against Germany.[55] While the Soviet Union did not abandon altogether its enmity towards the Western European powers, the USSR shifted its foreign policy in the direction of supporting the *status quo* in Europe and Africa.[56] The demands of the Soviet *rapprochement* with the West required a dramatic reorientation of strategy, and the Comintern's policy in the colonial world reflected this transition.

When the Seventh Comintern Congress met in Moscow in July and August 1935, its primary task was to enact a programme which called for cooperation against the Nazi menace. Edward Wilson observed that:

Never before, in fact, had Comintern policy been so obviously molded to correspond to calculations of Soviet national interest. Primed for almost a decade to pursue the solitary course of proletarian orthodoxy, world communism at the time of the Seventh Congress was, in effect, routed onto the cooperative path of anti-fascist coalition. Recognising the threat posed by Nazi Germany, the Seventh Congress formally abandoned the 'united front from below' approach, replacing it with a policy of relatively indiscriminate cooperation with elements sympathetic to the anti-fascist cause.[57]

The new 'popular front' strategy was explained in the 26 October 1935 issue of *Umsebenzi*, the official paper of the CPSA.[58] Although the Party had eschewed cooperation with several mass organisations since 1928, loyal communists were now enjoined to participate in all movements which proclaimed to be anti-fascist. These broad, anti-fascist popular movements included the National Liberty League Against Fascism and War and the South African Friends of the Soviet Union. (For a description of the latter organisation, refer to the chapter on diplomatic relations.)[59] However, information about specific Comintern instructions to the CPSA was sparse during this period. Yet, those articles which did appear made scant reference to the plight of Africans in South Africa, but rather concentrated upon 'the task of bringing together progressive opinion in an effort to stem the pro-Nazi tendencies which have already shown themselves in the majority party, the United Party, and the openly fascist party, the Nationalist Party'.[60] A dramatic example of Moscow's move away from revolutionary activism in Africa was the Comintern's decision to cease its support for the International Trade Union Committee of Negro Workers (ITUC–NW) led by George Padmore. Padmore claimed that this action was taken 'in order not to offend the British Foreign Office which has been bringing pressure to bear on Soviet diplomacy because of the tremendous indignation which our work has aroused among the Negro masses in Africa'.[61] In short, the Comintern's *volte-face* in favour of a more conservative approach to the question of colonial revolution marked the end of revolutionary left-wing tactics.

The Molotov–Ribbentrop Pact of August 1939 between the Soviet Union and Nazi Germany demanded the discontinuation of strident anti-fascist propaganda and once again the complete reorientation of Comintern policy. From cooperation with social democrats and reformists in the struggle against Nazi tyranny, the Comintern now asked its adherents to adopt an anti-war policy. The change in policy came a month after the signing of the Nazi–Soviet Pact, and the conflict in Europe was portrayed 'in its character and essence . . . on the part of both warring sides, an imperialist, unjust war . . .'[62] The abrupt change in strategy was reflected in Comintern policy towards South Africa. In an article written before the pact in

World News and Views, Bell Keats supported the war against Germany and criticised Malan for his support of Hitler. Keats described it as a 'base betrayal of the true ideals of Afrikaaners'.[63] Yet, two months later, Keats declared that the struggle was between two rival imperial powers, and the CPSA did not support either side.[64]

Hitler's attack of 22 June 1941 on his erstwhile ally in the Soviet Union required an immediate and abrupt break from the Comintern policy of the previous two years. The German thrust into Russia transformed the imperialist war into a struggle for survival for the USSR. A hallmark of Soviet policy since the establishment of the Comintern was the slogan that negroes from Africa and the United States would be used as 'cannon-fodder', as in the First World War, in an imperialist intervention against the Soviet Union.[65] In 1941, however, with the very existence of the Soviet Union threatened, the participation of black Africans was encouraged in the struggle against the fascist invaders.[66] In South Africa, propaganda against non-European military recruitment was replaced with the slogan: 'Arm the non-European soldiers'.[67] Y. M. Dadoo, a prominent South African communist of the period, switched from bitter criticisms of the Union government's policy of recruiting non-Europeans into the army to equally vociferous demands that armed Africans should be used in the war against the fascists. Indeed, the war in Europe which weeks before was described as 'not the negroes' war', now required the active involvement of blacks everywhere to save the socialist homeland. The requirements of Soviet foreign policy made it necessary to mute the revolutionary drums during the 1941–3 period, but the virtually complete subordination of the Comintern to these requirements is striking.[68] Indeed, in the few years preceding the Comintern's dissolution in 1943, its official journals were almost barren of material on colonial revolution.

The Comintern was formally dissolved on 22 May 1943, shortly after its headquarters had been moved from Moscow to Ufa, the capital of the Bashir Autonomous Soviet Socialist Republic. The primary reason given for its dissolution was the growing contradiction between the seat of communist authority, or 'directing center' in Moscow, and the 'fundamental differences of the historical paths of development of the separate countries of the world'.[69] The Comintern controlled the destiny of the CPSA for nearly 25 years and left a profound impression upon South African radical politics. What is the legacy of Comintern policy in South Africa?

The dissolution of the Comintern marked the end of the most blatant period of Soviet involvement with resistance politics in South Africa. However, the Comintern's intervention into South African affairs has left its mark. In retrospect, the now underground South African Communist Party is critical of much of the early Comintern programme, characterising the controversial slogan of 'an independent native South African republic' as 'not suitable' to local conditions.[70] The harshest criticism has been reserved for the Comintern's backing of the purges in the 1930s. One writer noted that 'the development of the Stalin cult in the Soviet Union . . . all but wrecked the party' and 'left a scar which will not soon be forgotten'.[71] Furthermore, the lack of sophistication and understanding in the Soviet approach to South Africa, coupled with several reorientations of Comintern policy, has hindered the success of the CPSA and sparked controversy about communist participation in the national liberation struggle.

Yet the Soviet Union, under the aegis of the Comintern, helped to shape the national liberation movement during this early period. The USSR was the first country to champion the plight of the politically disenfranchised population in South Africa, and this propensity to look at Africa in human terms should not be dismissed. The fact that Comintern intransigence and militancy often hurt the reputation of the USSR does not detract from the material and moral support that has been rendered by the USSR since the very inception of Soviet power. Although practical aid from the USSR, such as funds and equipment, was simply not advertised in Comintern publications, Soviet assistance was undeniably useful. Even the Bolshevisation of the Party in the 1930s, which allowed a 'sectarian ultraleft group' to come into control, also helped to infuse a tradition of discipline and loyalty in the CPSA.[72] Soviet material assistance and organisational strategy were to become increasingly important to the CPSA after 1950 when the party was forced to continue its work underground.

V

In the years directly following the 'Great Patriotic War', Soviet energies were confined primarily to repairing their war-ravaged economy. The USSR's involvement in South African politics declined accordingly, and Soviet proclamations calling for national liberation

appeared to be motivated more by rhetorical than practical considerations. The USSR returned to a strict 'two-camp' view of the world,
and Moscow stressed the leading role of Communist parties in the
national liberation movements of the Third World.[73] With the abolition of the Comintern, the Soviet Union's coordination of the international communist movement changed appreciably. The new
relationship between the Soviet Union and national communist parties became more secretive and less open to outside scrutiny. There
were no longer Comintern publications providing details about the
proceedings of party conferences. Party contacts tended now to be
more direct and private, outside the formalised and stultifying Comintern structure.[74] Soviet relations with South African communists
were no exception to this general rule. Apart from the renewed
Soviet commitment to a multiracial approach to South Africa's
problems, there is little information in the available literature about
the nature or level of Soviet involvement in radical politics after the
war. Indeed, from 1950 onwards, it becomes increasingly difficult to
point to evidence linking the USSR to the national liberation movement.

One of the important motivations for renewed secrecy in the world
communist movement was the growing repression of communist
parties by host governments. In 1948, the Nationalists swept to power
in South Africa on an anti-communist platform and the Malan
government introduced the Suppression of Communism Act in 1950.
Also in 1950, the government confiscated several bundles of mail
posted to South Africa from the USSR (this included a large amount
of Marxist theoretical literature on imperialism and colonial
revolution).[75]

Faced with increasing government opposition and the imminent
prospect of being declared an outlawed organisation, the Party disbanded on 20 June 1950, before the Act was passed by Parliament.[76] At the time of its dissolution, the CPSA could claim over 3000
members, among them approximately 1200 blacks.[77] Still, white members were at the top of the party hierarchy and were generally
more sophisticated in their understanding of Marxist theory. The
Party had emerged from the Second World War with the highest level
of public support in its history and a representative sitting in Parliament. This situation changed dramatically with the arrival in power
of the Nationalists, and the Party was faced with the dilemma of
whether to disband permanently or regroup in some clandestine
form.

Several Party members opted to regroup as an underground organisation, and in the early 1950s the underground South African Communist Party (SACP) was inaugurated. Moses Kotane, the General Secretary of the CPSA, instructed party members to infiltrate a variety of 'front' and national organisations. These were the multiracial South African Congress of Trade Unions (SACTU), the whites-only Congress of Democrats (COD), the Southern African Coloured Peoples Organisation, the South African Indian Congress, and the African National Congress. These organisations were loosely grouped in what was collectively termed the Congress Alliance.[78] The ANC was singled out in particular as an organisation which communists should take all necessary efforts to infiltrate.[79] However, the ANC had displayed an historically ambivalent attitude towards the Soviet Union and the CPSA. Some ANC leaders such as James Gumede, who after his visit to Moscow in 1927 returned to South Africa a committed communist, accepted Party members into the ranks of the ANC. Others, such as the tribal chiefs, opposed any system which sought to overthrow traditional rule and were suspicious of communist participation in ANC affairs. Nevertheless, large numbers of communists joined the ANC in the period after the Party was banned, though publicly, communists denied all association with the fronts and the ANC.

Apparently, the CPSA still received and acted on instructions from Moscow after the dissolution of the Comintern. Jordan Ngubane, a former Party member, described the relationship in these terms:

> The inner nonracial core of real communists, with headquarters in Johannesburg, was in direct communication with the [Communist Party] of the Soviet Union, partly through agents in Lourenço Marques, London, and more recently Dar-es-Salaam. The members of the core joined a number of 'national' organizations of Africans, Indians, Coloureds, and Whites, which in turn belonged to a bigger alliance called the Congress [Alliance] . . .[80]

There were other indications, too, that the Soviet Union still exerted its influence on the affairs of the SACP. Even during the period of increasing government repression which culminated in the 1956 Treason Trial, several radical publications and pamphlets, such as *Fighting Talk*, *Liberation* and the *New Age*, gave strong editorial support to the USSR. For instance, the Congress Alliance and the underground SACP applauded Soviet actions in Hungary in 1956, took a pro-Soviet stance on the issue of the Korean War, criticised American hydrogen bomb tests in the South Pacific, and condemned North Atlantic Treaty Organisation (NATO) manoeuvres in Western Europe.[81]

Soviet influence over the SACP and white participation in the national liberation movement led some members of the ANC to break from the organisation and establish the Pan-Africanist Congress (PAC) on 5 April 1959. The PAC, with its organisational roots in Anton Lemede's Youth League of the ANC, criticised ANC moderates for their 'collaboration with white oppressors' and for submitting to 'foreign domination and foreign leadership' imposed by the USSR.[82] The PAC's leaders, Robert Sobukwe, Potlako Leballo and Peter Molotsi, were profoundly influenced by George Padmore's conception of pan-Africanism which to them offered an alternative to the brand of communism promulgated by the SACP and the USSR. This split of the national liberation movement into black nationalist and multiracial divisions was characteristic of the militant period of resistance in the 1960s.

With the death of Stalin and the emergence of Khrushchev as his successor by 1956, the USSR officially moved away from its previous 'two-camp' approach to foreign policy. Khrushchev initiated a dynamic new Soviet policy towards the developing nations and began in earnest to woo the newly-independent states of Africa. At the Twentieth Congress of the CPSU in February 1956, Khrushchev declared that the shift in the balance of power in favour of the 'world camp of socialism' would encourage a rapid acceleration in the liberation of colonial peoples and offer new hope to national liberation movements.[83] Yet, the Soviet Union's African policy during the 1956–60 period was directed primarily towards the Arab states of the Northern Maghreb.[84] It was not until after the Sharpeville massacre of 1960 that the Soviet Union began to participate more actively in the militant campaign against white minority rule in South Africa.

VI

The Soviet Union's role in the national liberation movement took on greater significance with the establishment of *Umkonto We Sizwe* (Spear of the Nation), the fighting wing of the Congress Alliance, in 1961. At a meeting of senior ANC leaders in June of that year, in the wake of the events at Sharpeville, the organisation abandoned its fifty-year tradition of non-violence.[85] Nelson Mandela explained during his courtroom trial in 1964 that after Sharpeville there was a popular realisation that the South African system was inherently violent and could not be transformed merely through non-violent means. Mandela noted that the decision was made to take up arms because 'all channels of peaceful protest had been barred to us' through the enactment of 'more and more repressive legislation'.[86] However, there were strict limitations placed on tactics: a sabotage campaign would be directed only against property, not persons. There was a general fear amongst Congress leaders that indiscriminate violence might provoke a violent racial clash in South Africa.[87]

The SACP was extremely reluctant to countenance an armed struggle in South Africa. Although Ghandian tactics had proven ineffective, staunch Party members opposed the initial decision to take up arms. Following the sabotage campaign of *Umkonto*, the isolated attacks of another group, the nearly all-white African Resistance Movement (ARM), and the violent attacks by the PAC, the majority of the SACP leadership went into exile. Those that remained, Denis Goldberg, Arthur Goldreich, Harold Wolpe, Bob Hepple and Lionel Bernstein among others, were arrested on a farm in Rivonia on 11 July 1963, allegedly planning further activities for *Umkonto*. By 1964, much of the senior leadership of the SACP and the ANC had fled the country. The strength of both organisations within South Africa was seriously diminished. Thus, the period of 'revolutionary exile politics' began with prominent resistance leaders travelling to Europe and other parts of Africa in search of support for their militant campaign against the white regime.[88]

By 1964, most South African communists exiled in London were in agreement concerning the necessity of waging an armed struggle in South Africa. Through the long-standing association of the SACP with the Communist Party of the Soviet Union (CPSU), *Umkonto We Sizwe* was assured of the material support of the Soviet Union and other socialist countries.[89] In 1963, before his capture at Rivonia, Arthur Goldreich had journeyed to Moscow to arrange military assistance from the Soviet bloc.[90] Arms, ammunition and some training personnel from the Soviet Union began to arrive in 1964 to newly-established ANC bases in Tanzania and Zambia.[91] The USSR also initiated a programme to train a cadre of South Africans in Soviet universities and at special military centres in Russia.[92] Although large sums of money were promised to the ANC by several African countries, Soviet assistance was to be rather more valuable than pan-African support in the period of armed struggle.

The increasing salience of the South African issue in Soviet foreign policy was apparent after 1960. Although the new Kosygin–Brezhnev leadership rejected Khrushchev's 'zero-sum' interpretation of colonial revolution (this being that a loss of Western influence necessarily rebounded in favour of the USSR), the Soviet Union attached greater significance to South Africa in its propaganda and at the United Nations (see the chapter on Soviet policy at the UN). The Soviet Union established the Africa Institute of the USSR Academy of Sciences in 1959, the Third African Department of the Soviet Foreign Ministry in 1962 (this department has responsibility for the countries of southern Africa), and the Africa Section of the CPSU International Department during the same period.[93] Soviet scholars and publicists also focused further attention on events in South Africa.[94] In addition, there was a greater awareness of the difficult theoretical questions involving race and class in Soviet literature about South Africa.[95]

Soviet support for the national liberation movement served to draw the issue of South Africa not only into the Cold War but into the Sino–Soviet split as well.[96] The relationship between the USSR and China from 1960 was characterised by mounting ideological friction, and this schism had dramatic consequences for the ANC and the PAC. The PAC, which enjoyed Chinese support in the 1960s, mounted strident attacks against the Congress Alliance because of its association with white communists. The PAC declared that 'Russian imperialists' had managed to 'capture and dominate' the ANC and Moscow was directing its offensive in southern Africa through 'African functionaries'.[97] For a time in the 1960s, Soviet writing on South Africa tended to give much attention to refuting these allegations. One Soviet Africanist described the PAC as a 'racist, chauvinist, arch-revolutionary, demagogic and anti-communist organization . . . which seeks support from imperialist circles on the basis of an imagined communist threat to South Africa'.[98] Professor I. Potekhin, a leading Soviet specialist on African questions, criticised the PAC for its 'vicious anti-communist propaganda'.[99]

There is some evidence to suggest that there has been some anti-communist feeling in the ANC. In 1968, four ANC guerrillas fled a military training camp in Tanzania to political asylum in Kenya. In a statement issued in Nairobi in 1969 the four dissidents pledged to 'resist all attempts to make South African revolutionaries tools of the lukewarm South African Communist Party or the Communist Party of the Soviet Union'. The document was also explicit concerning the dominance of the Soviet line in ANC policy: 'Whoever spoke against the Kremlin and its policies was branded as a deviate Maoist and revisionist, or alternatively an imperialist, and branded a fifth columnist, who was against the liberation of South Africa.'[100] Although the ANC's Morogoro Conference in Tanzania during 1969 is said to have resolved many of the problems which led to dissension in the ranks of the national liberation movement, the role of white communists in the ANC is still a source of some controversy.

In fact, the position of the South African communists was improved and legitimised at the Morogoro Conference. The ANC–Communist Party alliance was given organisational expression in the establishment of a Revolutionary Council with authority to direct *Umkonto* and the armed struggle. Several white and black communists were appointed to the National Executive Committee and the Revolutionary Council. Indeed, Joe Slovo, a key military strategist and white Communist Party member, was elected as a member of the ANC leadership itself. The final conference statement also reaffirmed and praised the role of the USSR in the struggle against white minority rule. It read: 'The pillars of the anti-imperialist movement are the Soviet Union and other socialist states.'[101] The SACP delegation to the CPSU Party Conference in 1969, led by J. B. Marks, also noted the complete alignment in world views between Soviet and South African communists. Marks, in a reference to the Sino–Soviet split, confessed he found the quarrels of other communists with the USSR 'rather difficult to understand'. Marks also criticised Chinese support for the PAC and hailed the Soviet Union 'as the citadel and mainstay of anti-imperialist forces everywhere'.[102]

Perhaps the affinity for the Soviet Union among the ANC leadership is not surprising given the difficulty in obtaining international assistance. Tom Lodge has written this about the relationship of the ANC with the USSR:

Despite the criticism it evoked the ANC's link with the SACP was of great value in this period. It was assured of a continual source of funds, equipment, training and diplomatic support – resources of a scale and quality its rivals could not hope to match. Soviet bloc-derived aid had, in the experience of African liberation movements, been proven to be more helpful than that obtained from any other source. Despite lavish promises the OAU donors have been fickle allies who, in any case, could themselves ill-afford their generosity. Chinese support for African movements has been meagre and unreliable; foreign policy reversals since the cultural revolution have made China an especially unpredictable source of support. Soviet aid, given the stability and continuity of the Soviet regime, has on the whole been more consistent and less subject to sudden changes of attitude than Chinese, American or African assistance. Moreover, its price, in the short term at least, has been a modest one. It costs African liberation movements little to align themselves loyally in favour of Soviet foreign policy. The alienation of the Chinese in 1964, when the ANC supported the USSR in the Sino–Soviet dispute, did the movement no significant harm. The ANC's endorsement of the Russian invasion of Czechoslovakia in 1968 was rather more offensive to its Western sympathisers, but by this stage it was clear that enthusiastic and committed Western backing for the cause of African liberation was a chimera. The only Western governments regularly prepared to give financial grants to African guerrillas have been the Scandinavians and the Dutch, and here the money has been given for non-military purposes. The only Western military support has been from the CIA to right-wing African movements and its effects have been disastrous for the recipients.[103]

The strategy and tactics of the ANC in exile have changed little since 1965. The collapse of the Portuguese African Empire in 1974 and the subsequent establishment of radical governments in Angola and Mozambique provided the ANC with greater support among the Front Line states. Yet, these gains have been partially offset by recent South African diplomacy. One of the important conditions of the 18 March 1984 Nkomati Accord required the FRELIMO government of Samora Machel to severely restrict the activities of the ANC in Mozambique. Subsequent reports suggest that Mozambique has complied with the conditions of the agreement (Joe Slovo was reportedly deported from Mozambique in April 1984). In the wake of the Soweto uprisings of 1976, thousands of black South Africans fled the country to join the ANC and undertake military training.[104] Although sabotage attacks in South Africa are on the increase, there has been no decisive escalation in the ANC's military campaign. However, the 15 May 1983 ANC bombing of government buildings in Pretoria led several commentators to believe that this attack signalled a shift in the tactics of the ANC.[105] In particular, some suggested that the younger members of the ANC, unsatisfied with the slow pace of the armed struggle, have adopted more militant tactics in the fight against white minority rule.[106] A bomb blast in downtown Durban following the signing of the Nkomati Accord lends some credence to this explanation, but the ANC has made no public statement suggesting a dramatic change in revolutionary strategy.

The Soviet Union, too, has remained consistent in its approach to South Africa since 1960. Soviet writers hail the ANC in alliance with the SACP as the sole legitimate liberation movement in South Africa. However, the USSR has established direct contacts with other indigenous groups (Soviet officials held several discussions with Gatsha Buthelezi in the United States in 1982). Soviet publicists also insist that, while trade union organisation and political education are necessary tasks, ultimate power can only be achieved through armed struggle.[107] Following the Soweto disturbances in 1976, one prominent Soviet Africanist claimed that 'the liberation struggle entered its decisive stage.'[108] Yet, most Soviet observers see a long struggle ahead, with the white regime holding on to power well into the 1990s.[109] Recent Soviet literature has stressed the need for a multi-racial approach to South Africa's problems and highlighted class rather than racial aspects of South African society.[110] Thus, the SACP, while generally supportive of Steve Biko's Black Consciousness Movement, warned that 'as a substitute for scientific social analysis [Marxism–Leninism], and as an alternative to the ideology of our liberation front, [Black Consciousness] becomes a harmful demagogic cliché . . . which weakens the cause of national liberation'.[111] Finally, the Soviet Union has committed itself to continue its military, financial and moral support for the national liberation struggle until majority rule is attained in South Africa.[112]

VII

To what degree can the Soviet Union exert its influence on the national liberation movement in South Africa? The United States' Senate Sub-Committee on Security and Terrorism chaired by Jeremiah Denton addressed this question during two months of lengthy and often controversial testimony in 1982. After interviewing several former ANC members, including Bartholomew Hlapane (who was later killed in Soweto) and Nokonono Delphine Kave, Senator Denton offered these recommendations about the relationship between Moscow and the ANC:

We may well sympathize with the original goal of the ANC to achieve democratic political rights and expanded freedoms for the black peoples of . . . South Africa. We cannot, however, delude ourselves that their purpose now is the achievement of those praiseworthy objectives. They have, from the testimony the sub-committee has received and from the statements and actions of its leaders, been deeply infiltrated by those who seek to advance the imperialistic ambitions of the Soviet Union.[113]

The official South African position is that the ANC is controlled by the USSR through white members of the SACP. Thomas Karis argues conversely that the ANC is a nationalist organisation which would govern a future South African Republic according to the principles enshrined in the Constitution of the United States. Soviet influence over the ANC, Karis claims, has been vastly overestimated by Denton and others.[114]

It is difficult to estimate the level of Soviet influence in the national liberation movement, but it probably lies somewhere between the two characterisations set forth by Denton on the one hand and Karis on the other. It is correct to speak of Soviet influence over the ANC, but clearly the USSR does not control the liberation movement in South Africa. There are indeed a few interlocking membership or 'organic links' between the ANC and the Communist Party, but the ideological differences between the ANC and the SACP are vast. Both the ANC and SACP acknowledge that the organisations are separate and independent from one another and that the ANC is the leader of the alliance. To assume that in any collaboration between African nationalists and white communists the latter will inevitably dominate is to underestimate the experience and sophistication of nationalist leaders. Walter Sisulu, a Secretary-General of the ANC from 1949 to 1954, was fond of retorting: 'cannot these people see that *we* might be using the Communists?'[115]

While it is true that South African Communists have a prominence vastly disproportionate to their numbers in the liberation movement, the size and influence of the SACP is, from many accounts, declining.[116] However, the ANC, without substantial Western support, will continue to look to the USSR for the provision of military assistance. It is inconceivable that the Soviet Union does not demand a *quid pro quo* from the ANC for this assistance.[117] Thus, with the Soviet Union providing the great majority of military aid (approximately 90 per cent), it can be reasonably expected that the USSR will continue to play a prominent role in the armed struggle.

The Soviet Union's involvement in the national liberation struggle in South Africa is a long-standing one. Soviet policy has on several occasions served to alienate the ANC and impede the national liberation process, but the USSR's relations with the liberation front in the contemporary period have shown flexibility and sophistication. Yet how this will influence Soviet strategy it is impossible to predict. Moscow's links with South African blacks have traditionally been through Soviet ties with the ANC and the SACP, and these ties will remain important. Undoubtedly, Soviet interest in national liberation in South Africa will continue, and as the racial situation in South Africa becomes critical, the Soviet role in the national liberation struggle will take on greater significance.

3 Soviet Diplomatic Relations with South Africa, 1942–56

A Soviet embassy in South Africa would help to further allied unity. (I. Maisky, Soviet Ambassador, London, 1942)

A Russian presence in South Africa could lead to propaganda, intrigue and even assassination. (Oswald Pirow, South African Parliamentarian, 1942)

What is the Russian Consulate doing here, with such a large staff numbering twenty or more? (D. F. Malan, South African Parliamentarian, 1947)

I

On 21 February 1942, the South African High Commissioner to the United Kingdom, Sidney F. Waterson, and the Soviet Ambassador and Minister Plenipotentiary to Great Britain, I. Maisky, signed an agreement which officially established diplomatic relations between the Union of South Africa and the Soviet Union.[1] This brief ceremony at South Africa House in Trafalgar Square marked the beginning of state to state relations which would last until 1956, with the departure of the Russian diplomats from South Africa after the closure of the Soviet embassy in Pretoria. Apart from a brief period of diplomatic contact between the Czarist government and the Union from 1912 to 1917 (W. L. J. Moore served as the Vice-Consul for Russia in Johannesburg with various other Russian representatives in Pretoria, Cape Town and Port Elizabeth until the successful conclusion of the Bolshevik Revolution when their official recognition was withdrawn),[2] the wartime alliance brought the Soviet and Union

48

governments together for the first time. However, despite the presence of a Soviet legation in South Africa, official contacts were never close. As a retired South African Foreign Service Officer with considerable contact with Soviet diplomatic personnel recalled it, 'relations were proper, even polite, but far from warm'.[3] Indeed, after the close of the war, relations began to deteriorate, becoming increasingly distant and stormy over time.

Although ostensibly allies during the Second World War, the Soviet Union and South Africa did not engage in any significant military collaboration, nor were they fighting the axis powers in the same parts of the world (South African forces served mainly in North Africa while Soviet troops fought desperately against the Nazi army in Russia and Eastern Europe). What then encouraged the Soviet leadership to approach South Africa, a country almost five thousand miles from its southernmost borders, on the issue of establishing official relations? Waterson, in a communication to Pretoria during his preliminary negotiations with Soviet officials in London concerning the conditions for establishing diplomatic contacts, presented the reasons Maisky offered for the Soviet overture:

> Maisky said that, in addition to the desirability of demonstrating allied unity and making contacts which could continue after the war, he thought that since Russia was likely to need increasingly large supplies of materials of all kinds for carrying on the war, Russian ships were likely to be calling at Union ports with increasing frequency to take Union products which would be bought either direct or more probably through the United Kingdom Corporation. It would be desirable for a Soviet representative primarily concerned with commercial and shipping matters, but with Consular-General rank, to be appointed at one of the Union's main ports, either Durban or Cape Town.[4]

The subsequent posting of Mr Ezhov Nicolaev, an expert in maritime affairs, as Soviet consul in Cape Town lends credence to this explanation.

However, while the reason for the Soviet initiative was hinted at by Maisky above, there is no evidence in either the South African External Affairs files nor the British Foreign Office documents, that the USSR explained their most important reason for establishing an official Soviet presence in the Union. After Hitler's attack against Russia on 22 June 1941, the USSR was suddenly and wholly unexpectantly ranged alongside the democracies fighting the common enemy. At once the Soviet Union became eligible for their share of American aid. (By the terms of the 11 March 1941 Act to Promote the Defense of the United States, the president was authorised to sell, exchange, lease, lend or transfer war goods and food to the value of $1.3 billion to any country whose defence was deemed vital to that of the United States.) In July, Roosevelt dispatched Harry Hopkins to Moscow for consultations with Stalin to determine which supplies would be necessary for the Soviet war effort. Subsequently, Hopkins' recommendations for a joint Anglo–American supply mission to the USSR were adopted by the Atlantic Conference on 12 August.[5] Soon after, supplies began to flow eastward: guns, tanks, planes and transport vehicles. By late September, war goods to the value of $41 million had reached the Soviet Union, and Roosevelt extended lend–lease to Russia to the amount of $1 billion on 30 October (by the end of the war, the value had risen to $11 billion). Thereafter, a steady and seemingly endless supply of war material crossed the seas, entering the USSR by way of Murmansk, Vladivostok, and the Persian Gulf.[6]

It was during the Moscow Conference, in the autumn of 1941, that American and Russian officials first agreed 'in principle' to operation *Frantic*, the code name for an American project to fly bombers from bases in southern USSR.[7] The Soviets were extremely reluctant to permit the United States to use airfields in Russian territory for the shuttle bombing of axis positions in the Balkans, but with the Siege of Leningrad and the increasingly desperate military situation, they cast aside their apprehensions and agreed to the conditions of *Frantic*. The plan was to ferry bombers on tankers with shelter-decks in convoy across the Atlantic, around the Cape of Good Hope into the Indian Ocean to Abadan, on the Persian Gulf in southern Iran. From here, the bombers would be partially assembled and taken overland across Iran by truck and train, through Armenia and Georgia, to airfields located in the Ukrainian cities of Poltava, Mirgorod and Pyrytic.[8] Over 350 heavy four-engine bombers of the Flying Fortress and Liberator class were to be carried by ship to the Soviet Union, and Cape Town was to be the only principal port of call on a voyage of nearly 10 000 miles. There, the bombers would be inspected for any damage suffered during the rough Atlantic passage and tankers would take on 100-octane aviation spirit in addition to other cargo bound for the USSR.

Operation *Frantic* was fully implemented in March 1944, and eighteen missions were flown against important strategic targets in

Germany. In addition to the bombers shipped for operation *Frantic*, the United States made available to the Soviet Union a further 200 bombers for delivery in August 1944. Some of these aircraft were ferried to Russia through the Persian Gulf to Abadan. During the period from 1 October 1941 to 17 August 1945 when lend–lease was terminated by President Truman, over 2500 ships carrying valuable war supplies were sent to the Soviet Union – a large number of which arrived in Iran by way of Cape Town.[9] Consequently, the establishment of an official Russian presence in South Africa, specifically the appointment of a Soviet diplomat in Cape Town to monitor the flow of lend–lease material through the port, was considered a high priority during the latter part of 1941.

Thus, Maisky was instructed in October 1941 to make discreet inquiries as to what the attitude of South Africa would be to a Soviet proposal calling for diplomatic relations. In September, Soviet officials had approached the High Commissioners from Canada and New Zealand about the advisability of establishing official contacts. The High Commissioners asked the British Foreign Office for advice on the matter, and Vincent Massey, the senior Canadian diplomat in London, informed Waterson of the Soviet interest in developing official ties with South Africa. After the initial conversation between Maisky and Waterson at the Soviet embassy in London on 24 October 1941, the South African Secretary of External Affairs in Pretoria, D. D. Forsyth, advised Waterson to contact the Foreign Office for consultation on the Soviet proposal.

II

The Union of South Africa was recognised to have what came to be called Dominion status in 1926 when the Balfour Committee of the Imperial Conference declared the dominion territories to be 'autonomous communities within the British Empire, equal and in no way subordinate to one another in any aspect of their internal or external affairs'.[10] Soon after, a Department of External Affairs was established on 1 June 1927. Although South Africa exerted a primary influence on the formulation of its domestic policy, the Union did not really have a foreign policy separate from Britain's in the Second World War.[11]

Decisions were essentially made in London with major political issues handled by direct communication between Smuts and Churchill, and the United Kingdom High Commissioner's Office in the

Union served as the primary channel for keeping the South African government informed of important wartime developments. Smuts, with his experience, standing and confidence in foreign affairs, frequently did not consult his own Department of External Affairs when formulating policy.[12] The identification of South Africa with British foreign policy goals was exceptionally strong during this period, owing partially to Smuts' personal sympathy with Britain and his impressive stature throughout the Commonwealth. Accordingly, on the occasion of Maisky's initiative to Waterson, Smuts advised Forsyth that the Union would adopt a line of policy in accordance with Great Britain.

The Foreign Office, after a brief period of consideration, notified Waterson of its recommendations on 6 November 1941, as follows:

> It will be remembered that early in 1936 we closed all consular posts in Soviet territory at the request of the Soviet Government. After the outbreak of the Soviet–German war it clearly became important for us to re-establish consular posts in Soviet Russia, and in July of this year we suggested to the Soviet Government that British Consulates should be opened in the Soviet Union. The Soviet Government, however, informed us in August that they had decided not to authorize the opening of further Foreign Consulates during the war, and we felt at that stage that it was not possible to press the matter, in view of Soviet preoccupation elsewhere. It is understood that the Soviet Government are now anxious to establish a Consulate in South Africa. We still attach great importance to the establishment of British Consulates in the Soviet Union, particularly at Vladivostok and Baku, and we feel that it would not be auspicious to take advantage of M. Maisky's approach and endeavour to persuade the Soviet Government to reconsider their attitude.[13]

With the blessings of the Foreign Office, the South Africans entered into negotiations with the Soviet Union on the conditions of diplomatic representation. Maisky expressed the desire of the Soviet government to appoint a diplomat of Ambassadorial rank in South Africa, but after consultation with Pretoria, Waterson informed him that 'this was out of the question while the war was on'. The head of the Soviet legation would be of Consul-General rank only. Maisky stressed that his government felt that official recognition would mark a turn in relations between the Soviet Union and South Africa which it hoped would be permanent, and he intimated that the Soviet authorities would again approach the Union on the question of upgrading relations after the conclusion of the war.

Smuts personally wanted an informal understanding with the Soviet Union that Russian diplomats would not carry on 'communist propaganda' among South Africa's native population. He envisaged an agreement along the lines of the 1921 protocol concluded between Great Britain and Soviet Russia to restrict foreign propaganda campaigns.[14] Apparently, Smuts received such an assurance from the Soviet authorities, for in a conversation with the British High Commissioner to South Africa in April 1943, he reportedly stated that 'the Soviet Union has agreed not to carry on propaganda in South Africa. Any manifestations of Communism here, whether good, bad or indifferent, were a local product'.[15] It was also agreed in the preliminary discussions that the question of South African diplomatic representation in the Soviet Union would be taken up after the war.[16] With these considerations settled, Forsyth cabled Waterson and advised him to inform Maisky that the Union government would agree to receive a Soviet Consul-General if a formal request were made.

Nearly three months passed between the agreement to establish diplomatic contacts and Prime Minister Smuts' announcement to Parliament on 17 March 1942 that the USSR would send a Consul-General to Pretoria. It was during these months that members of the opposition Nationalist Party learned of Smuts' intention to allow the Soviet Union an official presence in the Union. Thus, the issue of the wartime alliance between South Africa and 'communistic Russia' was drawn into the already raging debate in the Union concerning participation in the Second World War. Prime Minister Smuts and his Union party believed deeply that South Africa should honour her obligations to Great Britain and the Commonwealth and fight side by side with the allies. Afrikanerdom was deeply divided politically, but the Nationalist Party was united in its opposition to South Africa's participation in 'England's War'.[17] Hertzog and Malan, the two most influential Afrikaner leaders of the period urged that South Africa adopt a policy of neutrality. The deeply rooted conviction of Afrikaner Nationalists that dominion status was not synonymous with absolute sovereignty, but was rather a shackle by which imperialists in Britain would drag South Africa into war, reinforced their strong desire to extricate themselves from the Commonwealth and declare a republic. The crisis in Britain, brought on by the war, would mean the disintegration of the Commonwealth and would serve to open the way at last for an Afrikaner republic.[18] However, Smuts insisted on an immediate declaration of war on Germany, which barely passed Parliament, and South Africa joined the struggle against Nazi Germany and its allies.

There was a good deal of sympathy among many young Afrikaners for Nazi Germany. The support rendered by Germany to the Boer republics, an exaggerated sense of German humiliation at Versailles, the appeal of Nazi doctrines of blood and race, all combined to instil in Afrikaner thought a predisposition towards friendship rather than enmity with the Third Reich. More importantly, the Nationalists were drawn towards the enemy of their own archenemy: Great Britain. These sentiments provoked some to challenge the government's policy of participation in the war. Principally, the *Ossewabrandwag* (meaning literally the ox-wagon night watch) and Oswald Pirow's New Order were authoritarian Afrikaner organisations founded along Nationalist-Socialist lines. Both groups were organised in commando-like bodies and many of their members were interned for anti-war activities deemed to be threatening to the interests of the state.[19]

It was Pirow who moved to create a 'select committee to enquire into and report upon Communistic activities in the Union' during an acrimonious debate in the House of Assembly on 10 February 1942. Pirow outlined his understanding of the 'doctrines of communism' and gave a short synopsis of Soviet history, highlighting the brutality of Stalin's purges during his presentation to the Assembly. Turning to the threat communism posed to South Africa, Pirow asserted that:

> The equality of black and white is one of the fundamental principles of communism because the equality of the whole proletariat, whether he be white or black or whatever his colour, is the first principle of communism. The Minister of Justice has a file dealing with these matters in his possession . . . . In 1929 Moscow officially informed the communists in South Africa [a reference to the Sixth Comintern Congress 'Black Republic' scheme] not only that the system of equality between [all races] must be introduced in South Africa, but that the future republic which they contemplated for South Africa must be a black republic where the nigger must have preference.

Turning to the recent decision by the government to allow an official Russian representation in the Union, Pirow contended that: 'Soviet embassies and other representative bodies are used deliberately . . .

to create trouble in the countries where they enjoy hospitality . . . the Communists through the consulates are deliberately intent on getting control of the trade unions in every country'. Finally, he warned that the acceptance of a Soviet ambassador in Pretoria would be an invitation to 'propaganda, intrigue and even assassination.'[20]

The United party, in response to Pirow, introduced an amendment urging the government to intensify its efforts to suppress all forms of subversive activity, but despite this move there was still considerable dissatisfaction among Afrikaners about the imminent arrival of a Soviet Consul-General in the Union.

There was concern in the Foreign Office about the growing anti-Russian sentiment in South Africa. The British High Commissioner in South Africa reported several bomb attacks in Pretoria carried out by militant Afrikaner groups during the early part of February. In one cable he specifically referred to Pirow's address to the Assembly. It read: 'Despite obvious Nazi inspiration and political opportunism Pirow's speech was effective propaganda and embarrassing to the Government especially in view of the recent representation by the combined Dutch Reformed Church about [the] Communist "menace".' The High Commissioner warned that: 'There is fertile soil, especially in the country area, for anti-Russian propaganda', and that Nationalist opposition 'would find useful material for a "Red Scare" in the suggestion that the Communists are out to establish a "Black Republic" in South Africa'. However, he concluded that 'pro-government opinion . . . is not likely to be shaken in support of the Russian Alliance it believes to be essential for victory'.[21]

Quite apart from the apprehension felt in certain Afrikaner circles, there were a number of groups in South Africa which greeted the news of the impending official Soviet representation in the Union with approval. The South African Communist Party, the Medical Aid for Russia Committee, the Jewish Workers Appeal and the South African Friends of the Soviet Union all supported the establishment of full diplomatic relations with the USSR.[22] The South African Friends of the Soviet Union (SAFSU) was founded in the late 1930s, and most of the former groups used the SAFSU forum during the early years of the war to appeal to the government for the 'need for diplomatic, economic and military relations' with the Soviet Union.[23] The SAFSU held public meetings during the war, often attended by crowds in the thousands, and there was considerable support for its activities among the English-speaking population. The organisation brought together a diverse group of people who, for a variety of reasons, sought closer ties with the Soviet Union. The SAFSU was not institutionally linked to the Communist Party though several communists, including Ruth First, were among its members. It was multiracial, in the sense that its membership included Indians, and when public meetings were held in Pretoria, these were on occasion attended by Smuts and members of his cabinet. Generally speaking, the SAFSU enjoyed support among the English speakers in the Union, and the task of raising money and medical supplies for the valiant Russian soldiers was considered a *cause célèbre* among the liberal establishment.

A number of Communist Party members were active in the South African Friends of the Soviet Union and its associated organisations. Although the Nationalist government would subsequently go to considerable lengths during the Treason Trial to prove that these bodies were communist front organisations, the activities of these groups, even with their communist members, were considered benign by the Union government in the early 1940s. The attitude of the Union party appears the more reasonable. While it is true that the South African Communist Party received Comintern instructions from July 1941 that every effort had to be expended to help the Soviet Union in its struggle with Nazi Germany,[24] it is unlikely that Smuts' decision to accept a Soviet Consul-General was in any way influenced by the pro-Soviet propaganda in the Union.[25] Merely, the SAFSU was a reflection of public and official attitudes of the USSR in South Africa during this period, and the communists were not alone in their admiration of Soviet achievements in the war.[26]

III

Whether the South African communists appreciably influenced opinion towards the USSR or not, Soviet officials were, nevertheless, pleased when Smuts officially announced in Parliament on 17 March 1942 the inception of diplomatic relations between Russia and the Union.[27] The establishment of a Soviet embassy in South Africa marked the first official presence of the USSR on the entire African continent. (Shortly thereafter, the Soviet Union would establish relations with Ethiopia, on 21 April 1943, and with Egypt, on 26 July 1943.)[28] On 1 April 1942, the Soviet embassy in London informed Waterson of their intention to appoint Nikolai Iakovlevich Demianov, former Assistant Chief of the Second European Department of the Peoples'

Commissariat of Foreign Affairs, as the Consul-General in Pretoria. Waterson duly requested information regarding Demianov from the British Embassy in Kuibyshev (during the Second World War, many foreign embassies were moved from Moscow to Kuibyshev, a city approximately 300 miles to the east). The British Ambassador to the USSR, Sir A. Clark Kerr, cabled in reply that Demianov had held the post of Counsellor at the Soviet Embassy in China at one point and that he was 'quite an agreeable person of unimposing appearance, no standing and small diplomatic or consular experience'.[29] After some delay, the South Africans concurred in Demianov's appointment, and arrangements were set in motion for the Soviet diplomats and family to make the long journey to South Africa.[30]

It would appear that the South Africans envisaged a much smaller contingent of diplomats to staff the Soviet embassy than the Russians had in mind. Maisky approached South Africa House in early April with a request for twenty official visas for Consular employees along with sixteen visas for their accompanying wives and children.[31] Maisky explained that this group represented but 'the first instalment of Soviet diplomats to embark for the Union'. Officials in Pretoria were fearful that the 'arrival of this horde may produce an embarrassing outcry in South Africa'. It was therefore suggested that Waterson 'should represent to Mr Maisky that, in the interest of good relations, the Soviet Government would be well advised to send a smaller number of Vortrekkers to the Union'. There was also much concern in South Africa about the probable composition of the group of diplomats. One British official noted of the Soviet congregation that: 'it is rather a formidable instalment which no doubt includes a number of NKVD people to look after the PCFA officials. The wives may be wives: but they may be disguised as such.'[32] With the concurrence of Maisky in London about the advisability against the Soviet group travelling *en masse*, an advance party of sixteen arrived in Durban by flying boat at the end of May 1942 to establish the first Soviet embassy in Africa.

The Soviet diplomats posted to the Union were surprisingly inactive during the war. For all of Smuts' and Maisky's pronouncements about the need for allied unity, there was very little expression of this in the relationship between South Africa and the Soviet Union. The large staff of the Pretoria embassy (numbering nearly forty-five, including dependants) led a particularly insular life, rarely venturing outside the fortress-like Soviet domicile at 496 Lanham Street. Forsyth, in his capacity as Secretary of External Affairs, only met with the Soviet Consul-General on rare occasions, and Russian diplomatic personnel seldom came into the Ministry of External Affairs.[33] In addition, the consular service provided by the Soviet Union was used only infrequently; apart from a group of medical personnel who travelled to Russia to assist the severely overburdened Soviet Red Cross, few South Africans journeyed to the USSR.[34]

The Soviets did host gala receptions complete with the finest Russian caviar and champagne during the 1940s which were highly regarded by the diplomatic community in South Africa and well attended by the liberal English-speaking population. These parties were often multiracial, to the dismay of the authorities, and prominent communists such as Abram Fischer, who was then a member of the Central Committee of the CPSA, were also present.

Outside of social functions, the Soviets were primarily interested in enemy ship movements in the South Atlantic and proved diligent in obtaining information of allied shipping losses.[35] A Soviet diplomatic courier made the trip from Cape Town to Pretoria nearly every week carrying information of lend–lease shipments to the USSR and news of recent U-boat sinkings.[36] However, there was no Union policy concerning the exchange of information with the Soviet authorities and each Russian request for shipping and military data was dealt with on an *ad hoc* basis. The Soviet Union had no military attaché stationed in Pretoria, and when the USSR required information concerning the naval war in the South Atlantic theatre, Soviet diplomats would first approach the British Foreign Office. The reasons for this were that the lines of communication between Moscow and London were faster and more developed than those between Pretoria and Moscow, and it was presumed by Soviet officials (correctly) that the Foreign Office had access to military intelligence which South Africa did not.

On 27 September 1943, Consul-General Demianov informed the authorities in Pretoria that he was returning to the Soviet Union. In his stead, the People's Commissariat of Foreign Affairs appointed Ivan Kornilovich Ziabkin.[37] Not long after his arrival, Ziabkin addressed a meeting of the SAFSU and toasted the recent Russian victories at Odessa, Tarnopol and in the Crimea.[38] However, despite the public celebrations of allied unity, it was during this period that the first hints of discord between South Africa and the USSR became apparent in their tenuous wartime alliance. The Soviet consulate lodged a series of complaints with the Ministry of External Affairs expressing their displeasure with the civilian and police guards which patrolled the grounds of the Soviet mission. Although the patrols appear to have been established initially to protect the Soviet embassy personnel rather than to observe their activities, the initiative was greeted with distrust by the Soviet authorities and the brusque Russian response helped to engender anti-Russian sentiment among officials in Pretoria.[39]

While 1944 saw a series of allied victories on every front, the final year of the war in Europe also brought a deterioration in relations between the Soviet Union and the Western democracies. The debate over German reparations and boundaries, differing views about eastern Europe's political future, the question of the appropriate French role in any new world order, and the many issues arising from the proposed creation of a powerful new international organisation, all posed thorny obstacles to further collaboration.[40] Indeed, as the allied armies converged on Germany from east and west, these several issues, still unresolved even after fruitful allied consultation at Tehran and Dumbarton Oaks, loomed ominously on the horizon promising a future rift in relations. This climate of misunderstanding, ill-feeling and suspicion had a discernible impact on both South Africa's external relations and on the heightening domestic debate about the nature of the threat posed by communism. Specifically, events in Europe caused a noticeable worsening in the already cool relations between the USSR and South Africa and added to the resurgent Nationalist Party's strident anti-communist campaign.

The growing tensions in Europe furnished the Nationalists with much grist for their mill. Eric Louw, who later was to become South Africa's first Minister of External Affairs, demanded in Parliament to know the present status of the Soviet legation in South Africa. Louw contended that the government had been negligent in its responsibility to monitor the activities of the Russian diplomats in Pretoria and Cape Town. Smuts, seeking to gain further details of the history of allied relations with the USSR so as to allay criticism of the Union's policy towards the Soviet Union, urgently requested information regarding Britain's decision to sever relations with Russia in 1927.[41] Forsyth cabled Smuts in Cape Town informing him that Great Britain broke off diplomatic contacts with the USSR 'on the grounds of alleged military espionage, subversive propaganda in the United Kingdom itself and in British overseas territories carried out by the personnel of certain Russian firms, the Russian Communist Party and the Third International and abuses of diplomats' privileges with the object of interfering in the domestic affairs of the United Kingdom in contravention of the Anglo–Russian Trade Agreement of 16 March 1921'.[42] Smuts and his Union government could do little more than watch the anti-communist movement gain momentum in South Africa.

There is evidence to suggest that Smuts himself came to regard the official Soviet presence in the Union with some trepidation, particularly because of the strong rallying point it provided Nationalist organisers, but it was not until the San Francisco Conference in April 1945 that he openly admitted his doubts about Soviet willingness to cooperate in the post-war world.[43] Smuts attended a number of wartime conferences, including several meetings of the British War Cabinet, and the allied plenary in San Francisco was his final important appearance on the international scene. The conference dealt mainly with the drafting of the United Nations Charter and Stalin dispatched Molotov to San Francisco (Stalin had initially appointed a lesser official from the Ministry of Foreign Affairs, the young Andrei Gromyko, to head the Soviet delegation). Molotov came to the conference hostile and suspicious and surrounded by a formidable bodyguard. His insistence on the right to exercise the veto, his demand for recognition of the Lublin Polish government, and his generally intransigent attitude created an unpleasant impression among many of the participants, including Smuts. Smuts saw too much evidence of an absence of cooperation and of seeds of discord to be optimistic about the future of the wartime alliance.

The last three years of Smuts' Union government, 1945–8, were marked by an increasing isolation of the Soviet embassy and its personnel. Meetings of the South African Friends of the Soviet Union became less frequent (their offices were now subject to searches by police), and the Soviets were far less active socially. Political relations also deteriorated after the abrupt termination of lend–lease in August 1945 and the decline of allied shipping to the Soviet Union around the Cape. Ziabkin returned to Moscow in March 1945 and was replaced by D. K. Afansiev.[44] Afansiev was in Pretoria just over a year before giving place to P. S. Atroshenko, who was to hold the post until August 1949.[45] Atroshenko arrived in South Africa to a far more hostile reception than his predecessor Demianov had four years before.

IV

The 1948 election which brought the Nationalists to power was decided largely on domestic concerns, but there were a number of external issues which received considerable attention.[46] Of these, the question of South African participation in the United Nations, the republic versus self-governing dominion debate, and the issue of communism in the Union were doubtless the most important, and the latter has particular relevance to this study.

Dr Malan and his associates seized on the issue of communist activity in the Union with renewed vigour and effectively used it to rally the *laager* to the Nationalist party. Malan decried in Parliament the Union government's lax attitude toward the Soviet presence in the Union and warned that Russian propaganda was more effective in South Africa than in other Western countries because 'we have here a large non-European population susceptible to Communist influences . . .'[47] On the same occasion, Louw commented in a similar vein that 'the Russian Consulate has one of the biggest staffs of any consulate . . . in South Africa, except that of the USA . . . what is the Russian Consulate doing here with such a large staff numbering twenty or more? Only £8 worth of trade, no subjects in the country – what are they doing in South Africa?'[48] Smuts responded by asserting that South Africa did indeed have 'a small Communist Party, in itself so small and insignificant that it means nothing as a party'.[49] Afrikanerdom rejected Smuts' appraisal of the threat posed by communism and embraced the Nationalist party's warnings of Soviet expansionist aims in Africa. Accordingly, the Nationalists surged to power in the 1948 election with the promise to expel the Soviet legation from South Africa.

Events in the United States and Canada during the late 1940s and early 1950s reinforced the already dominant anti-communist consensus in South Africa. The Cold War had come into full force in American politics. The communist victory in China energised the right wing of the Republican Party, and anti-communist hysteria was rife. While the Truman administration only warned of the dangers of communist subversion in other countries, several congressional committees made fantastic allegations of widespread communist subversion within the United States. Senator Joseph McCarthy went so far as to declare that the State Department and Army were filled with communists.[50] In Canada, a Royal Commission Report concerning the activities of Soviet diplomats in the country concluded with a warning about Russian espionage and the existence of a powerful NKVD organisation in Canada. Both the Royal Commission Study and the many reports of the House of Representatives Committee on Un-American Activities received wide coverage in the South African media and during Parliamentary debates.[51]

The newly elected Nationalist government first approached the United States for information about Soviet activity in South Africa in April 1948. Subsequently, the American embassy in Pretoria provided the Ministry of External Affairs and the CID of South African police with information pertaining to individuals and organisations suspected of subversive activities.[52] American leaders shared South African fears about Soviet world ambitions and this kind of collaboration seems all the more plausible given the alignment of worldviews among leaders in Washington and Pretoria. The Nationalists also set up an Executive Committee on coming to power to investigate communist activity in the Union which ultimately led to the state adopting the Suppression of Communism Act in 1950. This piece of legislation effectively outlawed the Communist Party and severely curtailed the activities of numerous radical organisations within the Union.[53]

Despite the Nationalists' bold initiatives in domestic affairs, the foreign policy of South Africa changed little in the immediate years following their 1948 election victory. The Nationalist Party was committed to a domestic policy of apartheid, but beyond a desire to withdraw from the Commonwealth and declare a Republic, Malan and his advisers came to power without a foreign policy agenda. Indeed, the Nationalist leaders were unprepared to handle the External Affairs portfolio with the foresight and adroitness that Smuts had exercised. Dr Malan had little expertise in the realm of foreign policy and depended heavily on the advice of D. D. Forsyth, who was asked to stay on as Secretary of External Affairs.[54] Eric Louw, the Minister of Economic Affairs in Malan's cabinet, also exerted a notable influence on the formulation of South African foreign policy from the very inception of Nationalist power. His most important role in this regard was in connection with the Union's relations with the Soviet Union.

Soon after the 1948 election, Malan's cabinet convened for a two-day session to discuss the whole question of South African policy towards the Soviet Union. Several sources cited Dr Malan as having 'communicated his decision to end formal diplomatic relations with the USSR to Mr Ernest Bevin at the British Foreign Office – not with a view to obtaining his approval but simply to maintain inter-Dominion agreement on Soviet policy'.[55] The Foreign Office apparently urged restraint, particularly after the recent crisis over Berlin, but officials at the Soviet consulate expected a breach in relations and were reportedly packed and ready to leave at short notice, in anticipation of their recall. However, despite the great clamour within the ranks of the Nationalist Party for government action to expel the Russian diplomats from the Union, no such action was taken at that time.

The South Africans did, however, continue their bellicose public denouncements of the USSR and the Soviet presence in Afrikanerdom. Eric Louw told an election meeting at Middleburg in the Transvaal during March 1949 that 'it had been established that thousands of communistic pamphlets being distributed among the natives in the Belgian Congo had emanated from the Soviet Consulate in Pretoria', and that the consulate was the centre for a 'communist propaganda campaign in Southern Africa'.[56] In reference to this alleged dissemination of material in the Belgian Congo, and to the claim that the Soviet legation was the focal point of a communist propaganda drive, Consul-General Atroshenko commented that 'what happened outside the Union, in the Belgian Congo or anywhere else, did not concern his office'.[57] Subsequently, in a prepared statement countering Louw's allegations, Atroshenko declared that these were 'nothing else but sheer fabrication'.[58] He further contended that the Soviet government was anxious to promote healthy economic relations between their two countries, and that South Africa could import many things from Russia, particularly machinery.[59]

The evidence suggests that there was no direct link between the Soviet consulate in Pretoria and local communist activity in the Congo such as Louw had asserted. Apparently, Louw received information while in Paris from an official he described as 'a prominent member of the Belgian delegation', that communist propaganda distributed in the Congo 'came from Pretoria'.[60] The young Arnaud de Borchgrave gave credence to this assertion with his article in the *New York Herald Tribune* concerning a study, shown to him by the same official, which dealt with 'Soviet methods of infiltration, agitation, propaganda, espionage and sabotage in the Congo'.[61] However, the South African Consul-General in Leopoldville, D. C. Marais van der Merwe, cabled Pretoria that:

the report from Brussels referred to an article supplied to the *New York Times* by Andre Moyen, who was very active in the resistance movement during the war and has since been a private detective in no way connected with the Belgian Security Service. His statements are incorrect and the Belgian Congo authorities have ignored the report. There is no Soviet Consulate in Brazzaville (contrary to a claim made in the report) and they give a little credence to his allegations against the USSR Consulate-General in Pretoria as to his statements concerning French equatorial Africa.[62]

Thus, Atroshenko's comments appear to reflect accurately the consulate's stated position of non-involvement *vis-à-vis* the Congo.

The South African Bureau of Police Affairs also launched an investigation into alleged links between Consul-General Atroshenko and Solly Sachs, who had been expelled from the Communist Party on a directive from Moscow in 1931. Sachs was the leader of the powerful Garment Workers' Union until 1952. The aim of the Police Commission was to establish evidence linking the Soviet legation to several strikes staged by the Garment Workers in 1948 and 1949. However, the report concluded that the only eye-witness of supposed meetings between Atroshenko and Sachs was described as 'old, illiterate, and apparently had a wild imagination'. The Ministry of External Affairs concluded grudgingly that 'the Police do not seem to have obtained any reliable information to show that Atroshenko acted improperly'.[63] Atroshenko's tenure as Consul-General saw the complete deterioration of relations between Moscow and Pretoria and on his departure from the Union in 1949 he merely commented: 'I have spent three years in South Africa, during which time I have become acquainted with your country and with the problems which are facing it'. He concluded with only a brief reference to 'some political difficulties and prejudices which exist in this country toward my country'.[64]

Regardless of the accuracy of reports emanating from Brussels, Pretoria or the Congo, the 'evidence' of Soviet wrongdoing was considered irrefutable by Nationalist leaders.[65] Officials in Pretoria took further steps to improve the surveillance of Soviet diplomatic personnel in the Union.[66] In addition, the Nationalist government moved to restrict any expansion of commercial contacts between South Africa and the Soviet Union. The Soviet Ministry of Foreign Affairs approached Pretoria in June 1950 about the possibility of appointing L. A. Afansiev to be the Soviet Commercial Attaché in South Africa. Forsyth replied tersely that, 'as trade between the Union and Russia is negligible and there is little prospect for an increase it is considered that no good purpose would be served by appointment of a Commercial Attaché'.[67] South Africa also rejected the nomination of B. I. Karavaev to head the Soviet legation in the Union after the departure of Atroshenko from Pretoria in August

1949.[68] Consequently, the post remained vacant with the Vice-Consul, A. A. Hrypunov, serving as the ranking official until 1952 when he was promoted to Consul-General.

The Russian consulate 'reminded one of a monastery' during the final four years of Soviet representation in the Union (1952–6), remarked a former high-ranking South African diplomat.[69] South African newspapers, both English and Afrikaans, were filled with dire warnings of the activities of Soviet agents within the African trade unions and among the underground communist party organisers.[70] By this time any trade union organisation or radical political agitation was synonymous with Soviet world revolutionary activity in the minds of many South African leaders. However, the staff at the Soviet embassy had been severely reduced to only two resident diplomats with a very modest support staff. How these few diplomats could play such a damaging role in South African politics was never fully explained by the Nationalists. During these final years, the Soviet representatives took virtually no part in the social life of Pretoria and rarely approached government officials in Pretoria about political matters. The Russian Whaling Fleet in the Antarctic set anchor briefly in Cape Town on several occasions during the early 1950s, and the factory-vessel *Slava* often carried official material from the consulate in South Africa on its return voyages from the southern oceans.[71] N. V. Ivanov was appointed Consul-General in November 1955, and he presided over the closing of the Soviet embassy in 1956.[72]

V

Eric Louw was appointed the first Minister of External Affairs in 1955 during Strijdom's term as Prime Minister, and one of his first official acts was to expel the residing Soviet legation from South Africa. Citing that Soviet diplomats had 'cultivated and maintained contact with subversive elements in the Union, particularly among the Bantu and Indian population' and that the consulate had 'served as a channel of communication between such elements and the authorities of Soviet Russia', Louw informed Parliament that the consular representation of the USSR was to be discontinued from 1 February 1956.[73] This move was part of a government anti-communist campaign which would culminate in the Treason Trial beginning later in 1956. The news came as a surprise to no one, and the Soviets quietly vacated their residence and returned to the USSR. Indeed, the only question was why the Nationalists had waited eight years to fulfil their 1948 election promise.

This reticence to act can, in part, be ascribed to the lack of experience of the Nationalist party in foreign affairs. It was not until Louw received the Foreign Minister's portfolio that South Africa began to move away from its dominion status within the Commonwealth and to assert itself more forcefully in international politics. Also, the 1955 Simonstown Accord with Britain allayed fears of political isolation and gave South African leaders the reassurance to discharge the Soviet Consul-General of his duties in the Union. In addition, the earlier decisions taken by Australia and Canada to curtail their relations with the Soviet Union no doubt encouraged the Nationalists to request Ivanov's withdrawal.[74]

Thus, the period of diplomatic relations between the Soviet Union and South Africa, 1942–56, came to a close. However, despite the loss of a diplomatic foothold in southern Africa, a new era in Soviet policy-making towards the Third World was underway. With the death of Stalin and ascendance of Khrushchev, the USSR began in earnest in 1955 to court the newly independent nations of Asia and Africa. Soviet leaders overcame the barrier Western diplomacy sought to interpose by the Baghdad Pact of Middle East nations and, with military and economic assistance, established an official presence in Egypt. Heads of State of India, Syria and Iran visited Moscow, and in the latter part of 1955 Khrushchev and Bulganin made an unprecedented and much publicised tour of India, Burma and Afghanistan. In addition, the USSR also began to play a more active role towards the new Third World nations in the United Nations and Soviet foreign aid was made available to several Afro-Asian states. Soviet political commentators followed developments in Algeria, Libya, Tunisia, Morocco and the Sudan during the latter part of the 1950s. Nevertheless, it should be noted that Soviet interest in sub-Sahara Africa was substantially lower compared with Soviet concern regarding the North African countries.[75] It was not until the wave of national independence swept across Black Africa in the early 1960s that Soviet leaders turned their attention more fully towards the former colonies of sub-Saharan Africa.

VI

How then can we explain the initial Soviet diplomatic foray into South Africa in 1942? The period of official relations with South Africa should be considered as an anomaly in the context of Soviet foreign policy towards Africa. The diplomatic, trade and to a degree the propaganda relations with South Africa during the 1940s and 1950s serve as the exception to Soviet policy towards the rest of the continent. Although the higher level of Soviet activity in South Africa is clear, there is an apparent contradiction between Soviet support for colonial revolution and the USSR's desire to establish friendly state-to-state relations. That the USSR acted simultaneously as a revolutionary and conservative power during this period complicates and discourages the search for an adequate definition of Soviet policy. Nevertheless, a few observations can be made concerning the nature of official Soviet policy in South Africa.

The establishment of diplomatic contacts had its genesis exclusively in the wartime alliance between South Africa and the Soviet Union. The South African Communist Party, on orders from the Comintern, was instructed to aid the war effort by campaigning for South African recognition of the USSR. After the dissolution of the Comintern in 1943, presumably as a gesture to the allies, the Soviet Union placed greater emphasis on state-to-state relations, and party relations temporarily declined in importance. A corollary to this shift was the increased interest shown in upgrading commercial contacts with South Africa. South Africa, possessing the most developed and diversified economy on the African continent, was a potential market for Soviet exports. In 1949, Soviet Consul-General Atroshenko approached officials in Pretoria about the possibility of an extension of trade between South Africa and the USSR.[76] Atroshenko proposed that the Soviet Union should send farm machinery to South Africa in exchange for certain raw materials. He also suggested the formation of a bilateral trade agreement which would allow these exchanges to be made on a barter basis.[77] Although Atroshenko's appeal was rebuffed, this initial move to increase Soviet commerce in South Africa preceded Soviet efforts to expand trade on the rest of the continent by five years. In addition, the Soviet leadership in the post-Stalin period focused on developing economic contacts in Africa as a prelude to broader political interaction.[78] However, in the case of South Africa, commercial contacts followed political initiatives.

Perhaps the explanation for the extraordinary nature of Soviet policy in South Africa lay in the fact that healthy official relations with the white regime were of greater importance than furthering the emancipation of the oppressed population. Indeed, it was not until 1950 with the Suppression of Communism Act that Soviet efforts to improve trade with South Africa were discontinued. Only after the deterioration in official relations did the USSR become a strident advocate of national liberation in South Africa. For instance, despite arguments to the contrary, there is little evidence which links the Soviet consulate to Communist Party functionaries or to the increase in trade union activity during the period of official relations. The consulate might have played a more active role in Khrushchev's bold Third World policy had the Soviets been allowed to stay beyond 1956. As it was, the South Africans terminated relations before the Soviet Union became involved actively in southern Africa.

This examination of official Soviet policy towards South Africa suggests a 'dual policies' approach to the diplomatic and propaganda spheres of Soviet foreign policy.[79] For example, while Soviet representatives at the United Nations criticised South Africa for its treatment of the Indian population, Soviet diplomats in Pretoria tried to negotiate a trade agreement with Union officials. After the onset of the Second World War, the well-being of the non-European population was clearly not of primary importance to the Soviet leadership in comparison with their zeal to establish relations with South Africa. The USSR has fervently advocated contradictory goals in South Africa, promoting diplomatic relations and trade while at the same time fomenting revolutionary change. Here, there is a good parallel with Soviet–German relations at the time the Nazis were eliminating the German Communist Party (KPD).[80] Soviet policy has always, whatever the ideological justification, served Soviet national interests, and the needs of the Soviet state have an absolute priority over any needs of foreign communism. In this, it was normal rather than extraordinary for the USSR to sacrifice revolutionary causes to short-term Soviet interests. Thus, a wartime alliance with South Africa was deemed useful by Soviet leaders for political and commercial reasons, and the Comintern diatribes against the white regime were temporarily replaced by appeals for communists to assist allied governments with the war effort.

Finally, it must be stressed that South Africa was not of great importance to the USSR during the period of official relations, despite the large contingent of Soviet officials stationed in Pretoria.

This is evident merely from examination of the Soviet diplomatic personnel assigned to South Africa. Apart from Ivanov and Karavaev, Russian officials appointed to South Africa had little diplomatic experience and their command of English was generally poor. In contrast, the recent ascendancy of southern Africa in Soviet policy is manifested by the high quality of diplomats posted to South Africa's neighbouring states. Recent ambassadorial appointments, such as Vladimir Cherednik in Zambia, Georgi Ter-Gazaryants in Zimbabwe, Valentin Vdovnin in Mozambique, and Nikolai Petrov in Botswana, illustrate this point.[81] The Soviet Union did not attach great significance to South Africa during the 1942–56 period; it was only after the Soviet legation departed from the Union that southern Africa began to play a more prominent role in the formulation and execution of Soviet foreign policy.

4 The Soviet Union, South Africa and the United Nations

The USSR has consistently supported, in the United Nations and in direct contact with the liberation movement, the struggle of the South African people against the apartheid regime. (Edwin Ogbu, Chairman of the United Nations Special Committee Against Apartheid, 1975)

The UN has been fully subverted by the Soviet Union. (Eric Louw, South African Minister for External Affairs, 1956)

The Soviet Union will continue to pursue a principled anti-apartheid policy at the United Nations. (Vladilen M. Vasev, Head of Third Africa Department, Soviet Ministry of Foreign Affairs, 23 April 1984, Moscow)

I

The Soviet Union has played a major role in the long-standing debate in the United Nations concerning the racial policies of the South African government. The issue of apartheid has offered the Soviet representatives to the world organisation an excellent opportunity to express their country's support for the national liberation movement of southern Africa and to draw attention to the gulf existing between Western and Black African policies toward the region. (Apartheid is one of the few issues on which there is now complete pan-African solidarity; therefore, it is appropriate to refer to Black Africa, or the Third World in general, as acting in unison on the South African issue at the UN.) If the question of South Africa has had a divisive influence on North–South relations, so too has it proven to be an important determinant in the formulation of Soviet policy in the Third World. Whether the Soviet Union has been successful in gaining influence in Africa by virtue of its prominent position in the anti-apartheid movement in the UN and whether Soviet activity in the world body has exacerbated the already strained relations between the West and the Third World over South Africa, are the subjects of this examination of the USSR's anti-apartheid policy at the United Nations.

This issue will be examined within the context of Soviet policy towards the Third World, because the question of apartheid in South Africa is intrinsically related to Soviet policy toward the Afro–Asian states. For this reason, careful attention will be given to the evolution of Soviet perceptions of the Third World in general and Black Africa in particular. While many South African policies have received considerable scrutiny from the United Nations – such as the treatment of Indians and the dispute over South West Africa – this study will focus on the issue of apartheid, as conflict over the former policies is due essentially to the existence of the latter.[1] To this extent, questions relating to Namibia and to Indian discrimination in South Africa will be addressed only in so far as these relate to the central issue of apartheid.[2] Further, it would be difficult to fathom Soviet behaviour in the UN concerning apartheid without a general understanding of the formation of Soviet attitudes and expectations about the appropriate role of the United Nations. For this reason, the enquiry will begin with a review of Soviet involvement in the world institution since its founding, concentrating on the increase in importance of the Third World and the corresponding rise in prominence of the anti-apartheid issue in Soviet foreign policy.

II

In general, the Soviet Union is selective in its support of, and participation in, international organisations. Multilateral institutions that exhibit a balanced international distribution of actors are organisations in which the USSR will actively participate.[3] Those perceived to be dominated by capitalist states, regardless of their claim to be supra-national, are either ignored, attacked or obstructed.[4] For example, the Soviet view of the League of Nations prior to 1934 was that of an organisation whose members were implacable foes of the USSR. The increase in Soviet participation in the United Nations after 1954 coincided with the emergence of new states on the international scene which shared an anti-Western predilection with the USSR. These non-aligned nations were judged by the Soviet leadership to be autonomous in their relations to their former colonial rulers and thus potential allies of the Soviet Union. However, the period of the most strident Soviet activism at the United Nations following 1956 was preceded by a decade of Russian involvement which was characterised by defensive and obstructionist policies.

Soviet participation in the United Nations has historically been motivated by a desire to prevent Western mobilisation of the world body against the USSR. During the early years of UN activity, the Soviet Union could depend on the support of only five members: Byelorussia, Ukraine, Poland, Yugoslavia and Czechoslovakia. With the socialist states in the numerical minority, Soviet perceptions of international organisations in the late 1940s and early 1950s were conditioned by a negative appraisal of the potential effectiveness of these institutions during a period of capitalist predominance. Owing to this minority position, the Soviet view of the UN was that its single important task was the preservation of peace and security.[5] More-over, the initial Soviet attitude was that UN operations should not be concerned with the promotion of international cooperation in dealing with economic and social problems.[6] Though the structural conditions during this period did not favour Soviet ambitions, Stalin considered that it was better to be inside the United Nations than to be outside and thus denied its world forum. Participation at least offered the possibility of forging defensive alliances based on common interests. However, at the height of the Cold War when the United States successfully manoeuvred to bypass the veto for UN action in Korea, Stalin might have recalled Lenin's warnings of the dangers of international organisations controlled by capitalists.[7] As Alexander Dallin observed, 'It is the problem of a state with a 'two-camp' world view trying to operate in a 'one world' organization'.[8]

Despite the many hazards, the Soviet leadership endeavoured to use the United Nations as a forum where competition between the two blocs could remain within the confines of 'peaceful coexistence'. The USSR attempted to protect their precarious position in the UN during the 1945–55 period by insisting on strict interpretation of those Charter provisions which protected minority rights. The veto in the Security Council provided the Soviet Union with an instrument to achieve this goal. For instance, the Soviet contention that the United Nations should not aspire to supra-national status reflected the defensive nature of Russian policy-making.[9] To the Soviet leaders, an enlargement of UN powers would mean at best a reinforcement of the *status quo*, and at worst a potential violation of Soviet security. As Inis Claude aptly surmised: 'The urge to enlarge the functions and powers of an international agency is characteristic of a majority mentality; the demands for restriction and inhibition, the outlook of a minority.'[10] Supra-nationalism during the Cold War years was considered to be an ominous threat to state sovereignty and, when invoked by Western representatives at the United Nations, to be a euphemism for outside intervention in Soviet affairs.

Given this apprehension of the perils associated with international organisations, it is little wonder that the Soviet Union had no Third World policy to speak of during their first decade at the UN. In the conditions of a divided world, the participation of smaller nations and Afro–Asian states in multilateral institutions was viewed with distrust by Soviet leaders. Stalin's own suspicions of colonial politics, partly due to his personal association with the ill-fated partnership between the Chinese Communist Party and the Kuomintang, caused him to regard the emerging Third World actors as merely 'bourgeois nation-alists', who were often dominated by wealthy capitalist states.[11] Nevertheless, Soviet representatives at the UN sought to exploit differences between the developed West and the newly independent territories of Asia and Africa by taking anti-Western stands on colonial issues. For instance, the Soviet Union condemned South African racial discrimination from the outset and supported the Indonesian independence movement. The Soviet Union and its East European allies denounced Great Britain in its quarrels with Sudan and Egypt and assailed French policies in Morocco, Syria and Lebanon.[12] This is not to say that the Soviet Union had no particular affinity for the fledgling Third World states, but rather that Soviet voting behaviour on Afro–Asian issues during this period was defensive and anti-Western in its inspiration.

Some suggest there were signs of Stalin himself rejecting the 'two-camp' thesis as early as 1952,[13] but it was not until after the emergence of Khrushchev as his undisputed successor in 1955 that the USSR began to play a more forceful role in the United Nations. At the Twentieth Congress of the CPSU in February 1956, Khrush-chev declared that because Soviet power was capable of deterring capitalist aggression, and because of the destructive nature of mod-ern warfare, the 'capitalist encirclement had been overcome'. For Khrushchev, this profound change in the balance of power in favour of the 'world camp of socialism' would encourage a rapid acceleration in the liberation of colonial peoples and offer new hope to national liberation movements.[14] Having previously launched a new foreign aid programme with a tour of developing countries in 1955, Khrushchev told the Party Congress of the gaining strength of the anti-imperialist movement in Latin America and of the recent victories of the progressive forces in Asia and Africa. An important publication on the Soviet role in the UN subsequently declared that 'profound changes took place in the United Nations Organization between 1957 and 1960, attesting to the fact that a new era in its history had begun'. Building on Khrushchev's thesis it further asserted that these changes, 'resulting from the admission into the UN of a large group of new members and, consequently, a serious shift of the balance of forces inside it', gave the Soviet Union the opportunity 'to place before the UN new tasks for which the objective conditions of their solution had now appeared'.[15]

The most prominent change in the UN after 1955 was the increase in membership of the Afro–Asian states which suggested a new distribution of influence in the world body. Between 1956 and 1966, forty-six new members were admitted to the United Nations. Of this group, thirty-four were African states and six were Asian. Hence, Africa became more salient to the USSR as more African states gained independence and joined the UN, and these new states precipitated a shift in Soviet attitudes. Indeed, the increasing Soviet activity in the organisation during this period suggests a realisation of the importance of these new actors in international politics. The USSR endeavoured to exploit 'the emerging anti-colonial consensus in the UN' and spoke out frequently against the evils of apartheid.[16] The traditional Soviet concern for sovereign equality and its opposition to supra-nationalism did not stop them from supporting General Assembly legislation calling for UN intervention in the domestic affairs of South Africa. After the reorientation of Soviet foreign policy in 1955, the USSR has consistently voted with the Afro–Asian bloc on issues related to colonialism and has tended 'to vote with the African group' more often than any Western power.[17] In addition, remarks made by Soviet representatives at the UN were frequently in support of Third World initiatives and resolutions. Thus, the USSR began to find itself voting more frequently than not with the winning coalition on anti-colonial legislation.

In response to the demands of the new Third World majority during this period, the USSR began to undertake more ambitious initiatives at the UN rather than merely criticising Western policies.

Unhampered by previous colonial interests in Africa, not interdependent with unpopular states such as South Africa, and with a model of rapid social and economic development attractive to many Third World elites, the Soviet delegates in the committees and agencies of the UN sought to identify themselves with anti-colonialism and anti-imperialism.[18] The Soviet Union also altered many of its positions characteristically associated with its earlier defensive diplomacy. The most pertinent example relevant to this study is the Soviet Union's flexible interpretation of the Charter concerning the issue of apartheid.[19] Due to deadlock in the Security Council on the question of implementing UN resolutions calling for collective action against South Africa, Soviet representatives have inferred that General Assembly predominance would be appropriate under certain circumstances. The principle of the 'rule of the majority', previously attacked and berated by the USSR as being patently unfair to the socialist community in the numerical minority, was sanctioned as an effective means of eradicating the last vestiges of colonialism in southern Africa.

The Soviet zeal for participation in the UN was not limited to support of Third World political objectives, such as the abolition of apartheid, but extended to issues of multilateral aid and economic development. Reversing Stalin's policy of non-participation in United Nations specialised agencies, the USSR re-entered the United Nations Economic Scientific and Cultural Organisation (UNESCO) and the International Labour Organisation (ILO) in 1954. Indeed, one of the most significant results of Khruschchev's abandonment of the 'two-camp' thesis was a more flexible approach to participation in UN agencies. While there were earlier indications of this change in Soviet attitudes, affiliation with the Expanded Programme for Technical Assistance (EPTA), the Special United Nations Fund for Economic Development (SUNFED), and the Economic Commission for Asia and the Far East (ECAFE) being cases in point,[20] it was not until the advent of Khrushchev that a notable reorientation of Soviet policy was apparent. This shift in policy culminated in the USSR's dramatic presentation in 1960 at the General Assembly, in its demand for increased representation on the UN committees, and in its call for greater participation in the social and economic agencies of the world body.

However, the period from 1960 was marked by several setbacks in Soviet foreign policy outside the UN which served to weaken

Khrushchev's position within the Politburo. The failure of the 1960 summit, another Berlin crisis and the subsequent erection of the wall, the eruption of the Sino–Soviet split, and the Cuban missile crisis all contributed to his removal from power.

Khrushchev's colleagues were critical of the conduct of his foreign policy outside the United Nations, but his successors also had reason for misgivings about Soviet policies inside the organisation as well.[21] The new Soviet leadership considered that Khrushchev was overly optimistic in his perceptions of the Afro–Asian states, and Brezhnev ultimately adopted a less ambitious policy towards the Third World in the UN. In time it became apparent that Moscow took a more conservative view of prospects for an eventful Soviet–Third World alignment[22], and consequently a more pessimistic view of the United Nations. Where Khrushchev proclaimed enthusiastically in his 6 January 1961 speech to the General Assembly that without the growth of Soviet power 'there could have been no question of the abolition of colonialism',[23] Brezhnev observed six years later, in contrast, that the USSR had achieved less than satisfactory results in 'the task of developing cooperation with states that have already cast off the colonial yoke'.[24]

The reasons for the Soviet retrenchment in the United Nations can only be alluded to briefly here. The disappointment over the Congo affair no doubt contributed to a reappraisal of Soviet policies, but the primary motivation lay in the USSR's opposition to various organisational changes in the world body. The expansion of the United Nations' activities during the decade following 1956 was largely in response to the new Afro–Asian majority and the corresponding increase in expenditures was looked upon with growing displeasure by the new, more pragmatic, Soviet leadership. Behind this Soviet dissatisfaction was a fundamental rejection of the zero–sum interpretation of UN politics. Namely, a loss of Western influence in the Third World did not necessarily rebound in a corresponding gain in the Soviet position among the Afro–Asian states. As the demands of the Third World nations mounted for the enlargement of UN functions and spending, and Soviet delegates began objecting to these 'excessive' requests for multilateral aid, technical assistance and capital development funds, Khruschev's dream of consolidating a 'united front' with the developing countries was forsaken.

Despite evidence of an increasing divergence in Soviet–Third World views on economic and aid issues under consideration at the UN during the 1964–8 period,[25] there were also indications of a growing Soviet support for Third World positions on 'colonial' questions, and particularly on the question of apartheid in South Africa. The USSR began to play a more active role in the various committees dealing with South Africa and was more clearly associated with the anti-apartheid movement in the UN and in the Organisation of African Unity (OAU). An examination of the voting record in the period following 1963 reveals an increasing number of resolutions condemning South Africa, coupled with a high level of Soviet voting 'success' in these various roll calls. ('Success' here is defined as voting with the majority.) The present importance the Soviet Union attaches to the anti-apartheid movement is exemplified by its participation in a recent UN-sponsored 'International Conference on Sanctions Against South Africa'. The Soviet, Ukrainian and Byelorussian delegations, together numbering nearly fifty, were the largest in attendance, and these delegates played an active role in the plenary discussions and working groups.[26]

Of what significance is this apparent Soviet–Third World alliance on the issue of apartheid? To answer this question, it will be useful to trace the history of the apartheid question at the UN from the initial debate concerning discrimination against Indians in South Africa to the situation as it stands today. In so doing, particular attention will be given to the historical evolution and present nature of Soviet policy on the South African debate at the UN.

III

One of the bitterest, most acrimonious, and least soluble debates confounding the United Nations for nearly forty years has been the one concerning the racial policies of the South African government. In 1946 at the first meeting of the General Assembly, South Africa's Indian policy was fiercely criticised by the Indian and Soviet delegates. Soon after the election of the National Party government in 1948 a second issue – that of apartheid, or separation of the races – was included in the UN agenda.[27] Since 1962, the question of Indian discrimination and the racial legislation affecting the black population of South Africa have been combined into the single issue of apartheid in all its complexities. All discussion concerning South Africa in the United Nations during the 1940s and 1950s took place in the General Assembly. The Sharpeville shootings in 1960, and the subsequent uproar among the new African members in the world body, brought the conduct of South Africa to the attention of the Security Council for the first time.[28] In the aftermath of Sharpeville, the 1962 General Assembly requested member states to break off diplomatic and economic relations with South Africa and created a permanent Special Committee on Apartheid 'to keep the racial policies of the Government of South Africa under review'.[29] In 1968 the General Assembly acted again to establish the Unit on Apartheid, which publishes a wide range of literature on the socio-economic consequences of South Africa's racial practices. Meanwhile, in the wake of independence, newly liberated African states founded the Organisation of African Unity in 1963, which located its Liberation Committee headquarters in Dar-es-Salaam.

Black Africa's impact on the United Nations increased after 1963, and a sense of urgency was injected into the international diplomatic campaign to eradicate apartheid from the African continent. Soon after the establishment of the Liberation Committee, thirty-two African states called on the Security Council to consider the potentially explosive situation in the Republic. The Security Council subsequently adopted a resolution recommending that an arms embargo be instituted against South Africa (with only France and Britain abstaining).[30] The African states, dissatisfied with the slow progress towards a solution to the problem, called on the Permanent Members to initiate more assertive international action. In response, the Security Council unanimously adopted a Norwegian-sponsored resolution proposing the establishment of a Group of Experts.[31] The group, chaired by Alva Myrdal and with Sir Hugh Foot serving as Rapporteur, published its report in April 1964. In its most notable recommendation, the Group of Experts called on the Security Council to consider the logistics of economic sanctions and the implementation of sanctions in the event of South African recalcitrance to abolish apartheid. Nearly two decades later, the report stands as possibly the most important document on the relationship between the international community and South Africa.[32]

The United Nations, with the urging of the Black African states, continued its denunciations of South Africa throughout the late 1960s, and in 1973 the General Assembly adopted a resolution to form an International Convention on the Suppression and Punishment of the Crime of Apartheid, declaring apartheid to be a 'crime against humanity' and making individuals, organisations and states 'legally' responsible for the continuation of apartheid. By 1980, fifty-eight states, including the Soviet Union, had agreed to be bound by the convention.[33] Since 1974 the representatives of the South African government have not been allowed to participate in the plenary sessions of the General Assembly, while the African National Congress and the Pan-African Congress (ANC and PAC) have been granted observer status in both the Special Committee on Apartheid and in the plenary sessions. Following the World Conference for Action Against Apartheid held in 1977, the General Assembly reaffirmed in 1979 the legitimacy of waging armed struggle against the apartheid regime. In additon, the General Assembly has on numerous occasions adopted resolutions calling on the Security Council to embargo the sale of all military equipment to South Africa, institute mandatory economic sanctions and to generally take more effective action on the issue of apartheid. However, due to the veto power of the Permanent Members, the Security Council has gone no further than reaffirming its abhorrence of apartheid and racism – with one important exception. After the death of Steve Biko and the suppression of the Black Consciousness Movement, the Security Council in 1977 unanimously voted for an arms embargo against South Africa, citing Chapter 7 of the UN Charter.[34]

The fact that the Security Council resolution specifically made reference to Chapter 7 Article 41 is important in that it was the first time such action was taken against a member state. However, the race issue in South Africa had long posed some fundamental questions in connection with the UN Charter. The South African government has historically claimed that its racial policies are strictly a domestic concern and, therefore, outside United Nations jurisdiction under Article 2 of the Charter. The Black African states have consistently held that South Africa has flagrantly violated its human rights obligations stipulated in the Charter, and that the existence of apartheid serves to so affect and offend other states as to constitute a threat to international peace and security. Each position is based on fundamental Charter principles, but there is a growing consensus, outside a handful of Western nations, that South Africa is a profoundly destabilising influence on the whole of southern Africa.

This brief survey of the United Nations deliberation on the question of apartheid illustrates the shift in majority opinion in the world organisation from merely verbal criticism to strongly worded resolutions demanding severe measures involving diplomatic, economic and military sanctions.[35] Indeed, since 1946 there have been several hundred major resolutions adopted in the General Assembly and several in the Security Council condemning apartheid. In addition, the Soviet Union is the major provider of material assistance to the liberation forces in Southern Africa. Nevertheless, a systematic examination of the voting record on resolutions pertaining to South Africa indicates a more complex Soviet policy than that which initially emerges from the record of UN proceedings on the apartheid issue.

On the broad aspects of apartheid, the General Assembly resolutions can generally be characterised as falling within one of five groups, requesting:

(1) South Africa to modify its policies or face expulsion from the world body;
(2) the formulation of specific committees to study the South African problem, disseminate information about apartheid, and to make recommendations concerning an appropriate course of action;
(3) the Security Council to authorise economic and military sanctions against South Africa;
(4) the Security Council to take action by all appropriate means, including the possible use of peacekeeping forces, to apply pressure on the South African government;
(5) member states to provide moral and material assistance to the national liberation movement in South Africa.

A review of Soviet positions on each of these resolutions will give a further indication of Soviet policy in the apartheid debate.

IV

The USSR has been an active participant in the anti-apartheid movement in the United Nations and Soviet delegates have supported virtually every resolution calling for South Africa to reform its discriminatory racial policies or be excluded from the UN. These initiatives were favoured by the Soviet Union during the late 1940s and early 1950s when, deriving from differing interpretations of the Charter, many members regarded these resolutions as controversial. In 1960, it was Khrushchev's proposal which led to the adoption of the Declaration on the Granting of Independence to Colonial Peoples and Countries,[36] and Soviet representatives played an important role in the formulation of the International Convention on the Suppression and Punishment of the Crime of Apartheid.[37] The USSR also favoured the resolutions which established several of the specialised committees which deal either exclusively or in part with the racial policies of South Africa. Some of these include: the Special Committee on Apartheid, the Special Committee on the Granting of Independence to Colonial Peoples and Countries, the Ad Hoc Committee on Sport and Apartheid, and the UN Working Group on Human Rights in South Africa. Soviet delegates have served on all these various committees, often holding senior positions during the last thirty-five years. For instance, Dmitri Z. Manuilsky was the Chairman of the Political Committee in 1946 when India first raised the question of racialism in South Africa, and Vladimir Martynenko has served as the Vice-Chairman of the Special Committee on Apartheid for several years. The Unit on Apartheid has also published a number of studies on South Africa authored by Soviet scholars: Professor J. P. Blishchenko of the State Institute for International Relations and Dr. A. Pokrovsky of the Africa Institute have both contributed papers to the Unit.

In addition to action taken in the General Assembly, the Security Council has also created two trust funds: the United Nations Trust Fund for South Africa and the UN Educational and Training Programme for South Africa. These funds are intended to provide legal aid and educational assistance for refugees or persons arrested or displaced because of the apartheid laws of the South African government. The funds are modest in relation to need, but the Scandanavian countries have been especially generous with their financial donations.[38] The USSR abstained in the voting on both initiatives to create these funds and the contributions of the Soviet Union have been very modest. Soviet abstentions on resolutions calling for an expansion of UN economic and social programmes can be attributed partially to the hesitation about the financial implications of such undertakings; the USSR wants to keep UN programmes and budgets within specific limits.[39] The Soviets undoubtedly prefer bilateral to multilateral arrangements for dispensing aid, as bilateral disposition offers the opportunity to negotiate a *quid pro quo*. The Soviet tendency has been to give verbal support to the work of the specialised committees, while opposing efforts to enlarge their mandate or budget. Or as one UN delegate observed, the Soviet Union is often 'the first to criticize and the last to pay'.[40]

While the work of the special committees is important in relation to the proceedings of the General Assembly, Security Council action is preferable to Assembly decision if strong measures are ever to be applied against South Africa. The Charter is more explicit in granting the power to impose sanctions to the Council rather than to the Assembly, and many observers agree that sweeping economic and political sanctions against South Africa would be the most effective pressure which could be applied toward forcing a change in policy. The Soviet Union has been one of the most vociferous supporters of the imposition of military and economic sanctions against South Africa in the Security Council, and it is this issue which has proven most difficult for South Africa's major trading partners. These principal trade partners – Great Britain, the United States, France and West Germany – oppose the imposition of universal economic sanctions, and effective Security Council action is impossible without their cooperation. Annually, the Soviet Union either sponsors or supports a resolution in the General Assembly calling on the Security Council to authorise general mandatory sanctions against South Africa. Invariably, one of the Western powers must cast a negative vote in the Council to kill the initiative.

Before the Security Council resolution in 1963 calling on all states to place an embargo upon the sale of military equipment to South Africa, the Soviet representatives to the world body criticised the Western powers for providing military equipment to the white regime. The Soviet delegate to the Special Political Committee in 1962 observed that South Africa would be unable to carry on its abhorrent racial policies if it did not enjoy the support of the West. He also presented evidence indicating that a substantial portion of NATO shipments to South Africa consisted of arms and ammunition.[41] The Western powers were thus step by step isolated as the chief suppliers of military hardware to, as well as the primary investors in, South Africa. In the wake of African independence, and worried about the prospects of losing influence in the Third World, the West reluctantly accepted a ban on the sale of arms to South Africa in 1963. Admittedly, neither the United States nor any major Western European power was prepared to view the situation in South Africa as a threat to international peace and security or to support collective measures under Chapter 7 of the Charter. However, the decision to accept an embargo upon the sale of arms was seen by Black Africa as a significant victory, and the Soviet Union regarded it as a success as well.

Since the 1963 resolution forbidding the sale of arms to South Africa, Soviet delegates have frequently chastised the Western powers for their continued collaboration with the South African regime. In

1965, Mr Morozov, the Soviet delegate to the Special Committee, asserted that the responsibility for the continuance of apartheid lay with the major commercial partners of South Africa, who were also supplying military equipment in direct violation of the UN.[42] The Africa Institute in Moscow has on occasion provided information concerning embargo infractions to the Committee on Apartheid. In addition, the World Peace Council, an organisation funded substantially by the Soviet Union, has published a detailed study which cites several arms transactions between South Africa and the West.[43] The USSR has effectively used the United Nations as a forum to expose and berate the West for their aversion to impose and adhere to sanctions, and Soviet representatives have highlighted the military links between NATO and South Africa.

However, there are indications that the Soviet Union is not the ardent champion of economic sanctions it touts itself to be. The USSR abstained in the 1966 Security Council vote which committed the UN to economic and military sanctions against Rhodesia under Articles 42 and 43 of Chapter 7. The Security Council initiated this course of action after determining that the situation created by the Rhodesian rebellion constituted a threat to international peace.[44] The Soviet delegation was conspicuously mute on this first occasion of the United Nations taking enforcement action, and there is evidence to indicate that Soviet authorities later imported embargoed Rhodesian chrome in strict violation of UN protocol. Indeed, with respect to the sanction issue, the Soviet Union has preferred to use the UN as a political forum to denounce the West, rather than as a medium for enforcement action. This is possibly due to a recognition that sanctions could be used against the USSR.

The Soviet Union has also been cautious and hesitant to give its support to the deployment of UN peacekeeping forces in southern Africa during a period of crisis. Indeed, Soviet enthusiasm for the use of UN forces in Africa was soured after the experience of the Congo peacekeeping effort, ONUC, initiated by Secretary-General Dag Hammarskjold in 1960 (the acronym ONUC follows the French word order).[45] The Soviet Union, in fact, withdrew its forces from the ONUC in protest over the failure of the United Nations to recognise the legitimacy of then Prime Minister Patrice Lumumba. The USSR contended that the introduction of UN troops into the beleaguered country strengthened the position of the Belgian imperialists and served to reinforce an unjust *status quo*. When the Soviet leadership determined that Hammarskjold's policies in the Congo were harmful to Russian interests they mounted an attack on him personally and upon the office of Secretary-General (Soviet representatives at the UN were said to have privately referred to Hammarskjold as the 'Secretary-Generalissimo' during the Congo crisis).

Asserting that no man is 'neutral', Khrushchev demanded in the General Assembly that Hammarskjold resign and that the single office be modified to a 'troika', or three-member collective executive body representing the socialist, western and 'neutralist' groups of states. Under this arrangement the vital interests of each bloc would be effectively safeguarded by vesting each member of the 'troika' with veto powers. Thus, the arena for political struggle would be broadened to include the Secretariat, and the 'independent authority' of the Secretary-General would be abandoned.[46] Hammarskjold refused the Soviet initiative and the General Assembly, with the support of the newly independent African states, upheld his position with an overwhelming vote of confidence. Hammarkjold's use of African troops for ONUC no doubt helped him to secure vital African support in the United Nations.[47]

It is difficult to imagine a situation in which peacekeeping forces might be introduced into South Africa. The major powers represented on the Security Council use the United Nations when it is in their respective interests to do so. For instance, the United States operated through the UN on the issue of Korea, but declined offers of UN assistance in settling the war in Vietnam. The same observations can be made of the Soviet Union. For reasons appropriate to its own interests in the region, the USSR did not support UN action in the Congo. The Soviet Union has given full support to the OAU demand for an economic blockade against South Africa, but it has committed itself against sending a UN military force to wrest control of Namibia from South Africa.[48] A developing consensus between the superpowers concerning the possible deployment of UN peacekeeping forces in South Africa appears unlikely.

This lack of a mutual commitment for the use of UN forces is undoubtedly influenced by differing perceptions about the appropriate role and objectives of peacekeeping operations. The United States has historically viewed the introduction of these forces as a means to promote stability and thus prevent the spread of communism. To the USSR, UN peacekeeping operations have served as a convenient agency for the pacification of conflicts that have become uncontrollable and thus dangerous to Soviet interests. These positions reflect substantive differences in the superpowers' conceptions of the proper role of peacekeeping forces in promoting change in the *status quo*. The Soviets have tended to interpret the American recourse to multilateral agencies as either a cover for unilateral military intervention or an attempt to shore up repressive and unpopular regimes. In the Soviet view, the United States, while desiring to minimise conflict with the introduction of UN forces, discourages legitimate changes in the *status quo*. Thus, the Soviet leadership would be likely to reject a UN operation which poses a threat to the national liberation process. In addition to divergent views about the goals of these endeavours, the issue of operational control of peacekeeping efforts serves to further impede Soviet–American collaboration in employing the multilateral option. The USSR, as mentioned above, is uncomfortable with the 'independent authority' of the Secretary-General, and Soviet representatives in the General Assembly assert that the Secretary-General, if he is to have the authority to act, must by Charter definition be part of a system in which the Soviet Union has a veto over actions it disapproves.[49]

The questions arising from peacekeeping expenses also pose significant obstacles for future United Nations military operations and indeed threaten the stability and viability of the organisation. The Soviet Union, along with a number of other countries, refused to make a financial contribution to both the United Nations Emergency Force (UNEF) established in 1956 and the UN Congo operation. Attempts made by the Secretary-General to appraise the costs of these operations on the same basis as the regular assessments met with strong resistance from the USSR and France. The situation approached a crisis point in the 1964 General Assembly session when the United States embarked upon an ill-considered legal crusade over the principle of collective financial responsibility (a provision of Article 19 of the Charter) in an attempt to coerce the Soviet Union into paying peacekeeping costs.[50] Despite the serious financial crisis facing the United Nations, the Russian delegate in the Security Council refused to depart from the oft-stated Soviet position that expenditures for military operations should not be the subject of binding decisions.[51] Quite the contrary, Soviet diplomats stressed that curtailing the discretionary budgetary powers of the United Nations would serve to allow member states the option to decline to pay for operations not to their liking. Ultimately, the United Nations adopted a system of voluntary contributions, although many of the financial difficulties arising from UN peacekeeping operations remain unresolved.

Related to the question of assessment is, of course, the issue of the magnitude of the costs incurred by peacekeeping ventures. The total United Nations costs of the UNEF from 1956 to 1967 was approximately $200 million, and the cost of the ONUC from 1960 until its withdrawal in 1964 was in excess of $400 million.[52] Some observers have suggested that the financial crisis brought on by peacekeeping is not primarily the result of an incapacity of the members to pay, but rather a result of their unwillingness to do so.[53] However, while it is true that political factors play a major role in the Soviet refusal to pay operation costs, financial considerations are doubtless important. The USSR is loath to expend large amounts of hard-earned foreign currency when the potential political rewards are unlikely to merit the financial outlay. (Payments for UN peacekeeping must be made in an international currency; payment in roubles is unacceptable.) A project undertaken by the Carnegie Endowment in 1964 on the feasibility of implementing collective measures against South Africa included a cost analysis of a hypothetical blockade operation. Based on US experience during the Cuban naval quarantine of 1962, the study estimated that a force of 50 warships and 300 aircraft would be required, at a cost of approximately $27.6 million a month.[54] These projected costs, quite apart from the political or logistical problems, might possibly deter the Soviet leadership from participating in any large-scale UN operation in South Africa.

What possible circumstances might encourage the USSR to override these considerations and make a commitment to collective action through the United Nations? Certainly the Soviet Union would consider supporting a UN operation if a conflict developed in the region, the severity of which posed an imminent threat to world peace. The Soviets would have to be convinced, however, that neither they nor the United States would stand to gain from a violent racial conflict. Despite their rivalry for power and influence, the superpowers have a stake in the avoidance of a war in which they would be actively engaged on opposing sides. In the protocol covering the basic principles of relations agreed upon at the 1972 Moscow summit meeting, the USA and the USSR acknowledged their 'special responsibility' to avert conflicts or situations arising which serve to increase international tensions.[55]

Nevertheless, the potential for direct superpower military intervention in South Africa is very real, and it is likely that the Soviet Union or the United States would turn to the United Nations only as a final resort. There appears to be a consensus among the major powers that the UN will never again undertake an assignment so large and ambitious as the Congo operation.[56] With many issues such as the cost and control of UN missions yet unresolved, and with no apparent commitment among the Permanent Members of the Security Council to make improvements in the multilateral peacekeeping procedure, the prospects for future operations are dim.

The South African situation presents a further obstacle to any joint action in that the two superpowers envisage dramatically different futures for the Republic. The West is at least publicly committed to political reform, while the Soviet Union supports the national liberation of the oppressed population and the violent overthrow of the apartheid regime. It is foreseeable, therefore, that resolutions calling for enforcement action in South Africa will continue to be blocked by default and deadlock in the Security Council. And one clear observation can be made from nearly forty years of UN activity: the organisation can operate effectively only when the two superpowers see it as serving a common interest. Such development of a 'community of interest' in South Africa between the USSR and USA appears remote.

The Soviet leadership, while wary of collective action, have strongly supported UN legislation calling on member states to provide moral and material support to national liberation groups in southern Africa. In 1969, the Soviet representative on the UN Special Political Committee, Mr Issraelian, requested that the General Assembly 'review its appeals for moral and material assistance to the national liberation movement in South Africa'.[57] In the same speech, he stated that the Soviet Union would increase its contributions to the struggle against apartheid and colonialism in southern Africa, thus making the most authoritative commitment to armed struggle to date. Indeed, the Soviet Union has been and continues to be the principal benefactor of the ANC, providing military equipment and training to insurgents fighting in the region.

It is undoubtedly this act of support which has helped the USSR to gain influence in Black Africa and has served to establish a certain legitimacy with the nations of the Third World. In 1975, the Chairman of the United Nations Special Committee against Apartheid, Mr Edwin Ogbu of Nigeria, visited the Soviet Union for a series of discussions on the South African issue. On his arrival in Moscow, Ogbu declared that the Soviet government has 'consistently supported, in the United Nations and in direct contact with the liberation movement, the struggle of the South African people against the apartheid regime'.[58] In his statement before the Soviet Afro–Asian

Solidarity Committee he added that the UN Unit on Apartheid had 'been informed by several leaders of the liberation movements and by the Secretariat of the Organization of African Unity that [Soviet] solidarity has not been in words but in concrete action – by providing very generous political and material assistance to the Southern African liberation movements in their struggle for self-determination and independence'.[59] It is because of the role it plays both as the chief benefactor of the national liberation movement in South Africa and as an outspoken antagonist of apartheid policies in international forums, that the Soviet Union enjoys a prominent position in the anti-apartheid movement in the UN.

There are a number of indicators, too, which point to an increase in the Soviet priority placed on the apartheid issue in the United Nations. Certainly the UN has offered the USSR a platform for exploiting existing divisions between the Third World and the West, and Soviet policy at the world body has been on the assumption of a fundamental antagonism between the industrialised West and the underdeveloped South. Yet, to the extent that the West has agreed to discuss the substantive North–South agenda on a New International Economic Order (NIEO), despite previous resistance to it, and to the extent that members of the Third World's 'Group of 77' have determined that they can often gain more in the short term by bargaining with the West than confronting it, West–South relations have become more complex and the antagonism muted.[60]

Third World political elites have come to view the process of negotiation and compromise with the West as essential to prosperity. Although Soviet participation in these negotiations is ensured by virtue of its membership in most multilateral institutions, the Soviet Union has neither defined the agenda nor played an important role in the discussions to date. This is due in part to the limited role the USSR is capable of playing in Third World economic development. The Soviet Union is virtually irrelevant to the development needs of the developing states. Consequently, the Soviet leaders have chosen to participate more actively in political disputes at the United Nations, in attempts to accentuate the areas of contention between the Third World and the West. Principal among these is the issue of South Africa, possibly the most divisive issue under consideration at the UN.

Since the late 1950s, there has been mounting Western concern that the USSR was reaping handsome dividends from its support of the African states on the question of apartheid. Recently, former American Secretary of Defense, Robert McNamara, expressed grave concern about the potential loss of American prestige in Africa in the event of a major conflict in southern Africa.[61] This brief examination of the General Assembly voting record on the South African issue would appear to warrant his concern. The Soviet Union and its East European allies have supported virtually every resolution condemning the South African government's racial policies.[62] Often the text of these resolutions contains severe criticisms of the major Western powers for either providing military assistance to, or for continuing to invest in, South Africa. The United States legation to the UN in 1978 went so far as to make public alleged trade statistics from the South African Department of Customs and Excise which indicated a modest amount of trade between the Republic and various East European states (East Germany, £850 000; Czechoslovakia, £1 900 000; Bulgaria, £250 000; Poland, £900 000).[63] The US representatives asserted that the intention was to discredit the Soviet bloc countries' 'holier than thou' position with respect to trade with South Africa.[64]

While Western statesmen are worried about an increase in Soviet influence among African states in the UN, many South African observers further contend that the world organisation has been fully subverted by the Soviet Union. The anti-colonial posture of the fledgling African states in the early 1960s was interpreted by the South African government as merely a subtle disguise cloaking the predominant position of the Soviet Union on the continent. South African leaders encouraged the view that the United Nations was an institutionalised version of a Soviet conspiracy to isolate and eventually destroy 'white civilisation' in Africa.[65] This tendency to equate nationalism with communism, to picture the overthrow of South Africa as central to Soviet expansionist aims, was and is today a recurring theme in parliamentary debates on foreign affairs. In this context, Eric Louw, the first South African Minister for External Affairs, declared in 1957 that 'because of the preponderant strength of the Bandung–Soviet bloc, I am not very optimistic about the future of the United Nations . . .'.[66] The comments of the late Prime Minister, Dr Verwoerd, are also representative of this belief:

> Both the western bloc and the communist bloc seek the support of the Afro–Asian bloc in the UN, and South Africa is landed in the position where both sides attack her. In this way the friendship of the Afro–Asian countries can be sought . . . without any doubt the attacks against us are created by the struggle of communism for world domination.[67]

Are the concerns expressed by these western and South African statesmen in any way warranted? Has the Soviet Union indeed gained notable influence in Black Africa because of its stand on the apartheid issue? Although the similar voting records of the socialist states and Black Africa on the question of South Africa would indicate a high level of concurrence, is there any evidence of a divergence of views on the subject? Are Soviet protests of solidarity with Black Africa merely rhetorical proclamations?

V

It is a formidable task to evaluate the relative success of Soviet policy towards South Africa in the United Nations. Certainly, the USSR has taken a position in the struggle over apartheid which is close to the one propounded by the Black African states. It is also clear from Soviet participation in the apartheid debate that, in terms of the perception of the political situation in South Africa, the Black African perspective tends to be more in alignment with the Soviet Union than with the West. Both the Soviet Union and Black Africa perceive South Africa to be the last remaining colonial regime in Africa, whereas the West views South Africa more as a conflict-ridden pluralist society. Whether this means that the Soviet Union is in the vanguard of the struggle to liberate South Africa, or whether the USSR has been successful in gaining substantial influence in the Third World, is far less clear. 'Success' in the anti-apartheid debate in the United Nations might be variously regarded as voting with the majority, mobilising the world body to take favourable action on initiatives important to the Soviet Union, or as developing relationships within the UN that manifest themselves in political alliances outside the organisation. This final expression of success is doubtless the most important, but political influence is a highly discrete quality which is difficult to determine and cannot be attributed solely to the Soviet position taken on any one of a range of issues at the United Nations. Nevertheless, a few observations can be made about the nature of winning coalitions in the General Assembly and about the effectiveness of Soviet policy on the apartheid issue.

In terms of siding with the majority, the Soviet Union has done so consistently on resolutions condemning South Africa, and the overall Soviet voting success at the UN can be attributed in large part to its support of anti-apartheid legislation. For example, at the 23rd Assembly session some 57 per cent of the roll-call votes in the plenary were on issues relating to South Africa, Southern Rhodesia, or the rights of dependent peoples, and nearly 70 per cent of the thirty-one successful Soviet votes in the plenum were in this category. A similar trend in Soviet voting on colonial questions can be noted in the committee proceedings. The USSR votes with the winning side most frequently in committees where declaratory pronouncements on apartheid, imperialism, or the plight of colonial peoples are standard (primarily the Third and Fourth Committees).[68] As Plano and Riggs contend, a country which votes anti-colonial and underdeveloped will usually be in the majority due to the predominant position of the Third World in the General Assembly.[69] Other studies conducted by Rowe and Manno indicate a high degree of Soviet voting success on issues relating to South Africa.[70] Thus, by siding with the majority on anti-apartheid resolutions, the Soviet Union has succeeded in identifying itself with the Black African position.

While it is clear that the Soviet Union has effectively identified itself with the Third World on colonial issues, the USSR has not had the same degree of success in generating coalitions on political and security matters.[71] A review of the Soviet record at the UN suggests that its gains in the Third World have been largely in areas of primary importance to the Afro–Asian states. There has been no corresponding Third World support for Soviet initiatives of particular consequence to the USSR. For instance, the majority of African states condemned the Soviet intervention into Czechoslovakia in a 1968 General Assembly draft resolution and, more recently, the Soviet Union has fared no better in attempting to gain support among the Third World for the Soviet incursion into Afghanistan. Seen from this perspective, voting trends on this issue do not represent a dramatic increase in Soviet influence in Black Africa. Indeed, there is little evidence of an increase in Black African support of Soviet positions in response to the favourable support the USSR has lent to the anti-apartheid movement in the UN.

It is interesting to recount the events of one occasion when these two issues – apartheid and Soviet political priorities – received joint consideration. The situation developed during a 1968 debate in the General Assembly concerning the proposed ousting of the Republic of South Africa from the United Nations Conference on Trade and Development (UNCTAD). When the resolution was presented to the plenary session the Soviet Union cast a negative vote, incurring the wrath of many of the African delegates in attendance. The Soviet delegate, in response to acrimonious criticism of his government's lack of support in the matter, asserted that the resolution contained inappropriate phraseology which was unacceptable to the USSR. He contended that in referring to 'members of the United Nations and members of the specialized agencies and of the International Atomic Energy Agency', the initiative was addressing West Germany but not East Germany. Thus, the resolution contained a 'discrimination against Socialist countries'.[72] When sharply criticised for taking issue with such an irrelevant point, the Soviet Union retorted that African states 'had no moral right' to lecture the USSR on the evils of apartheid. He further insisted that, while the Soviet Union was resolutely opposed to racial discrimination in South Africa, the USSR must also oppose discrimination in the UN against its 'own brothers'.[73] Clearly it was more important for the Soviet Union to get East Germany into the UN than to get South Africa out of it, a position not held by the majority of the Third World.[74]

To a large extent it is true that the position of the Western powers has declined due to their uncritical attitudes towards South Africa, but the Soviet Union, in contrast, has not emerged as a 'leader' of Black Africa on the question of apartheid. Rather, the USSR is behaving more as a 'follower' of the Third World, particularly on colonial and race issues in which its stake is marginal. Seen in this light, voting trends in the UN are more a reflection of Soviet efforts to curry favour with the African nations, than a representation of a dramatic increase in Soviet influence in Black Africa.[75] The USSR has, to a limited degree, been able to exploit tensions between South Africa and the Atlantic Community, and more importantly between the West and Black Africa. However, it has been the Black African states who have most effectively used the United Nations as a forum to bring pressure to bear on the Western powers as well as the Soviet Union to support anti-apartheid legislation. Although the non-aligned Afro–Asian states reject superpower rivalry and hail the UN as a means of lessening Cold War tensions, they are not averse to exploiting East–West competition in order to further Third World goals. As Khrushchev aptly surmised, the very existence of the Soviet Union has compelled the Western powers 'to make concessions in their relations with the underdeveloped countries'.[76] Indeed, the most impressive anti-apartheid legislation was adopted during the early 1960s when, due to the Cold War, the impact of the fledgling African states was at its peak.[77] In subsequent years, Western and

Soviet responsiveness to African pressures in the United Nations has steadily declined.[78]

The Soviet Union has been content to use the UN to criticise the Western powers for their role in perpetuating apartheid and has generally resisted efforts to inaugurate an ambitious collective action campaign in South Africa. In the event of a crisis in the region, it is likely that the USSR, if it were to become involved, would do so outside the framework of the United Nations. The existing alignment between the Soviet Union and Black Africa on the South African issue is based on convergent, not common, interests. Hence, there are probably limits to which the Soviet Union is willing to cooperate with the anti-apartheid movement. At some point in the intensifying struggle in South Africa, it is probable that Soviet interests will diverge from those of Black Africa, and the USSR will behave more as a superpower than as a 'follower' of the Third World on the issue of apartheid.

5 Minerals: The Soviet–South African Nexus

We have of course no reason for concealing this arrangement other than the Russians prefer not to receive any public attention for obvious reasons . . . we paid the Soviet Union more than half a billion dollars last year. (Harry Oppenheimer, 1978)

Such reports [of collusion with South Africa] employ the techniques of Dr Goebbels, who understood that a lie must be monstrous to be believed. . . . These reports are cooked up in Western kitchens of disinformation on the orders of Western intelligence services to discredit the peace-loving Soviet Union in the eyes of Africa. (*Isvestiya*, 1981)

When we are victorious on a world scale I think we shall use gold for the purpose of building public lavatories in the streets of some of the largest cities in the world. . . . Meanwhile, we must save the gold in the Soviet Union, sell it at the highest price, buy goods with it at the lowest price. When you live among wolves, you must howl like a wolf. (Lenin, 1921)

I

There are many tenets associated with the perceived or presumed Soviet threat to South Africa, but perhaps the dilemma posed by the unique Soviet/South African minerals nexus has received more attention than any other of these. South Africa possesses significant reserves of several 'critical' minerals – chromium, manganese, vanadium, gold and the platinum group metals – which are important to

TABLE 5.1 *World mine production and reserves of four key minerals*

Mineral	United States (%)	South Africa (%)	Soviet Union (%)*
Chromium:			
production	—	33.0	24.5
reserves	—	66.4	2.9
Manganese:			
production	—	20.9	45.8
reserves	—	37.2	50.7
Vanadium:			
production	17.6	42.3	27.9
reserves	0.7	49.4	45.9
Platinum:			
production	0.1	47.5	47.5
reserves	0.1	73.2	25.1

* The Soviet Union production and reserve percentages for chromium and manganese include production and reserve figures for all the Soviet bloc countries.

SOURCE US Bureau of Mines, *Mineral Commodity Summaries 1980* as taken from *South Africa: Time Running Out*, p. 312.

the economies of the industrialised democracies.[1] This reliance on South Africa, an international pariah, for mineral supplies is compounded by the fact that the Soviet Union is the other major world producer of each of these critical natural resources (see Table 5.1). The Soviet Union and South Africa are also identified as important producers of several non-critical minerals, notably gem-quality diamonds. Because these various minerals are important to industry and often have military applications, South Africa has come to be regarded in strategic parlance as the 'Persian Gulf of minerals' and also, due to the Soviet's 'Damoclean Sword' held over the Republic, the 'Achilles' heel of the West'.[2]

Indeed, the predominance of the Soviet Union in world production of these minerals has led numerous commentators to suggest that the Soviet Union has embarked upon a policy of 'resource denial' to the West by fomenting revolution and civil strife in southern Africa. The USSR and its East European and Cuban surrogates, it is asserted, could undermine the economic strength of the Atlantic Community by denying it key raw materials. And any general denial of Western access to foreign resources could serve to suspend economic growth in Western Europe and Japan for many years, pending radical improvements in the technology for exploiting indigenous resources.'[3] Other advocates of this viewpoint, writing in the wake of the OPEC experience, articulate the fear that a black-ruled Marxist South Africa might collaborate with the Soviet Union in a minerals cabal against Western nations. These convictions are present in much of the literature concerning the strategic significance of South Africa and, taken together, this litany of Soviet intentions represents the conventional wisdom about the impetus of the USSR's actions on the southern continent.

While it is true that the Soviet Union and South Africa currently provide the lion's share of several key minerals, it will be argued that the above list of Soviet objectives is based upon an inaccurate appraisal of Soviet minerals policy *vis-à-vis* South Africa. The USSR, to date, has followed an expedient course of action in commercial mineral transactions with South Africa. Its economic relationship with South Africa does not suggest a strategy of 'resource supply disruption' to the West.[4] On the contrary, the Soviet strategy, if indeed the diverse mineral marketing and production arrangements can be said to compose a unified strategy, includes collaboration with the white South African regime for the marketing of diamonds, gold and platinum. There has even been speculation about possible cooperation on mining expertise and metals technology. Furthermore, the Soviet Union has given no indication, in its commercial dealings, of wishing to alter its present arrangements with the racialist regime. This is not meant to suggest that the Soviet Union would eschew policy choices which might conceivably threaten the West with a disruption of its mineral supply, but rather that there are other considerations in the formulation of Soviet policy which are of paramount importance. Certainly the overthrow of the white minority government is an ultimate goal of Soviet foreign policy, but this does not mean that all Soviet activities involving South Africa are designed or implemented with this objective in mind. Profitability, not revolutionary activism, appears to be the motivation behind its economic activity.

This situation raises some interesting questions not only about the conditions of this secretive association but also concerning the nature of Soviet foreign policy. To what extent do the Soviet Union and South Africa collude in the marketing of various minerals? Does this clandestine economic interaction have any relevance to the overt, hostile political relationship? Are Soviet political and economic policies towards South Africa coordinated? How does the USSR reconcile its commercial connections to white South Africa with its support for national liberation in the region? What effects might this marketing relationship have upon the future price and supply of various minerals? Despite these areas of commercial cooperation between the RSA and the USSR, is the Soviet Union's long-term objective to cut off the Western supply of South Africa's strategic minerals? Would the Soviet Union's primary goal in advancing a supply disruption scheme be to deny vital materials to the West or rather, because of the growing shortfall in domestic mineral production in the USSR, to gain access for itself to a new source of supply?

This chapter will examine the areas of cooperation in the mining and marketing of diamonds, gold and platinum. Particular attention will be given to Soviet thinking on the rationale for its 'dual policies'[5] approach to national liberation on the one hand and mineral marketing on the other. Accordingly, the Soviet interpretation of 'peaceful coexistence' and the theoretical justifications of cooperation with South Africa will be reviewed. Further, the issue of the alleged Soviet 'strategy of denial' policy will be addressed in greater detail. Specifically, the historical debate surrounding the notion of a resource war actively initiated by the Soviet Union will be discussed with particular reference to the situation in southern Africa. Western vulnerability to such a disruption of South African-supplied minerals will also be considered. Through the development of these themes, an alternative interpretation of the motivations determining Soviet minerals policy will emerge. It should be noted, however, that this work does not profess to present an exhaustive or comprehensive examination of Soviet minerals policy, nor a quantitative exposition on the economics of mining, and South African mining will be discussed only when it is relevant to the central issues of enquiry. This study focuses only on those raw materials marketed exclusively, or in large part, by South Africa and the USSR and on the issues, both political and economic, which arise from this situation.

Before beginning this examination, it is necessary to mention a few words about sources. There are a number of inevitable problems confronting a researcher delving into the clandestine relationship existing between the USSR and the RSA. First and foremost of these is that these contacts are shrouded in secrecy and both countries wish this situation to persist. Consequently, evidence substantiating collusion is difficult to establish. Indeed, Soviet production figures for precious and strategic minerals are not made public. For instance, no total gold production figures have been released since 1928 and, after A. P. Serebrovsky, Stalin's head of the *Glavzoloto* vanished during the purges of 1937, 'a monumental silence has fallen over the whole question of Russian gold production and reserves.'.[6] A 1947 decree instituted the death penalty as punishment for anyone convicted of revealing information on gold reserves, or even for collecting newspaper clippings which could be collated to reveal such figures. There was a brief period of official disclosures of mining statistics after Khrushchev's call for more public statistics at the twentieth party Congress in 1956. However, in recent years there has been a move towards renewed secrecy.[7] Much of the same sort of secrecy exists for platinum, chromium, vanadium and diamond production as well.

Consequently the subject of this chapter is one where techniques of both detective Sovietology and investigative research are necessary. There are a handful of Western experts, notably Michael Kaser, Theodore Shabad and V. V. Strishkov, who examine a wide variety of both published and unpublished material in their estimations of Soviet mineral production.[8] This work serves as a starting point for the study of Soviet and South African mining. Obtaining information from both Soviet and South African sources was complicated by undue disclosures made in the BBC's *Panorama* piece entitled 'South African Gold and Diamonds – The Kremlin Connection' which have provoked even greater secrecy on the part of the mining and banking officials involved with these transactions.[9] Nevertheless, the evidence presented in this chapter is based upon material garnered from a range of both Soviet and Western sources.

It is perhaps surprising that there is a degree of cooperation between the Soviet Union and South Africa, given the political hostility which exists between these two countries. Since 1956 there have been no official diplomatic contacts between them and trade has been negligible.[10] However, through an accident of nature and politics, most of the world's supplies of gold, diamonds and platinum are found beneath the earth of these two countries which are the most bitter of political enemies. Earnings from mineral exports are uniquely important to the Soviet and South African economies and despite their outspoken antagonism for one another, both sides have an overriding interest in obtaining the highest prices for their mineral sales. High-level contacts between South African corporations, principally De Beers and Anglo-American, and the various Soviet mining ministries and foreign trade agencies in charge of mineral production and marketing, have helped keep world prices as high as possible. The venues for these discussions range from informal meetings at the annual Platinum Dinner held at the Savoy Hotel in

London to discreet negotiating sessions between Soviet and South African delegations in Moscow and Kimberley, South Africa. This clandestine relationship exists for the marketing of diamonds, gold and platinum, and these secret links are an important yet neglected aspect of the relationship between the RSA and the USSR.

II

The most extensive and well-established area of cooperation exists for the marketing of gem diamonds, and the explanation for the collaboration between the Soviet Union and South Africa lies in understanding the operating practice of De Beers Consolidated Mines of South Africa. De Beers, first under the direction of Sir Ernest Oppenheimer and later his son Harry Oppenheimer, has moved in the last eighty years to build up its monopoly position in the marketing of gem-quality stones.[11] Through its practice of buying up rough-cut stones throughout the world and controlling the amount of diamonds released on to the market at any one time, De Beers has proved to be the most successful cartel in the annals of modern commerce. The De Beers system of restricting and allocating diamonds handles over 80 per cent of the world's gem-quality diamonds. While the price of other commodities such as silver, gold, platinum, rubber and grains fluctuate wildly in response to a myriad of economic variables, diamonds have, until quite recently, continued to rise in value each year (for instance, in 1970, an average-quality one carat diamond sold for about £700; ten years later the same diamond was worth over £10 000 – an increase of over 1000 per cent). The intricate marketing arrangements and sophisticated supply-restraining practices evolved by the De Beers Corporation have been termed by Edward J. Epstein 'the diamond invention'.[12] Epstein writes:

> The diamond invention was an ingenious scheme for sustaining the value of diamonds in an uncertain world. To begin with, it involved gaining control over the production of all the important diamond mines in the world. Next, a system was devised for allocating this controlled supply of gems to a select number of diamond cutters who all agreed to abide by certain rules intended to ensure that the quantity of finished diamonds available at any given time never exceeded the public's demand for them. Finally, a set of subtle, but

effective, incentives were devised for regulating the behaviour of all the people who served and ultimately profited from the system. The invention had a wide array of diverse parts; these included a hugh stockpile of uncut diamonds in a vault in London; a billion-dollar cash hoard deposited in banks in Europe; a private intelligence network operating out of advertising agencies, brokers and distributors; corporate fronts in Africa for concealing massive diamond purchases; and private treaties with nations establishing quotas for annual production. The invention is far more than merely a monopoly for fixing diamond prices; it is a mechanism for converting tiny crystals of carbon into universally recognized tokens of wealth, power and romance.[13]

This 'ingenious scheme' for creating and sustaining the value of diamonds was threatened by the discovery of gem-quality stones in the Soviet Union. The USSR had, in fact, a history of contact with De Beers before the discovery of diamonds in Siberia in the 1950s. Immediately following the Bolshevik revolution in 1918, South African producers purchased large quantities of cut diamonds which flooded on to the market from Russia, as the new revolutionary government sold confiscated jewellery to raise foreign exchange.[14] In the post-Second World War period, the Soviet Union imported its entire supply of industrial diamonds from South Africa. These diamonds were used in drill bits for the exploration of oil and gas, were necessary in the production of precision-tooled parts and to draw out fine wire, and were essential for grinding machine tools and armaments. If the supply of these diamonds were ever cut off, several sectors of the badly war-damaged economy would be significantly impaired. Stalin, realising that the USSR was particularly vulnerable to an embargo, ordered in 1947 that Soviet geologists and scientists set about to relieve the USSR's exploitability either by discovering a domestic source of diamonds or by perfecting a process for diamond manufacture in the laboratory.[15]

A vast programme of prospecting was initiated. The primary region searched was the Siberian plateau in Yakutia province (now Yakut ASSR) near the Yenisei and Lena rivers – an area which Soviet geologists discovered resembled South African geological formations.[16] After several unsuccessful years of prospecting in the region, two Soviet geologists Larissa Popugayeva and Yuri Khabardin discovered first the Zarnitsa field and then the Mir diamond field along the Vilyuy river. The Mir field was determined to have an exceptionally high diamond content and Soviet planners in Moscow immediately ordered a crash programme to begin production.[17] With an average January temperature of −50°F, this area of 'the Pole of Cold' as it is sometimes called, posed immense engineering problems. Despite the incredibly harsh conditions at the mine site, Soviet engineers laboured successfully to excavate the diamond-bearing kimberlite ore.[18] The entire process of diamond recovery was complicated by the extreme cold and it was several years before the Soviet Union was ready to market its diamonds to the West. Although Stalin initiated the Soviet diamond industry in order to generate a domestic source of industrial diamonds, there is considerable debate among Western experts as to whether the Mir mine yields industrial-grade diamonds. However, it is certain that gem-quality stones from Yakutia began to appear on international markets in 1959.[19]

The mining operation in Siberia was placed under the local responsibility of *Yakutalmaz*, and this 'diamond trust' was organised within the Ministry of Non-ferrous Metallurgy in Moscow. The ministry's central division, named *Glavzoloto*, was (and still is) presided over by V.P. Berezin and it directed all diamond, gold and platinum mining. The export of diamonds in the early 1960s was encouraged by the Ministry of Foreign Trade because of the potential for earning valuable foreign exchange.[20] Indeed, in 1968 Viktor I. Tikhonov, the head of the Mirny Diamond Administration, boasted, 'we call ourselves the country's foreign exchange department'.[21]

It appeared that South Africa's control of the world supply of diamonds would be destroyed when the De Beers' intelligence network positively identified the vast potential of the Siberian discovery. Oppenheimer reasoned that if the Soviet Union ever attempted to market their diamonds independently of De Beers, the world price would plummet. He, therefore, moved boldly to bring the Soviet Union into the cartel arrangement. It was 1957 and South Africa had just broken off diplomatic relations with the Soviet Union because of alleged Soviet complicity with communist organisations in the Union (refer to the chapter on official relations for a description of the termination in official relations). The prospects of an agreement were unpromising. Oppenheimer dispatched his cousin Sir Philip Oppenheimer to Moscow to make the case for Soviet participation in the De Beers system.[22] The South African proposal called for De Beers to buy up the entire Soviet production of gem-quality diamonds for a price that would be renegotiated annually. These diamonds, in turn, would be marketed through the Central Selling Organisation (CSO) network. This arrangement proved suitable to the Soviets and Sir Philip returned to London with a secret contract to market all Soviet diamonds to the West, the full conditions of which have never been disclosed.[23]

Since the official policy of the USSR supported the national liberation struggle against South Africa and Soviet representatives at the United Nations castigated the West because of continued economic links with the racialist regime, the USSR insisted from the outset that De Beers deny the existence of any commercial relationship. In this, Oppenheimer was only too happy to oblige. However, after the Sharpeville shootings in 1960 it was politically impossible for the Russians to be seen to do business with South Africa. In the 1963 annual report of the Chairman, Oppenheimer noted that 'on account of Russian support for the boycotting of trade with South Africa, our contract to buy Russian diamonds has not been renewed'.[24] In actuality, the marketing arrangement was never severed but rather continued unabated in ever greater sophistication and secrecy. Indeed, in 1978 Oppenheimer stated that South Africa has 'no reason for concealing this arrangement other than that the Russians prefer not to receive any public attention for obvious reasons'.[25]

Although the full provisions of the marketing arrangement are subject to speculation, there is much about the relationship which is known. For instance, Soviet negotiators from the diamond-trading organisation along with officials of the Soviet Ministry of Foreign Trade meet yearly with De Beers executives to hammer out the terms of the diamond contract. These are often intense sessions during which the South Africans must, through a process of cajoling and negotiation, establish the amount of Soviet diamonds which will be made available to the Central Selling Organisation and at what price. The De Beers officials begin at a disadvantage, much as Western arms control negotiators do, because the South Africans have only Western estimates of Soviet production to work with. The Soviet officials refuse to offer any figures of Soviet production and will only make general corrections of erroneous De Beers estimates. Sir Philip Oppenheimer or his nephew Nicholas Oppenheimer often take part in these proceedings, and on several occasions Sir Philip has visited Moscow on behalf of De Beers. The Soviets are nearly always represented by Boris Sergeev, the deputy president of the Diamond and Platinum Trading Organisation in Moscow. A recent meeting between the Soviets and South Africans took place at Brougham Castle in Banbury, Oxfordshire. Apparently, the USSR has each

year demanded ever larger payments in exchange for their participation in the diamond cartel, and these ultimata have placed a great
financial burden on De Beers.[26]

Indeed, Soviet production was far greater than anyone at De Beers
imagined it would be, reaching 2–3 million gem-carats a year by
1965.[27] In 1978, Harry Oppenheimer stated that De Beers had paid
the Soviet Union more than $500 million during the course of 1977.[28]
By all accounts, De Beers' payments have increased in recent years.
This suggests that De Beers has provided the USSR with its single
largest source of hard currency; only petroleum and gold provided
more export earnings. Although there is some evidence of a wane in
Soviet diamond mining recently, the operation to date has furnished
the USSR with an important and reliable source of foreign currency.

In addition to the large payments of foreign capital specified in the
marketing contract, De Beers also provides the USSR with certain
varieties of industrial-grade diamonds which apparently are not
found in the Siberian mines. Also, there is some indication that the
Soviet Union, who pioneered the X-ray technique of diamond sort-
ing, has provided details of this technology to De Beers for use at
their African mine sites. Furthermore, in 1976 it was agreed that a
group of De Beers executives would be allowed to examine one
Siberian mine. The Soviet Union acceded to the South Africans' visit
on the condition that Soviet geologists be allowed to observe De
Beers' mines in southern Africa. Subsequently, a Soviet mining
engineer named Georgi Smernoff was attached to the Letseng mine
in Lesotho for two years as a 'consultant' to De Beers. De Beers in
1982 also blocked publication of British government figures on shipments of diamonds to London from the Soviet Union, thereby adding
another layer of secrecy around the highly discreet international
movement of diamonds.[29] Finally, there are persistent rumours that
the marketing arrangements specify that the USSR use its influence
in Angola to persuade the MPLA regime to remain within the De
Beers/Central Selling Organisation network to market their rough-
cut diamonds.[30]

There has been speculation from time to time that, possibly because of the USSR's own ambitions in southern Africa, the Soviet
Union might seek to upset the cartel and thus bankrupt De Beers. De
Beers' publications have attempted to calm these fears and in 1971
the annual review explained that: 'the Soviet authorities appear to
accept that the industry they have been at great pains to develop and
establish would founder if the market for diamonds in the Western

world were undermined or were not held in strong hands . . .'[31] It is clear that the Central Selling Organisation is extremely vulnerable to any change in Soviet policy and it remains in the power of the USSR to preserve or destroy the South African controlled system of restricting and allocating the supply of diamonds on the world market. The prospects, however, for continued Soviet participation in the Central Selling Organisation are high, according to several sources familiar with Soviet diamond policy. Oppenheimer has commented that he could 'see no conceivable reason why [the USSR] would want to abandon such a profitable arrangement'.[32] One Soviet official in answer to a question about potential threats to the De Beers' monopoly went so far as to suggest that the Soviet Union 'would never cut down the tree'.[33]

In short, there has been a high degree of cooperation between De Beers and the USSR for the marketing of Soviet diamonds to the West. Their relationship, which has spanned nearly thirty years, requires periodic consultation between Soviet officials and De Beers executives and these contacts have become a familiar and ritualised part of the diamond industry. The marketing contract, which is renewed annually, provides the Soviet Union with a steady and substantial supply of hard currency as well as certain varieties of industrial diamonds not found in the Siberian mines. Moreover, there has been a degree of technology sharing and interaction between mining engineers which has furthered cooperation and invariably proved invaluable to both parties. Finally, although there is speculation that the Soviet Union might in the future attempt to bypass the De Beers system and market their product directly to the West, most diamond experts are confident that the prospects for continued Soviet participation in the diamond cartel are high.[34] Thus, it is likely that the USSR will continue its commercial relationship with De Beers and the Central Selling Organisation for the foreseeable future.

III

The question of the relationship between the USSR and the RSA over gold is more complicated and potentially more important than Soviet participation in the De Beers marketing system. However, it is probable that any association concerning gold grew out of contacts already established for diamonds. Gold plays a unique role in the international monetary system and, despite the abandonment of the Gold Standard, it still remains the only universally accepted medium of exchange. Gold also has important applications in industry and, more recently, its price fluctuations serve as a sort of barometer of political tensions. (This relationship was ironically borne out in August 1981 when, during the South African incursion into Angola, a number of Soviet advisers were killed in the fighting. The resultant tension in international relations boosted both gold producers' fortunes.) The Soviet Union and South Africa mine perhaps 75 per cent of the world's gold, and together they provide the vast majority of gold traded each year on Western bullion markets.[35] Indeed, gold sales are essential to both their economies. It would be going too far to suggest that there is outright collusion between the two major producers to influence the price of gold, but covert contacts exist for the marketing of bullion and these undoubtedly provide both countries with valuable information and contribute to what economists term 'orderly marketing'.[36] However, consultation between the Soviet Union and South Africa over gold is far more discreet than for diamond marketing, and there is no formalised marketing arrangement similar to the Central Selling Organisation. To understand the relationship better, it will be helpful briefly to review the gold economy in greater detail, with particular reference to Soviet gold policy.

Since the appearance of large shipments of gold bars bearing the hammer and sickle inscription on the international bullion market after the death of Stalin, there has been unceasing speculation in the West about the Soviet government's gold policy. Stalin himself initiated the Soviet gold industry in 1927 with the establishment of *Glavzoloto*, or Gold Trust, and the appointment of A.P. Serebrovsky as head of the new state company (Serebrovsky was in charge of the oil industry until 1926).[37] With the use of forced labour to exploit the significant Siberian reserves, Soviet gold production surged ahead in the 1930s.[38] While Stalin chose to husband his gold reserves and financed his meagre imports with other commodity exports – notably lumber, oil and wheat – Khrushchev adopted a more liberal policy towards gold sales to the West. In the years 1953–65 it is estimated that the USSR sold nearly 3000 tons of gold on the London and Paris bullion markets, thus seriously depleting Soviet reserves.[39] Production declined in the late 1950s and early 1960s to probably no more than 120 to 150 tons annually, due largely to the decrease in flow of political prisoners to the Siberian mines after the closure of the

forced-labour camps.[40] Gold production rose sharply in the early
1970s and the predominance of the Siberian gold fields was eclipsed
with the development of a major new mining area in the Central
Asian province of Uzbekistan named Muruntau.[41] Muruntau is believed to be the largest gold mine in the world and along with newly
exploited reserves at Zod mine in Armenia,[42] the Soviet Union's
current annual production is estimated to be somewhere between
250–380 tonnes depending on the source.

In the absence of official production figures, the quest for determining the true level of Soviet gold production is arduously pursued
by a host of individuals, intelligence agencies, Western mining companies, consulting firms and bullion houses. These studies bring to
bear a wide variety of sources – reconnaissance satellite photographs,
ore samples and printed Soviet references – in their investigations of
Soviet mining. The speculation began when John Littlepage, an
American mining engineer who spent the period 1928 to 1937 working for Serebrovsky's *Glavzoloto*, wrote in his book, *In Search of
Soviet Gold* that not only was Russia comfortably ahead of the
United States and Canada in production, but that the Soviet Union
had the potential to overtake South Africa.[43] During the 1930–55
period of high Siberian production, Western estimates of gold production were based largely upon prisoner accounts from the prison
labour camps.[44] The Central Intelligence Agency, possibly due to
information supplied by KGB defector Oleg Penkovsky, dramatically
reduced its estimate of Soviet gold production to a range of 135–155
tonnes in 1964. Presently, the most widely accepted figures are
provided by the US Bureau of Mines, the Central Intelligence
Agency (CIA), and Consolidated Gold Fields.[45] Soviet gold sales to
the West give some indication of overall production, but the exact
totals remain elusive. Through the publications of the above groups
and the analysis of yearly Soviet gold sales to the West, a much
clearer picture of the organisation, extraction and marketing of
Soviet gold has emerged in the last decade. Yet, the precise figure of
total Soviet production is a closely guarded state secret. V. P. Berezin, the director of *Glavzoloto*, confided to Michael Beckett, the
executive director of Consolidated Gold Fields, that only two people
in the Soviet Union know the total Soviet production of gold and he
was not one of them.[46]

Within the USSR the overall direction of gold, diamond and
platinum mining is determined by the Ministry of Non-ferrous Metallurgy, which has been presided over for several years by V. P.

Berezin.[47] *Glavzoloto* and the Primary Administration of Gold and Rare Metals are required to meet established production targets cited in the Five Year Plan.[48] With a few exceptions such as Muruntau which is independently operated, there are fourteen regional *zolotos*, or trusts, that supervise the discovery, exploitation and recovery of primary gold deposits within set geographical boundaries. For instance, *Severovostokzoloto* is responsible for the alluvial deposits located near Magadan on the USSR's far eastern shores. Vneshtorgbank in Moscow and Wozchod Handelsbank in Zurich are responsible for the external sale of gold bullion, and perhaps the most tangible clues of alleged Soviet complicity with South Africa occur in the marketing of Soviet bullion.

In South Africa, gold has been the key to economic and industrial development and, amongst all the South African mining houses, it is Harry Oppenheimer's Anglo–American Corporation which is the dominant actor. In reference to Anglo–American's primacy in the gold world, Timothy Greene has written:

> The Anglo empire directly administers nine gold mines, producing just over 40 per cent of South Africa's gold, but its embrace actually extends much further. Anglo has a 41.3 per cent holding in Johannesburg Consolidated Investments, which controls two medium-sized gold mines (Anglo's sister company De Beers, that colossus astride the diamond business, also holds 9.1 per cent of JCI.) Besides enjoying a 10.8 per cent stake in Gold Fields of South Africa (GFSA), the Anglo–De Beers stable has the largest shareholding, 28.9 per cent, in Consolidated Gold Fields, the London mining house that in turn has 48 per cent of GFSA. This spider's web indirectly involves Anglo with two-thirds of South Africa's gold output. And, just for good measure, the mining giant has small holdings in two other important houses: Barlow Rand (formerly Rand Mines) and General Mining.[49]

Gold sales are controlled by the government in both the Soviet Union and South Africa. In South Africa, the mining houses are legally bound to sell their gold through the Reserve Bank, acting for the South African Ministry of Finance. Prior to 1965, the USSR marketed the majority of its gold through the Moscow Narodny Bank in London, but since that time most gold sales have been handled by Vneshtorgbank, the Bank for Foreign Trade in Moscow and through its Western subsidiary, the Wozchod Handelsbank in Zurich.[50] Both countries release their gold on to the market in Zurich through the Swiss Gold Pool, a collection of prominent Swiss banks. It is in Zurich where the timing of sales is crucial. Historically, there has always been concern that the Soviets might 'dump' gold in an emergency to raise hard currency.[51] On the contrary, however, the Soviet's Wozchod bank has often acted to support a falling market by making substantial purchases. The Soviet Union also has anticipated poor grain harvests and made the necessary gold sale to finance purchases before the official announcement that grain imports were required. In short, the Soviets are 'very shrewd and business-like', according to an executive board member of the Swiss Bank Corporation.[52] The similarity in gold policies of the Soviet Union and South Africa is also noteworthy. Both the USSR and the RSA support a strong monetary role for gold and each markets gold coins to private buyers (Chervontsi and Krugerands).

The question of collusion between South Africa and the Soviet Union to coordinate gold sales has been raised in several publications and, indeed, both sides have strong incentives to coordinate their marketing policies.[53] For South Africa, the price of gold determines her economic future. Every $10 drop in the world gold price costs South Africa $200 million a year. Soviet sales provide the political leadership with a major source of hard currency to finance food imports and high technology purchases from the West. Yet Moscow and Pretoria adopt different marketing tactics for their product. South Africa is far more dependent on bullion sales than the USSR: gold contributed to more than 50 per cent of South African exports, against less than 10 per cent for the Soviet Union in 1981.[54] South Africa maintains a reasonably steady flow of supplies while the Soviet Union often sells in sporadic bursts. This is frequently referred to by gold traders as South Africa providing the 'hard core' while the 'Russians play it at the top'.[55] Despite the common interest in maintaining a profitable and stable market relationship, it is nearly an impossible task to positively document even one case of overt collaboration.

However, there is considerable speculation about possible cooperation between the two. Herbert Baschnagel of the Swiss Bank Corporation has stated that he 'would imagine it is in the interests of the two major producers to find a common stand . . . definitely'.[56] A top Anglo–American executive remarked that: 'Zurich is where both sides can hear about each other's intentions. The South Africans and the Russians use the same bankers here, because Switzerland is the middle man we can all trust'.[57] Dennis Etheredge, Director of Anglo–

American's Gold Division, denies the existence of any sort of collusive arrangement, but pointed out that 'if the bankers in Zurich or London were to say to the South African bank, "Look the Russians are heavy in the market", that would cause the South Africans to hold back'.[58] In an in-house report compiled by the South African Chamber of Mines entitled *Soviet Foreign Trade Policy and its Implications for South Africa's Mining Sector*, this relationship between the gold sellers is referred to as 'collusive price leadership', whereby market forces encourage the adoption of similar sales policies.[59] Ian Wright, a former Consolidated Gold Fields executive, believes conversely that contacts with the Soviets, such as Gordon Waddell's mission to Moscow, were about 'the price of gold and whether it was possible to conduct an orderly market along the same lines as De Beers has done so well in diamonds'.[60] There are even persistent rumours that the South African Reserve Bank handles some Russian accounts.[61] Nevertheless, there is no general consensus among participants and observers about the issue of coordinated marketing.

There are, though, numerous examples of communication between the Soviets and South Africans over gold. For instance, Michael Beckett, executive director of Consolidated Gold Fields (in which Anglo–American has controlling stock), visited Moscow with two other Consgold officials in September 1980.[62] Beckett and his associates were entertained by the Soviet Foreign Trade Bank and their stated goal was to accumulate information on Soviet gold activities for use in the company's annual bullion study. During these meetings and in subsequent ones, there was considerable discussion about broadening contacts to include exchange of views on mining techniques and metallurgy. Significantly, the Soviets have developed technological expertise of interest to the South Africans. Anglo–American was interested to obtain the patent on a Soviet perfected pulp-in-resin technique for separating gold from its by-products.[63] There was even discussion about licensing a transaction in Argentina to avoid detection.[64] Further, early in 1981 there were regular meetings between Wozchod bank officials and top executives from Anglo–American. Finally, Mike Brown, chief economist for the South African Chamber of Mines, stated that 'in the past Narodny economists have had discussions with Chamber people'.[65]

There is no doubt of the existence of consultation between the two countries concerning all aspects of gold exploration, production and marketing, but the function of these discussions appears to have more to do with each side trying to determine the other's intentions than with codifying some sort of selling arrangement. Because of the secrecy surrounding gold in the Soviet Union and the strict penalties imposed for failing to meet standards, the Soviet mining officials and trade bank representatives are notoriously tight-lipped on the subject of gold.[66] Also, while the marketing of diamonds is managed exclusively by private companies in South Africa, the South African government controls the marketing of gold at the Reserve Bank. The existence of such extreme animosity between the two governments on official levels, particularly among the ruling Afrikaner elite, probably means that contacts are limited to the timing of gold sales in Zurich. In summary, the relationship between the two countries on the gold issue might best be termed 'a meeting of competitors',[67] and any contacts fostered in this atmosphere of mutual suspicion are limited by necessity and design.

IV

The possibility of cooperation between the USSR and South Africa in the production and marketing of platinum group metals is not a new idea.[68] Indeed, there is some evidence to suggest that South Africa seriously considered entering into a commercial relationship with the Soviet government in 1926 for the purposes of controlling the platinum market. Professor Paul Kovaloff, Vice-Director of the Mining Bureau in the Soviet government, and Professor Lipovski, Chairman of the Ural Division of the Soviet Geological Committee, visited South Africa during 1926 for the express purpose of convincing the South African authorities of the necessity of establishing 'a trading and controlling organization' to 'reconcile the limited requirements of the platinum market with the obvious over-production of platinum [in South Africa and the Soviet Union]'.[69] Because of new platinum ore discoveries in South Africa during the early 1920s, and due to the increase in Soviet production of platinum, the Soviet representatives were concerned that, taken together, Soviet and South African production might have disastrous effects on the fragile platinum market. In the Soviet view, 'limiting the annual supply of platinum to the actual demand of the market' was necessary to preserve the platinum industry. Kovaloff argued that: 'If South Africa would join Russia [in a marketing organisation], both countries together would control nearly 75 per cent of the prospective supply of platinum, and would . . . be able to exercise an effective control of the market'.[70]

With few modifications, this very same situation currently exists for the platinum industry. South Africa and the Soviet Union supply nearly 95 per cent of the world's platinum and together completely dominate the international platinum market. The free market price of platinum in the past four years has fluctuated wildly, soaring to over $1000 an ounce in 1980 and then dipping to below $300 an ounce during 1983.[71] Speculation about a possible marketing arrangement between the two major producers was fuelled when Gordon Waddell was seen in Moscow in the company of Soviet trade officials. Waddell, an executive of the Anglo–American Corporation, is chairman of Rustenburg Platinum Holdings of South Africa, the world's leading platinum producer. In the interests of achieving a stable market for both countries, Waddell is reputed to have sought a tacit agreement from the USSR not to accept a free-market price substantially under the South African contracted prices. (South Africa producers sell their platinum on a contract basis, often to industrial buyers, while the Soviet Union sells its product on the free market. South Africa is generally considered a steady supplier in contrast to the Soviet Union's periodic and intermittent sales to the West.) In dealings over platinum, as in gold, there are numerous contacts between senior officials from both countries, but the existence of a marketing agreement is subject to debate.

The uncertain nature of the relationship between South Africa and the Soviet Union is compounded by questions arising from the major decrease in Soviet platinum exports during the Tenth Five Year Plan period. Western experts are in general agreement that Soviet platinum group metals production has either increased or remained constant during the past seven years.[72] Daniel Fine, however, maintains that Soviet production has actually declined since 1977.[73] Daniel S. Papp accurately summarises the discussion in the Western literature about the recent developments in Soviet platinum production and marketing:

As might be expected, several explanations exist as to the cause of the precipitous drop in Soviet platinum group metals exports. One view holds that greater sophistication in the Soviet chemical, petrochemical, glass fibre and electronics industries has increased domestic demand for platinum and necessitated export reductions. Another view maintains that placer deposits in the Kola Peninsula and Ural Mountains are being exhausted, while a third argues that dredges have simply been removed from platinum production and moved to gold sites. A fourth interpretation is that serious production problems have cropped up at Norilsk, including a possible shaft collapse which temporarily stopped production. (These last three views would also seem to argue that total platinum group metals production has decreased.) A final, more cynical view posits that the USSR is simply stockpiling platinum group metals with the possible intention of capturing a dominant role in the future world market, and then increase prices as it attempted to do in the palladium market during the mid-1970s.

Whatever the cause, it is evident that the USSR is not a reliable source of platinum group metals exports. While it is reasonably safe to assume that there is no danger of platinum group metals depletion in the USSR, it must also be realized that in the worst of all possible worlds, Soviet demand for platinum may be growing rapidly even while production is falling.[74]

Because the USSR is the world's largest producer of platinum group metals, it is reasonably safe to assume that there is no dangerous shortfall in Soviet production. However, it is possible that the domestic demand for platinum is rising more rapidly than in the past. Too little is known about the Soviet platinum industry to warrant any further conclusion.

The Soviet platinum industry is also a subject of interest to South Africa, and recently Rustenburg Platinum convened an in-house study group to look at the future of platinum production in the USSR.[75] There have been a number of private meetings between mining executives of Rustenburg and the Soviet Diamond and Platinum Trading Organisation in Oslo and Hong Kong concerning the recent poor market for platinum.[76] Furthermore, Soviet and South African mining officials meet annually each May at the Savoy Hotel in London for the Platinum Dinner. Gordon Waddell is often in attendance and in 1980 he sat next to Boris Osipov, the London representative of the Soviet Diamond and Platinum Trading Organisation.[77] Harry Oppenheimer was a dinner guest in 1981 along with Eugene Manakhov of the Soviet Ministry of Foreign Trade.[78] Significantly, all major American automobile manufacturers have contracts with Rustenburg or Impala Platinum (South Africa) to buy platinum for use in catalytic converters. Because the Soviet Union has been absent from the international platinum market since 1977, there are persistent rumours that South African companies covertly market Soviet platinum to the West.[79] Specifically, Ayrton Metals, a subsidiary of Impala Platinum, serves as a large trading house for the marketing of platinum, and many observers believe Ayrton has in the past handled some Soviet production.[80]

The level of cooperation between the two in platinum affairs is probably somewhere between that of diamonds and gold. Yet, because of the industrial applications of platinum, Soviet leaders are certainly more concerned with meeting domestic needs than with obtaining a limited amount of foreign currency from platinum sales to the West.[81] Unquestionably, Soviet priorities here are with securing mineral self-sufficiency and it is likely that this demand would take precedence over any sort of marketing arrangement with South Africa.

In addition to consultation and collaboration among South African and Soviet officials over the marketing of diamonds, gold and platinum, there is also evidence of minor contacts in the marketing of chromium and karakul pelt furs (it is known that the USSR imported chromite from Rhodesia in violation of the UN embargo).[82] For instance, the USSR and South West Africa are the two largest exporters of karakul pelts and in November 1981, at the behest of the Soviet Union, there was a meeting of the two principal producers in London.[83] The Soviet Union was represented by the Director of the Soviet Leather, Fur and Hides Export Agency and the Chairman of the Namibian Karakul Board was the South African delegate.[84]

V

The irony of this Byzantine commercial relationship between the Soviet Union and South Africa is reflected by a curious coincidence which occured during Gordon Waddell's stay in Moscow. While Waddell was meeting with officials from the Soviet Ministry of Foreign Trade, President Brezhnev was conferring with President Samora Machel of Mozambique, who was on an official state visit to the Soviet Union. Indeed, there is a dualism in Soviet policy towards South Africa: the Soviet Union is an ardent supporter of the national liberation struggle for the oppressed population in South Africa and at the same time maintains clandestine commercial contacts with the white minority regime. This situation raises some important questions about the motivations and formulation of Soviet foreign policy. How does the Soviet Union rationalise the apparent contradictions in its political and economic policies towards South Africa? Does the cooperation exhibited in commercial affairs in any way influence the political relationship?

The foundations of Soviet trade policy were laid by Lenin when he observed in an essay published in 1921 entitled *The Importance of Gold Now and After the Complete Victory of Socialism* that 'when we are victorious on a world scale I think we shall use gold for the purpose of building public lavatories in the streets of some of the largest cities of the world'. However, until that time, Lenin urged that: 'we must save the gold in [Russia], sell it at the highest price, buy goods with it at the lowest price. When you live among wolves, you must howl like a wolf'.[85] Indeed, this metaphor accurately depicts the Soviet policy guiding mineral sales to the West during the past thirty years. Cooperation with South Africa to expedite this policy has never been ruled out or made taboo in Soviet Marxism-Leninism. Commercial relations such as these are necessary to strengthen the Soviet Union (and thus in the long-term, to help further the victory of communism and the final defeat of capitalism) and gain legitimacy, in Soviet theory, by the doctrine of peaceful coexistence.[86]

However, in the case of South Africa, there is the problem of the possible tension arising from the Soviet need to maintain commercial contacts with South Africa on the one hand and the Soviet doctrine of national liberation on the other. Yet, there are several references in Soviet literature which condone such compromises.[87] Lenin proclaimed that 'the task of a truly revolutionary party is not to declare that it is impossible to renounce all compromises, but to be able, through all compromises, when they are unavoidable, to remain true to its principles . . .'[88] Stalin sanctioned the need for the Soviet Union to make such compromises by drawing a distinction between strategic and tactical policies. While strategic policies are by definition long-term and in close accordance with the dictates of ideology, tactical policies are short-term, subordinate to and designed to serve strategic goals.[89] In Soviet Marxist–Leninist theory, there can be tactical compromises, but never strategic ones. Accordingly, collaboration with South Africa for the marketing of minerals is deemed a tactical compromise. This commercial arrangement helps to provide a valuable supply of hard currency to the USSR and thus reinforces the foundations of the Soviet state. In the Soviet view, this strengthening of the Soviet Union is actually seen to strengthen revolutionary forces and promote the ultimate national liberation of South Africa because of the identity of interests between the USSR and the world revolutionary movement. To a cynical observer this might appear, however, to be nothing more than a triumph of pragmatism over ideology, whereby two seemingly contradictory policies, each serving Soviet national interests, are followed independently of one another.[90]

Soviet officials, themselves, rarely use such theoretical arguments as advanced above to justify the economic relationship between South Africa and the Soviet Union. Indeed, official notification of Soviet involvement with South Africa, no matter what the justification, would do incalculable harm to the USSR's standing in Black Africa and chosen role as chief proponent of national liberation and majority rule in South Africa. *Isvestiya* dismissed accusations of collusion: 'our country has no contacts of any kind with South Africa, the racialist citadel of apartheid'.[91] When confronted with evidence of Soviet/South African consultations in mineral matters, Soviet representatives have instead chosen to make a distinction between South African business and government. Anatoli Gromyko, Director of the African Institute of the USSR's Academy of Sciences, stated that 'the Soviet Union has contacts with the cartel which deals in diamonds, which is not to be confused with official government ties with South Africa'.[92] Vladimir Bykov, Soviet Deputy-Ambassador in London during 1981, initially dismissed assertions of a covert relationship. He stated that 'from time to time some circles in the West try to make fabrications about alleged relations between Soviet Union and South Africa but . . . we have none'.[93] Presented with evidence of Soviet participation in the De Beers cartel and Gordon Waddell's trip to Moscow, Bykov would only say that there were no 'bilateral relations between South Africa and the Soviet Union' and that 'in South Africa there are a lot of multinational corporations and companies and the company in question is named Anglo–American. This means that British and American capital is involved and [Waddell] represents in Moscow, British and American capital'.[94] He concluded by asserting that charges of complicity 'are made deliberately, purposely to divide the Soviet Union and African countries'.[95]

Does this commercial interaction influence the openly antagonistic political relationship? One Consgold executive stated that contacts between South Africa and the Soviet Union over minerals were 'firmly based in economic realities', and that controversial political subjects were avoided.[96] While it is inconceivable that the Soviet and South African governments are not privy to these meetings, discussion of them is likely to be confined to issues directly related to mining. Anglo–American, the English-speaking internationalist mining house is the most important corporation in South Africa, and Harry Oppenheimer, its former director, has some influence within the South African government. In the USSR, the Ministry of Foreign Trade and the other various state organisations and banks which manage these mineral exports are allowed an unusual degree of autonomy of action in their efforts to gain export earnings for the state. Thus, both groups enjoy privileged positions in their respective governments and, due to the importance of their commercial undertakings, each are allowed discreetly to meet with the enemy. In Soviet theory, trade and politics are inseparable in foreign policy and, in principle, no commercial undertaking takes place unless it is deemed to make a contribution to Soviet objectives. Thus, by strengthening the Soviet economy, Soviet cooperation with South Africa serves a political goal. In this sense, there is an interplay between economics and politics, but it would be ascribing to the USSR and the RSA more subtlety of purpose to suggest that the atmosphere of hostility between them has been muted through these clandestine meetings.

While the evidence suggesting a link between the Soviet Union and South Africa for the marketing of various minerals has been virtually ignored in the literature concerning South African security, the issues raised by the purported Soviet threat to South African strategic minerals such as chromium, manganese and platinum, have received considerable attention in the West. Together, the Soviet Union and South Africa dominate world production for each of these critical resources and the production and reserves figures, presented without explanation, suggest a worrying reliance on these two foreign suppliers. South Africa accounts for perhaps 35 per cent of current world production and possibly 70 per cent of total world chromite reserves. The RSA provides the United States with 35 per cent of its total ore needs and 75 per cent of its ferrochrome requirements. Significantly, Western Europe is even more heavily dependent on South African supplies of chromite.[97] South Africa also produces 20 per cent of the world's manganese ore, and the Republic possesses nearly 95 per cent of all manganese found outside the Soviet bloc. The USSR is the world's largest producer of manganese and the Atlantic Community

TABLE 5.2   *Critical minerals and their uses*

Mineral	Major uses and characteristics
Chromium	An alloying element in steel and iron (especially resistant to corrosion and oxidation). Used in the production of stainless steel, nickel–chromium heating elements, pigments, catalysts, refractories, and in the plating of metals.
Manganese	Principal uses in the production of steel, aluminium, cast iron, and in dry cell batteries and certain chemicals.
Vanadium	An alloy in steels and non-ferrous metals, especially important for jet engines and airframes.
Gold	Used as a metal or metal alloy in jewellery, transistor connections, computers, the aerospace industry, dentistry, glass and coinage. Also used as a store of value.
Platinum	Used as a catalyst in the chemical, petroleum refining and automotive industries. Used as a corrosion-resistant material in the chemical, electrical, glass and medical industries.

SOURCE   Adapted from United States Bureau of Mines, 'Mineral Facts and Problems', *USBM Bulletin*, no. 667 (1976) p. 1259

currently meets approximately 40 per cent of their requirements from South African imports.[98] In platinum, South Africa produces 45 per cent of total world production and possesses in excess of 70 per cent of world platinum reserves. Again, the USSR is the other major producer of the platinum group metals, and most non-South African reserves are found inside the Soviet Union.[99] All of these minerals have important industrial and military applications and are vital to Western economies (see Table 5.2).

VI

Taking together South Africa's sizeable contribution to world mineral production, the West's dependency on a few vital minerals and the Soviet Union's position as the primary alternate supplier, it is not surprising that both American and South African observers see the primary thrust of Soviet policy as attempting to disrupt the supply of South African minerals to the industrialised democracies.[100] South Africa has been termed the 'Persian Gulf of minerals' and Soviet policy toward the Republic described as a 'strategy of denial'.[101]

United States Congressman, David Marriot, warned that: 'if the Soviet Union in their efforts in Southern Africa would team up with those [Marxist] nations in Southern Africa, we could have the entire Western world shut down in approximately six months'.[102] Others argue that South Africa will be the site of a Soviet-initiated 'resource war'. Former American Secretary of State, Alexander Haig, told a House of Representatives sub-committee that the United States and her allies were entering 'an era of resource wars', and because of Soviet adventurism in the region, southern Africa was its primary theatre.[103] Van Rensburg has contended that 'it is becoming increasingly clear that a major Soviet objective in Southern Africa is to obtain access to its enormous reserves of raw materials, or preferably control over these resources'.[104] Due partially to the increase in Soviet activism in the region since 1974, 'worst case scenarios for Southern Africa are being reconsidered as distinct possibilities'.[105]

There are two quite distinct worries expressed in the above statements. One concerns the fear of being beholden to the Soviet Union in the event of a disruption in South African supply; the second has to do with the fear of a Soviet/South African cabal to control mineral prices and supplies if a revolutionary regime aligned with the Soviet Union were to achieve power in South Africa.[106] In the first instance, there is an implicit assumption of Western vulnerability to a potential 'loss' of South African minerals should the Soviet Union succeed in promoting regional strife and cutting off South African supply. It will be argued that these presumed objectives of the USSR in southern Africa and the perceived consequences of Soviet policy for the Atlantic Community are based upon inaccurate and facile reasoning. Despite the conventional wisdom that a revolutionary transformation of South African politics would jeopardise the West's access to strategic minerals, neither logic nor experience supports this belief.

However, the notion of a 'resource war' in southern Africa should not be dismissed out of hand. Indeed, competition for scarce resources has been a recurring theme in much of the literature concerning the West's growing dependence on imported materials.[107] The reliance on a potential enemy, the Soviet Union, for defence related materials, the dangers of mineral exhaustion and the perils of resource diplomacy, have all been discussed by economic warfare theorists such as C. Fred Bergsten, Charles C. Abbott, Admiral R. H. Hillenkoetter, and George Kennan since the beginning of the Cold War.[108] Further, since 1945 there are at least two examples of the Soviet Union attempting to use its predominance in mineral production to gain economic leverage. After the US decision to license East–West trade in 1948, the Soviet Union notified Western governments of impending cutbacks in mineral shipments. Although in 1947 the United States depended upon the USSR for 31 per cent of its imported manganese, 47 per cent of imported chromite, and 57 per cent of imported platinum, the US was able to take countermeasures and circumvent any serious supply disruption.[109] During the 1970s, the Soviet Union contributed over half the world's open market palladium supplies and, possibly following the OPEC example, sought again to gain advantage through its mineral transactions. With such a dominant market share, the USSR attempted to double the price of its palladium exports. This resulted in large inventory liquidations by major Western consumers and months of depressed prices for freely-traded palladium.[110] Thus, both Soviet attempts to employ its commodity power failed.

The issue of Soviet mineral diplomacy has been closely linked with the question of the USSR's mineral self-sufficiency. The Soviet Union has long been regarded as a country rich in natural resources with little need for external sources of supply. An important study published in 1934, *The Strategy of Raw Materials*, concluded that of all the major powers, only the USSR could hope to be self-sufficient in mineral production.[111] A later study cautiously stated that while the 'Soviets have been unable to meet their own ambitious goals', their 'peacetime internal needs can probably be met from domestic output'.[112] However, the author was careful to qualify this conclusion by pointing out that the mineral requirements of the Soviet Union's East European satellites could jeopardise the Soviet Union's mineral independence. Indeed, because of increased demand for mineral resources in the Soviet Union and East Europe, the USSR has begun to look beyond the bounds of domestic production. Many Western analysts believe that the Soviet Union is now facing a shortage of many of its domestic minerals.[113] One Central Intelligence Agency report speculated that imports of lead and zinc may be necessary during the 1980s and many other studies have predicted growing shortfalls of various magnitudes in Soviet production of manganese, chromite, bauxite, cobalt and titanium.[114] The Soviet Union has made several notable references to this situation in recent publications. *The Basic Guidelines for the Social and Economic Development of the USSR for 1981–85 and the Period up to 1990*, which outlines the Eleventh Five Year Plan, attributes the shortfall in production to: depletion of old mineral deposits; the transfer of main centres of mining to Siberia; outdated extractive technologies; and industrial waste.[115] Further, the distinguished Soviet economist, Oleg Bogomolov, writing in the theoretical journal, *Kommunist*, warned Comecon that the USSR would be unable to guarantee unlimited supplies of raw materials to East Europe in the coming decade.[116] To remedy the situation, Kremlin planners have proclaimed the development of Soviet mining and industry a primary goal of this decade.

Daniel S. Papp offers a valuable overview of the current Soviet natural resource situation:

> The USSR has already purchased aluminium and bauxite, chromium, cobalt, iron and steel products, lead, titanium and zinc on the world market. In some cases, purchases have been out of necessity, in others because of cost, location or political factors. Soviet exports of high quality aluminium, chromium, iron ore, lead, manganese, platinum, titanium and zinc have either been drastically reduced or halted, and Soviet reportage of production statistics of all the surveyed materials except iron has ceased. Gold exports remain erratic. Something is clearly taking place in the non-fuel mineral industries in the USSR . . . Soviet non-fuel mineral industries are beset by problems which have no simple solutions. Whether these industries can provide requisite quantities of raw materials for the Soviet economy throughout the 1980s is an open question. While no definite conclusions can safely be drawn about Soviet mineral surplus or scarcity during the 1980s it is evident that the margin of self-sufficiency which the USSR enjoys in many of the mineral commodities surveyed above is a narrow and narrowing one.
>
> In several of the cases examined, increased consumption rates and declining rates of growth of mineral output have all but eliminated the margin of self-sufficiency. Thus, the USSR must almost inevitably import bauxite, cobalt, and titanium in the near-term future, and external sources of chromium, lead and zinc may also be necessary. It is reasonably safe to conclude that these six minerals will be imported because of the inability of the Soviet mineral industry to keep pace with growth in demand.[117]

Not enough is known about the current condition of the Soviet mining industry to warrant observations any more definitive than these.

How does the Soviet position *vis-à-vis* mineral production relate to the question of a Soviet inspired 'strategy of denial' directed against southern Africa? The alleged gravity of the decline in Soviet mineral production has been duly acknowledged in the resource war scenarios concerning southern Africa. Before the appearance of intelligence reports in 1976 speculating about Soviet dependency on certain mineral imports, Western strategists took the view that the chief goal of the USSR was to deny valuable resources to the West. For instance, Van Rensburg wrote that 'while the USSR is well endowed with most vital raw materials and has used them to earn foreign exchange, it is increasingly attempting to conserve those resources and buy elsewhere to preserve its self-sufficiency in times of crisis'.[118] Patrick Wall also noted that 'the USSR has, of course, little need of South Africa's minerals for its own use as it is largely self-sufficient' in domestic production.[119] So prior to forecasts of a slowdown in Soviet production, the main thrust of Soviet diplomacy was apparently to disrupt the supply of materials emanating from South Africa. Since the appearance of reports questioning Soviet long-term self-sufficiency for various resources, the motivation of the USSR is now reputed to lie in obtaining for itself the vast supply of South African minerals to relieve Soviet deficiencies. For example, James Arnold Miller explains that the goal of the Soviet Union is to 'gain effective control over Southern Africa' for its mineral resources so as 'to supplement domestic production'.[120] The apparent transition in Soviet goals in South Africa from simply denying minerals to the West towards 'stealing' minerals from the West is sudden, yet this alleged conversion in Soviet objectives is merely an artificial distinction posed by Western analysts.

Western observers often cite Major General A. N. Logovskia's work entitled *Strategiya i Ekonomika (Strategy and Economics)* as evidence of Soviet intentions to disrupt mineral supplies from southern Africa. Logovskia, writing in 1961, noted that the Western capitalist system depended on imported sources of cheap raw materials – notably chrome, platinum and nickel – from its colonial holdings in Asia and Africa. This dependence of the industrialised West on natural resources from the colonial areas he termed the 'weak-link principle' and asserted that if the newly independent nations of Africa would sever this exploitive relationship it would weaken the international predominance of the West and accordingly strengthen the USSR's world position. The Soviet leadership were optimistic that the national liberation process which was sweeping the developing world would favour the forces of socialism and promote Soviet influence in the Third World. Much of Soviet theoretical literature during Khrushchev's rule was characterised by an assumption of a burgeoning Soviet/Third World alliance in international affairs built upon an emerging identity of interests between the developing world and the USSR. However, by 1964 conservative Kremlin planners considered that Khrushchev was overly optimistic in his appraisals of the Afro–Asian states, and the new Soviet leadership adopted a less ambitious policy towards the Third World.

In time it became apparent that Moscow took a more conservative view of the prospects of an eventful Soviet–Third World alignment, as many of the newly independent states continued in 'neo-colonialist' relationships with their former colonial masters. This sense of reappraisal and caution towards the Afro–Asian states is apparent in Soviet writings since the ousting of Khrushchev. More recently, there is a conspicuous absence of suggestions in current Soviet theory that the Third World should deny valuable resources to the West or offer them at exhorbitant prices.[121] Indeed, in Kosygin's 1976 speech to UNCTAD V, the principal role assigned to the developing countries in the global economy amounted to providing raw materials at stable and equitable prices.[122] These more current and pragmatic Soviet sentiments are rarely, if ever, reflected in Western accounts.

The fact that the USSR is in the midst of a massive effort to unlock the vast mineral resources of Siberia suggests that the Kremlin seeks to avoid a raw materials shortfall by boosting domestic production. The USSR does trade for various minerals on international markets and there is Soviet concern that the less developed countries should keep producing the resources necessary for fuelling the advanced economies, including those of East Europe. Christopher Coker has made note, in this regard, of the increasing minerals exports from the newly independent countries of southern Africa to East Europe.[123] Genrikh A. Trofimenko of the Institute of US and Canada Studies, refutes the assumption that the chief aim of Soviet foreign policy in the developing regions is 'cutting the jugular vein' of the West, because it 'would lead to rapid escalation of a Soviet–American conflict . . .'[124] Further, it would be unreasonable for the USSR to place too much emphasis on gaining access to minerals vital to its economy from a region as politically uncertain as southern Africa. Indeed, Seth Singleton has observed that 'certainly the Soviets would be happy to control the world's supply of chromite and platinum and much of the manganese, gold and diamonds. But these possibilities are not their basic motivation'.[125] In short, the overriding objectives of the Soviet Union in supporting national liberation in southern Africa are political rather than economic.

However, should the USSR become actively engaged in a conflict in southern Africa and in the process block Western access to South African minerals, what consequences would the Atlantic Community face? The question of Western vulnerability to just such a potential cut-off has been treated in great detail in two separate reports: the Sub-committee on African Affairs of the United States Senate Study (commissioned by the Congressional Research Service) entitled *Imports of Minerals from South Africa by the United States and the OPEC Countries* and the Rockefeller Foundation Study Commission on US Policy Toward Southern Africa.

The conclusion of the former report was that 'South African minerals are of significant, but not critical, importance to the West. It is fortunate in the case of each of the critical minerals imported from South Africa, means are available for dealing with an interruption without depending on the Soviet Union as an alternate supplier'.[126] The Rockefeller Commission reviewed the supply situation with respect to several critical minerals, but it in no case found a supply problem which could not be obviated with planning and foresight.[127] Suggestions to help alleviate potential problems included: increasing stockpiles; developing a national minerals policy; diversifying sources of supply; and encouraging allies to take similar steps.[128] One of the principal findings of the Senate study included an observation that 'although various mineral supply interruption scenarios can be imagined . . . a long-lasting and complete cut-off of South African minerals seems the least likely possibility'.[129] The reason given for this is that 'South Africa's economic health is heavily dependent on trade with the United States and other OECD countries and on investment it receives from them. Because of this interdependence, a South African decision to deny minerals to the OECD countries is highly unlikely . . .'[130] The Rockefeller Commission report concluded that 'stoppages, if they should occur, are likely to be partial, intermittent and short term'.[131]

It is often overlooked in any discussions of Western dependence on South African natural resources that South Africa itself is dependent on its mineral transactions with the Atlantic Community. For instance, in 1982 the South African mining industry accounted for over 60 per cent of South African export earnings.[132] Indeed, mineral exports are essential to the continued prosperity of South Africa. Larry Bowman has poignantly questioned 'can anyone foresee the circumstances when *any* South African government would be in a position to forego these massive earnings ($25.6 billion in 1980)?'.[133] Robert M. Price has argued persuasively:

No South African government, however radical, could afford to forgo the revenues earned by mineral exports, and the only significant market for South African minerals is the United States and its allies. Thus, any government in power in South Africa, whatever its ideology, would be locked into selling its industrial raw materials to the West just as the West is locked into buying them.

This would be especially true for a radical South African government, which would, one must assume, attempt to satisfy the social welfare demands of the population to a greater degree than the present minority government does. The resources to pay an enlarged welfare bill – for education, health facilities, housing and the like – would have to come out of the overall economic expansion and given the nature of the South African economy, such an expansion would entail as one of its crucial elements an increase in export earnings. Thus a radical regime in South Africa, interested in increasing its foreign exchange earnings, would be motivated to expand the export of its minerals, not the reverse.

Moreover, increasing mineral export earnings would require increased mining production, which would force a radical regime in South Africa to seek external capital, technology and management resources. Even the present economic system, controlled by the dominant minority, relies heavily on external capital and technology. How much more reliant would a new regime be – having to answer to a much larger support base and therefore more earnestly needing economic expansion? Because the Soviet Union demonstrates neither the ability nor the willingness to subsidize an economy like South Africa's (as it has the less developed and less sophisticated Cuban economy), there would simply be no alternative but to turn to the West for the needed capital technology and management.[134]

The experience of newly liberated Mozambique, Angola and Zimbabwe would tend to support this thesis. Certainly the priority given in Zimbabwe and Angola to consolidating mineral exports to the West during the immediate post-independence period underscores this observation. In Angola, the ruling MPLA regime from the outset declared its intention to seek diversified Western involvement in its economy. The Gulf Oil Corporation dominates petroleum production in the Cabinda enclave and provides the vast majority of Angola's foreign exchange and government revenue.[135] Diamang, Angola's diamond production corporation is operating within the

Central Selling Organisation marketing system and the major diamond mines in the north-east of the country are operated by De Beers.[136] Claims such as made by Robert Hanks that, 'the fall of Angola to Marxists . . . placed that country's assets at the exclusive disposal of Moscow' are patently absurd.[137] Close political relations between the Soviet Union and African states do not portend a move away from close economic ties with the West. In fact, a feature common to all states of southern Africa is their continuing interest in attracting Western investment for the development of mining. The South African Development Coordinating Conference (SADCC) programme is a plea for further integration of the southern African constellation of states into the global economy. This dependence on Western investment and technology will doubtless continue in the future.

Concern about a future minerals cartel between a future South African government and the Soviet Union should be tempered by the realisation that collaboration already exists between the two for the marketing of various minerals. The value of diamonds, platinum and gold on international markets has declined precipitously during the past few years and the best years of the De Beers cartel are certainly in the past.[138] Marketing restraint has been the key to continued profits for South Africa and the Soviet Union in international commodity markets and a radical regime in South Africa, striving to increase its export earnings, would be inclined to increase mineral exports, not the reverse. This could prove disastrous for the market value of diamonds and platinum and play havoc with the world gold price. Raymond Vernon has written about the feasibility of establishing a minerals cartel that 'a substantial volume can only be a necessary condition, not a sufficient one, for purposefully influencing world markets. First, a country must have discretionary power in the decision whether to trade. A nation that badly needs the imports or exports it undertakes . . . can hardly be said to have much commodity power.'[139] In this sense, it is possible that the appearance of an avowedly Marxist regime in South Africa would not be in the best economic interests of the Soviet Union. Indeed, the USSR has a commercial interest, albeit an uncertain one, in the preservation of the *status quo* and the continuation of clandestine marketing contacts. This situation is not dissimilar to the USSR's Western adversaries: the interest in change in South Africa is balanced by a desire for continued profitable commercial relations. While projections about the nature of future cooperation between the Soviet Union and South

Africa can only be speculative, there has already been a long history of collaboration which cannot be ignored.

In conclusion, the notion of a Soviet-inspired resource war in southern Africa cannot be substantiated. Although the assertions of a Soviet 'strategy of denial' have had a considerable impact, generating extensive discussion and controversy, if one looks beyond the rhetoric emanating from all sides and observes the actual minerals policy of the Soviet government, a more pragmatic natural resources policy emerges. Cooperation with South Africa for the marketing of various minerals, a steady preoccupation with ensuring Soviet self-sufficiency in mineral supply through increasing domestic production, the recent Soviet experience in international commodity markets, all point to a conservative 'business as usual' economic strategy.[140] Should a revolution occur in South Africa and a radical government come to power, the proper conditions for an effective cartel or a cut-off in mineral supplies to the West are probably not present. The Soviet Union's objectives in promoting the national liberation movement in Southern Africa are, in large part if not exclusively, political rather than economic. It is more likely that considerations of profitability and security of supply, rather than revolutionary activism, determine the USSR's mineral policy and accordingly its commercial relationship with South Africa.

6 Soviet Espionage in South Africa

The Russians are such novices in Africa (Graham Greene, *The Human Factor*)

Possibly the biggest spy since Philby (a reference to Commodore Gerhardt in the South African Parliament, 1984)

The Soviets do not hesitate to send their men, repeatedly, as it turned out, and at great cost and risk, to spy on us in Africa (Prime Minister P. W. Botha, 1981)

I

With the discovery in 1983 that a high ranking South African naval officer, Commodore Dieter Gerhardt, was spying for the Soviet Union, the issue of Soviet espionage activities on the southern continent has gained greater significance. South Africa has, since the apprehension of a Soviet intelligence officer in 1967, almost gleefully held up captured Soviet spies as evidence of the USSR's policy of 'total onslaught' against the Republic. However, the uncovering of a Soviet agent within the South African military elite, who in his position enjoyed unhindered access to the most sensitive government secrets, has caused considerable embarrassment and worry in Pretoria. The apparent laxness of South African security precautions, the unknown extent to which South African secrets have been compromised by Gerhardt's revelations, and the fear that other such senior officials could possibly be working in the service of the Soviet Union, have resulted in a heightened concern about the nature of Soviet espionage activities in South Africa.

What are the intentions and capabilities of Soviet clandestine operators in South Africa? What priority does South Africa hold in the hierarchy of Soviet intelligence activities? What role does Soviet espionage play in the overall policy of the USSR towards South Africa?

Soviet clandestine operations in South Africa, as exhibited by the Gerhardt affair, are worthy of consideration and the limited available information can offer clues to the motivation of Soviet policy towards South Africa. The USSR has no diplomatic representatives in South Africa and thus the Soviet Union's tools of statecraft are severely limited and clandestine operatives are of manifest importance. Indeed, the acquisition of intelligence appears to be the prime function of the KGB in South Africa.

There are inevitable difficulties faced when delving into the clandestine world of espionage. This is a murky area of limited significance to any academic investigation where complexity and perplexity abound. There is often no apparent relationship between official policy and clandestine operations beyond the obvious intentions of both to serve the ultimate interests of the state. Covert activity follows a peculiar logic and dynamism, regardless of chills and thaws in the Cold War struggle between the Soviet Union and the West. While several studies examine the KGB's espionage activities on the international scene with a reasonable amount of thoroughness and precision, none provides a convincing picture of the KGB's role in the formulation and execution of Soviet foreign policy.[1] This is especially true with regard to defining the tasks of Soviet intelligence in South Africa.

This chapter will attempt to overcome this dearth of information and penchant for secrecy and focus on the activities of the Soviet secret service in South Africa, according particular attention to the intelligence work and clandestine operations of the KGB inside South Africa. Of course, we know only of the activities of agents that have been apprehended and nothing of those still at large, yet the information available about captured spies in South Africa merits scrutiny. Through the examination of available material – official papers, government studies, parliamentary debates, relevant journal articles and books, press accounts, and interviews – the record of Soviet clandestine operations will be reviewed, and observations concerning the objectives of Soviet agents in the Republic will be duly advanced.

There are undoubtedly KGB operatives who hold positions within a number of Soviet-supported institutions which deal with South Africa. These include the Soviet Committee for Solidarity with Asian and African Countries, the World Peace Council, the World Federation of Trade Unions, and Radio Peace and Progress to name but a few. Yet, the International Department of the Central Committee of the Communist Party of the Soviet Union, rather than the KGB, derives and implements policy for these organisations. It is appropriate here, to differentiate between the International Department's propaganda activities and the KGB's espionage undertakings, though this distinction is often blurred. The KGB plays a secondary and obscure role in the process, and thus Soviet intelligence activities in this sphere are beyond the scope of this enquiry.

It is important to preface this discussion further with the supposition that, unlike those who suggest that the KGB's operations in South Africa give credence to the notion of a Soviet directed 'grand strategy' against the Republic, it is the view of the author that such instruments of policy as the employment of agents are not unusual or surprising, and that these activities in themselves do not represent evidence of a Soviet grand strategy in southern Africa. Furthermore, the national liberation struggle to eliminate apartheid and establish black majority rule will continue unabated, regardless of the activities of Soviet clandestine agents in the Republic. The dark and Byzantine world of spying has little relevance to the powerful social and political forces in South African society which will ultimately determine South Africa's future. With these objectives and caveats noted, the main subject of enquiry can be addressed.

II

The carrying out of espionage and intelligence gathering by the Soviet Union is undertaken by the First Directorate of the Committee for State Security (Komitet Gosudarstvennoy Bezopasnosti), or KGB.[2] The First Chief Directorate is organised into at least twelve departments of which the Ninth Department is responsible for the English-speaking countries of Africa. The section of the Ninth Department which deals with operations against South Africa is apparently the largest and accorded a significant degree of importance.[3] The Chief Intelligence Directorate of the Soviet General Staff, or GRU, is also involved in intelligence operations, though the primary focus of its activities continues to be acquiring information of relevance to the military. Included in this broad category is the GRU's task of overseeing all Soviet satellite reconnaissance and technical means of verification. The GRU has recently coordinated its activities more closely with Directorate T of the KGB which is responsible for collecting scientific and technological intelligence in the industrialised countries.[4] It is the KGB, and to a far lesser degree the GRU, which directs Soviet covert operations against South Africa.

The issue of Soviet espionage in South Africa is not a new phenomenon. Indeed, the fear of Soviet clandestine activity was a major concern in Prime Minister Jan Smuts decision to establish diplomatic relations with the Soviet Union in 1942, and allegations of Soviet espionage in South Africa precipitated the break in official contacts in 1956.[5]

The South African fears concerning the clandestine activities of Soviet diplomats in Pretoria have been documented in the chapter on official relations. Both the Union and Nationalist leaders were fearful of 'the ruthlessness and efficiency of the Russian agents serving in South Africa'.[6] Although there was never any substantive evidence linking the Soviet consulate to any sort of communist activity or espionage in the Union, Eric Louw, South Africa's first Minister of External Affairs, expelled the Soviet legation from South Africa on the grounds that the embassy was a hive of espionage and subversion.[7]

The wave of national independence sweeping across Black Africa in the late 1950s and early 1960s coupled with the rise in prominence of the USSR on the continent, was greeted with concern in Pretoria. Government leaders decried the increase of Soviet influence in the newly liberated black nations and warned of a coming Soviet-directed insurgency intent on toppling the white order in South Africa. This purported communist challenge to South Africa gained credibility in the Republic (South Africa declared itself a Republic in 1961) with the announcement of the capture of KGB official Yuri Nikolaevich Loginov, alias Edmund Trinka, in Johannesburg during 1967.

III

The first Soviet spy to be apprehended in South Africa, Loginov's capture was made public by Prime Minister Vorster in a Statement to Parliament on 9 September 1967. Loginov's arrest was reputedly engineered by the then head of the Bureau of State Security (BOSS), General Hendrik Van den Bergh. Loginov had spent a total of less than eight months in Johannesburg before his capture. Both BOSS and the CIA interrogated Loginov, and he apparently provided his captors with a wide range of information. General Van den Bergh stated that during his interrogation Loginov divulged to the Security Police details about Soviet clandestine activities in twenty-three countries.[8] Loginov also described in some detail his responsibilities and training as a KGB operative.

A highly educated and privileged son of a Party functionary, Loginov devoted much of his adult life to a strict regime of KGB training. During the course of his questioning, Loginov revealed that he had spent nearly eight years in preparation for missions outside the USSR. He spoke English fluently with a pronounced American accent and was familiar with American customs and expressions. He had an impressive knowledge of North American geography and was familiar with the United States' system of government.[9] In order that he could gain employment, once in the West, Loginov was trained as a welder, a book-keeper and a travel writer. Previous to being sent to South Africa, Loginov was involved in Soviet intelligence operations in Egypt.[10]

There is, however, a lack of consensus concerning Loginov's activities while in South Africa. John Barron has written that: 'While in Johannesburg he gathered intelligence against South Africa, but he was mostly concerned with examining locales, scenes, and history that were to be part of the background the KGB had created for him'.[11] Yet, Loginov was reputedly involved in something more than simply creating an artificial background for himself while in South Africa. Rogers and Cervanka suggest that the Soviet Union had placed a high premium on obtaining information about South Africa's nuclear plans and Loginov was dispatched to South Africa to discover the status of the Republic's atomic programme.[12] They argue that: 'There have been indications that the Soviets have used agents on the ground in South Africa as well as satellite reconnaissance to get hold of this information; in fact it was reported by a Chinese source that a mysterious exchange of agents involving West Germans held by Soviets and a single Soviet agent, Victor Loginov, was connected with their priority concern with South Africa's nuclear plans.'[13] Barbara Carr, who produced a book about the affair with the assistance of the South African Security Police, wrote that Loginov was charged by his superiors to 'make every effort to get information about the extent of South African nuclear research'.[14]

The Soviet Union has indeed shown a real interest in exposing South Africa's nuclear weapons procurement programme. In 1977 Soviet reconnaissance satellites detected a possible South African nuclear testing site in the Kalahari desert, and Soviet President Leonid Brezhnev announced in Tass that 'according to information reaching here, work is now nearing completion in the South African Republic for the creation of the nuclear weapon and preparations are being held for carrying out tests'.[15] It is also true that Loginov was exchanged in 1969 for ten West German agents held by the Soviet Union.[16] Taken together these would tend to support the assertion that Loginov was involved in gathering classified information pertaining to South Africa's nuclear programme.

It was not until 1981 that a Soviet spy was again captured in South Africa. KGB Major Aleksei Michailovitch Kozlov, a senior intelligence operative, was apparently arrested in Johannesburg during the course of his fourth visit to Southern Africa. In an address to Parliament, Prime Minister P. W. Botha described Kozlov's mission as to 'assess the damage caused by the activities of other organs of his government . . . which train and arm terrorist groups like the ANC, SWAPO and others in southern Africa'. Botha claimed that during his interrogation, Kozlov admitted that he was sent to determine the effectiveness of the ANC inside South Africa because several Soviet analysts believed that the organisation's claims abroad did not justify the money and energy spent on it by Moscow. Kozlov is reputed to have reported to his superiors in Moscow that 'representatives of the ANC were unable to convince him that the ANC had indeed been responsible for the Soweto disturbances during 1976', and that 'ANC leaders were squandering Soviet aid unnecessarily'. Furthermore, Kozlov is purported to have passed along his observations that 'he found no visible support' for SWAPO and that Samuel Nujoma could only hope to win an election in Namibia on the condition that SWAPO organisers intimidated the voting population. Finally, contrary to a popular belief among Soviet Africanists that 'South Africa was a volcano which could be expected to erupt any minute', Kozlov is said to have reported back to Moscow that he found no evidence of political instability in South Africa.[17]

Prime Minister Botha did not explain the circumstances surrounding Major Kozlov's arrest and the statement he made before Parliament was the only official information revealed concerning Kozlov's activities in the Republic. It was later reported in the press that Major Kozlov was arrested in July 1980 at Jan Smuts Airport on his return from Windhoek. In May 1982, after being held for over 18 months, Kozlov was exchanged for what were described as 'eight very important Western intelligence agents' held by the USSR.[18] The

International Red Cross was widely reported in the press as the mediator between the Soviet and South African governments.[19] However, according to information obtained from the Red Cross, the USSR approached South Africa about the possibility of a spy exchange and throughout the subsequent negotiations, 'South African and Soviet authorities dealt directly with each other'.[20] Indeed, Dr Neil Barnard, the Director of the newly reconstituted National Intelligence Service (NIS) was recently praised by Prime Minister Botha for his role in negotiating with the KGB for Kozlov's exchange.[21]

Botha's allegations in Parliament about Kozlov's activities and reports back to Moscow must be treated with caution. Indeed, this collection of both plausible and unlikely testimony warrants suspicion. While it is possible that Kozlov ascertained that resources from Moscow were mis-spent by the ANC, it is inconceivable that he travelled throughout Namibia on at least two occasions and found 'no visible support' for SWAPO. Furthermore, P. W. Botha's decision to divulge details of a case with clear implications for South African national security is in itself unusual. It can be reasonably assumed that Kozlov was an important KGB operative sent to South Africa to observe the internal organisation and activities of SWAPO and the ANC, but beyond this, it is difficult to accept the official South African version of Kozlov's clandestine mission. However, it is true, as Botha notes, that Kozlov's capture does give an indication that the 'Soviets do not hesitate to send their men, repeatedly, as it turned out, and at great cost and risk, to spy on us in Africa.'[22]

IV

The most recent and spectacular case of Soviet espionage was uncovered with the apprehension of Commodore Dieter Gerhardt of the South African navy. The former commanding officer of the Simonstown naval dockyard, Commodore Gerhardt, and his Swiss-born wife were convicted of high treason in the Cape Supreme Court on 29 December 1983. Commodore Gerhardt was the first Soviet agent captured in South Africa who was recruited by the KGB (Gerhardt apparently initially offered his services to the USSR for ideological reasons, but was later tempted and recruited by the KGB with the lure of financial rewards). The arrest of Commodore Gerhardt was announced by Prime Minister Botha on 26 January 1983 on the eve of the annual visit to the Simonstown base by the foreign press corps.[23] Commodore Gerhardt, aged 47 at the time of his arrest, appeared the very model of a successful naval officer. Tall, balding and highly intelligent, with an intense, abrasive manner, Gerhardt travelled in high South African defence and government circles and was personally acquainted with Prime Minister Botha.[24] Accusations that Gerhardt had spied for the Soviet Union over a period of more than twenty years caused a sensation in South Africa and resulted in widespread suspicion that there were other highly-placed Soviet spies operating in the government, army and air force.[25]

Although the announcement of Gerhardt's capture was made in South Africa at the end of January 1983, the Commodore was actually detained three weeks earlier in New York in a joint operation conducted by the Central Intelligence Agency, the Federal Bureau of Investigation and MI5. These agencies, acting on information revealed in several documents from the African department of the Soviet Foreign Ministry provided by a Soviet defector, had scrutinised Gerhardt's activities for some time before his arrest. Commodore Gerhardt was in the United States for a six-month course in advanced mathematics at Syracuse University and was apprehended in his hotel room by a man he took to be a fellow student on the course, but who was in fact an undercover FBI agent.[26]

The evening of his apprehension, Gerhardt was flown to Washington in a government aircraft and subsequently interrogated by the CIA for eleven days. During his interrogation in the United States he is reputed to have made a confession while wired to a lie detector device. He was then flown back to South Africa under escort where Prime Minister Botha announced that Gerhardt had been arrested under Section 29 of the Internal Security Act on charges of treason.[27] Commodore Gerhardt was the first serving officer in the South African military to be tried for treason and news of his capture shocked the navy, since with fewer than 700 officers in the entire service, he was known to most of the defence establishment. There was initial incredulity that an officer of such seniority could have spied for a period of over twenty years in a country where there are no diplomatic links with any Warsaw Pact nation.

The Gerhardt trial lasted four months and most of it was held *in camera* at the request of the prosecution. Gerhardt was charged and convicted of spying for the Soviet Union and the full judgment was delivered by the Judge President of the Cape, Mr Justice Murrik on

29 December 1983. Commodore Gerhardt admitted travelling to Moscow on five separate occasions in the previous twenty-one years. The circumstances surrounding Gerhardt's recruitment by the Soviet Union were not made public although he spent several years in Great Britain during the period 1958–64, first in a naval training programme and later as a naval attaché at the South African Embassy in London. The prosecution argued that the Gerhardts had used ' "dead letter boxes", radio transmissions, couriers, and personal visits to communicate with Soviet agents and supply information about armaments, weapons systems, and public security'.[28] In exchange, Commodore Gerhardt is alleged to have been paid $325 000 for his reports.[29] Commodore Gerhardt was sentenced to life imprisonment and his wife received a ten-year sentence for her complicity.

According to Defense Department sources in Washington, Commodore Gerhardt passed on details of American, British and French contingency plans to use the Simonstown base and back-up facilities in the event of an East–West conflict in the Indian Ocean or South Atlantic.[30] As commander of the Simonstown dock he oversaw the refitting and refurbishment of most of South Africa's fleet and was in a position to provide the USSR with technical information about electronic and weapons systems – those of South African manufacture as well as equipment modified from Israeli, French and other Western designs – that would be of interest to Moscow. Commodore Gerhardt was intimately acquainted with the tracking capabilities of the underground maritime command and communications centre at Silvermine near Simonstown. As a senior official in the office of Force Development in the South African Ministry of Defence during 1979, he had unhindered access to most military secrets.[31] Gerhardt is also said to have divulged details about the reserve stocks of naval fuel and stores held at Simonstown by Western navies in case of an emergency. Furthermore, the prosecution during his trial argued that Gerhardt was able to monitor British naval movements during the Falklands conflict and relay this information to Moscow. There is also evidence to suggest that Gerhardt provided details concerning high level contacts between South Africa and various South Atlantic states for the possible establishment of a South Atlantic security organisation.[32]

Gerhardt's defence attorneys during the trial argued that the Commodore's treachery did not jeopardise South African security, because the information he was able to acquire was of limited value to the Soviet Union.[33] While the USSR may have little use for South

African military secrets, evidence of collaboration between the RSA and the West concerning details of contingency plans and military cooperation would undoubtedly be of some interest to the Soviet military. Regardless, Gerhardt's revelations cannot be dismissed as unimportant.

In short, Gerhardt had access to a wide range of information directly related to South Africa's national security. A senior South African naval officer commented that Gerhardt 'knew everything', and Robert Cabelly, special envoy to Assistant Secretary of State for African Affairs, Chester Crocker, stated that Gerhardt's treachery was 'extremely damaging to Western interests'.[34] Another American diplomat stated that Gerhardt's arrest 'was felt in Moscow'.[35] As a result of Gerhardt's testimony, the South African Defence Forces have initiated an exhaustive review of policy, projects and security measures in view of secrets now believed to be in Soviet hands. Gerhardt's arrest also led to the capture of KGB agent Mikhail Vassilievich Nikolayev in Zurich, who was allegedly there to collect information from Mrs Ruth Gerhardt.[36]

In addition to the exposure of KGB agent Nikolayev, Gerhardt's capture has led to the discovery that South Africa has been a key link in the smuggling of advanced Western technology to the USSR. Richard Muller, a West German businessman formerly based in Cape Town, had for several years purchased sophisticated electronics equipment and computers from the United States which, after shipment through South Africa and Sweden, ultimately arrived in the Soviet Union.[37] Muller has been linked with Commodore Gerhardt and Western intelligence services claim that Muller was the local KGB liaison officer in South Africa directing the activities of Gerhardt until the time of his arrest. However, the relationship between the two is subject to speculation. The CIA sent two agents to South Africa after Gerhardt's arrest to investigate Muller's movements and activities. The existence of the high technology trade route operating through South Africa was made public on 21 December 1983 with the seizure in Sweden of a VAX–11–782 computer bound for the Soviet Union.[38] The VAX–11–782 is valued at $2 million and manufactured by Digital Equipment Corporation in the United States. This highly sophisticated computer if appropriated by the USSR 'would significantly improve the Soviet microelectronic manufacturing capability and would have an important and pervasive effect on Soviet military technology', according to Professor Seymour E. Goodman of the University of Arizona.[39]

After a joint investigation conducted by the South African police and the United States Customs Department officials, it was announced that Muller's companies – Optronix, Integrated Time, Semitronik and Microelectronic Research Institute – operated as 'storefronts' for pirating high technology imports to the USSR. According to US customs spokesmen involved with 'Operation Exodus', a government investigation to limit high technology smuggling to the USSR, Muller had been previously indicted in California during 1979 for illegally exporting semiconductor manufacturing equipment to the Soviet Union and was wanted for questioning on three continents.[40] The investigations resulted in the seizure of a large amount of advanced equipment (over 60 tonnes) in Sweden and West Germany which was purchased in the United States and shipped through Cape Town. This discovery was termed the 'tip of the iceberg' and US customs officials and Western diplomats speculate that South Africa has been used as a transit point for shipments of high technology to Moscow for several years.

This incident illustrates clearly that South Africa has served as an important link in the smuggling of advanced Western technology to the Soviet Union and that KGB operations to acquire microelectronic equipment and computers from the West have multiplied in recent years.[41] The South African connection is also interesting in that the KGB has chosen to establish a clandestine commercial relationship with a country the USSR officially reviles. However, the attraction of using South Africa for these transactions is obvious: the stigma attached to trading with South Africa tends to keep paperwork detailing the conditions of a commercial agreement to a minimum.[42] This also points to the ever-increasing sophistication of KGB techniques for acquiring advanced Western technology. The association of a highly placed, long-term Soviet agent like Commodore Gerhardt with this scheme is a testament to the importance attached to industrial espionage in Moscow.

Another aspect of Soviet espionage activity directed against South Africa was described in the Committee on Intelligence hearings of the House of Representatives on Soviet Active Measures.[43] The term 'Active Measures', as defined by the Committee, includes propaganda and influence operations designed to affect public opinion. Active measures are often spoken of in an intelligence context to distinguish between espionage operations and propaganda activities. A primary goal of Soviet active measure campaigns is to 'demonstrate that the United States is an aggressive "colonialist" and "im-

perialist" power'.[44] A favourite method of the KGB for achieving this
objective is to leak forged documents to newspapers and governments. These forgeries often implicate the United States in unsa-
voury deeds with unpopular regimes.

In the case of Soviet active measures directed against South Africa
the Committee produced several forged documents detailing high-
level contacts between the United States and South Africa. These
documents included: a Presidential Review Memorandum on the
necessity of close political ties with South Africa which states that
'the failure of US strategy in South Africa would adversely affect
American standing throughout the world'; and a letter from an
American aviation firm detailing the conditions by which American
military pilots would serve with the South African Air Force.[45] These
forgeries clearly portray the United States and South Africa as acting
in collusion with one another in political and military matters.

V

It is apparent from this examination of Soviet espionage that the
USSR has accorded a notable degree of importance to operations
against the Republic. While KGB activity in South Africa does not
carry the prominence of Soviet espionage operations in Western
Europe or the United States, South Africa is a focal point of clandestine enterprise in Africa. Since the closure of the Soviet embassy in
Pretoria in 1956, it has been impossible for KGB officers to operate
under 'legal' diplomatic cover. Yet, the Soviet Union has continued,
repeatedly and often at great risk, to dispatch operatives to, and
recruit agents in, South Africa. This willingness to commit financial
resources and manpower for covert action in South Africa was
positively confirmed with the capture of Commodore Gerhardt. Yet
the abilities and training of these agents should not be exaggerated;
all three displayed remarkable ineptitude in the course of their
operations.[46]

The objectives of the KGB in South Africa are, as far as can be
deduced from the examination of available information, five-fold.
First, the KGB has actively monitored the activities and effectiveness
of ANC and SACP underground operations in South Africa. Second,
Soviet agents have placed a priority on gathering information concerning the South African Defence Forces, military cooperation
between South Africa and other Western powers, and details of the

Simonstown and Silvermine naval facilities. Third, the Soviet Union has followed the progress of South Africa's nuclear programme with great interest. Fourth, the KGB has displayed great ingenuity by smuggling large shipments of restricted electronics equipment and computers through South Africa to the USSR. Finally, the KGB has sought to establish the degree of cooperation which exists between South Africa and various South American states. It would be exceedingly difficult to rank the relative importance to the KGB of each of these endeavours. Yet, the interest of the USSR, particularly in highlighting military and commercial cooperation between South Africa and the West, is manifested in Soviet literature and official statements on South Africa.

This brief study has also revealed some corollary information concerning espionage in South Africa. The Soviet and South African governments have apparently dealt with each other directly on at least one occasion to arrange an exchange of captured agents. Furthermore, the degree of collaboration between BOSS and other Western intelligence agencies, the CIA in particular, in this area of Soviet espionage is exceptionally high. Gordon Winter wrote in his controversial exposé that: 'The relationship between British intelligence and BOSS is basically simple. They feed each other information about known Communists in both countries, as do other countries in the West. . . . the attitude of all these countries is that the real fight is East versus West, Communism versus Capitalism'.[47] Former CIA officer John Stockwell has also noted that 'the CIA has traditionally sympathized with South Africa and enjoyed close liaison with BOSS'.[48] These observations ring true, and as Soviet interest in South Africa has not waned, further cooperation will doubtless continue.

7 The Soviet Union and the Contemporary Political Situation in Southern Africa

Soviet leaders have an interest in impeding Western access to the raw materials and minerals in Southern Africa and in disrupting Western use of the sea lanes around the Southern end of the continent. (David Albright, 1982)

The whole idea of Russian submarines starving the West into submission by a strategy of protracted interdiction or blockade was . . . absurdly nineteenth century in its conception.' (R. W. Johnson, 1977)

If the USSR would interdict Western shipping in the Indian Ocean . . . this would lead to a rapid escalation of a Soviet–American conflict. (Genrikh A. Trofimenko, 1981)

I

Southern Africa was the scene of increased Soviet interest and activity in the 1970s. With the collapse of the Portuguese African Empire in 1974 and the attainment of national independence in Mozambique and Angola, Soviet policy towards the region has taken on a new significance. The period has also witnessed Soviet diplomatic and political initiatives in Zimbabwe, Zambia and Namibia and other countries in southern Africa. The purpose of this chapter is to provide a brief overview of Soviet policy towards southern Africa in

140

he contemporary period. Particular attention will be devoted to ecent developments in the region which have had an impact upon he shaping of Soviet policy for South Africa. Moreover, there will be n examination of the Soviet naval presence in the Indian Ocean and n the South Atlantic. The implications of these maritime forces for he formulation and execution of Soviet policy against the Republic vill also be reviewed. Finally, there will be a related discussion oncerning Western perceptions of Soviet involvement in the region.

The People's Republics of Angola and Mozambique are the USSR's oldest surviving allies in Black Africa. Both countries are regarded by soviet theorists not only as 'socialist-oriented' states but also as nations where 'scientific socialism' is the official ideology.[1] Angola and Mozambique have signed long-term security pacts with the soviet Union, and Soviet military equipment and personnel provide he basis for their national defence. The current relationship of the soviet Union to these front-line states will be examined in the ollowing section.

It should be stressed at the outset that the dramatic escalation of soviet involvement in southern Africa which characterised the 1970s vas unforeseen by Western Sovietologists. Most observers forecast pragmatic moderation and peaceful competition in Soviet activity in he Third World. Robert Legvold, the noted American commentator on Soviet involvement in Africa, stated in 1970 that: 'The Soviet Union is not given to political and ideological adventures, nor is it villing to distribute its resources liberally to achieve modestly im-proved positions in areas of declining importance such as Black Africa.'[2] Yet, in 1975 the Soviet Union intervened directly with Cuba n the Angolan Civil War to support the Popular Movement for the Liberation of Angola (MPLA).[3] While the planning of this operation and the decision-making process are beyond the scope of this study, it can be noted that the USSR displayed a willingness to assist militarily a local client in a region where the Soviet Union had no compelling strategic interest and no history of significant military involvement.[4] In this, the operation was unprecedented. For the first time the USSR demonstrated its ability to project power decisively thousands of miles from the Soviet mainland. Also, due to South African ntervention in Angola, the joint Soviet and Cuban actions were supported by a majority of African states.[5]

The MPLA's military victory over rival liberation organisations, he Front for the National Liberation of Angola (FNLA) and the Union for the Total Independence of Angola (UNITA), and the

South African army did not end Soviet or Cuban involvement i
Angola. Currently, the MPLA is supported by approximately 25 00
Cuban troops and roughly 500 Soviet military advisers and instru
tors. In 1976 Agostinho Neto, then President of Angola, flew t
Moscow to sign a Treaty of Friendship and Cooperation with th
Soviet Union. At the behest of Moscow, Neto transformed th
MPLA into a Marxist–Leninist party. Also in 1976, Neto preside
over a plenary meeting of the newly established Central Committe
which launched the 'transition to socialism'.[6] While there has bee
some suggestion that the USSR was involved with the abortive cou
attempt led by Nito Alves in 1977, the Soviet Union probably was nc
associated directly with Alves' unsuccessful undertaking. Presider
Dos Santos, who assumed power after the death of Neto, is cour
selled by Soviet advisers in Luanda.

Certainly the most important article of the twenty-year Friendshi
Treaty, and indeed the most notable aspect of Soviet–Angola re
lations, concerns military ties. The Treaty specifies that both cour
tries shall work to develop cooperation in the military sphere 'in th
interests of strengthening their defense capacity'. Weapons ship
ments from the USSR to Angola include jet fighters, tanks an
sophisticated anti-aircraft missiles.[7] With the renewal of South Afr
can military incursions into southern Angola in 1977 and the reviv
of Jonas Savimbi's UNITA, the Soviet Union stepped up its arm
transfers to Luanda. On 12 January 1984, an announcement by th
Soviet news agency Tass stated that defence assistance was ir
creasing.[8] Yet, little specific information has been revealed about th
type and quantity of arms shipments.[9] It is clear that despite thes
reported increases in military deliveries, Soviet assistance has nc
been sufficient to secure the MPLA's faltering position in Angola. I
this respect, Soviet aid has been primarily defensive, to guard again
the capture of Luanda or the vital oil-producing enclave of Cabind

After South African motorised units again crossed Angola's south
ern frontier in December 1983, the USSR issued a strongly worde
condemnation of the attack. The USSR called for 'urgent and cor
certed international efforts' to halt South Africa's 'aggression again
the freedom loving peoples of Africa'.[10] However, the statemer
avoided mention of the Soviet–Angolan Treaty, nor did it indicat
any specific Soviet actions on behalf of the MPLA to curb Sout
Africa's incursions. This communiqué was interpreted in the West a
an indication that the USSR was disinclined towards any furthe
direct involvement in Angola.[11]

Measured against Soviet military support to Angola, which is second only to that given to Ethiopia in Black Africa, the USSR has received only modest strategic, political and economic returns. While the Soviet Union has acquired airport facilities for long-range military reconnaissance flights over the South Atlantic to monitor Western shipping, the MPLA has to date resisted Soviet requests for a naval or submarine base.[12] Politically, the Soviet Union has made no claims about the 'irreversibility' of socialism in Angola, and Soviet Africanists acknowledge there are divisions within the MPLA which seek to lessen the USSR's influence. With the recent spate of diplomacy between South Africa and the front-line states culminating in the Nkomati Accord, coupled with the decisive new phase in the international negotiations for Namibian independence, the Soviet position in Angola is uncertain. Compounding Angola's military and political challenges are severe economic problems which the Soviet Union is unwilling or unable to help alleviate. The USSR exports mainly heavy machinery and transport equipment to Angola and imports mainly coffee. Angola's trade deficit with the USSR is striking (Soviet exports in 1983 amounted to about £150 million, while imports reached just £2 million).[13] Soviet aid contributions have been meagre and Russian commentators indicate that 'in the current situation, security considerations take precedence over economic matters – greater attention will be given to the economy when order is restored'.[14] Moreover, the USSR did not encourage Angola to join Comecon. The USSR and Angola signed a ten-year economic agreement in 1982, but significant extensions of Soviet economic aid have not as yet materialised.[15] The asymmetry in Soviet involvement in Angola, particularly the USSR's propensity to commit military rather than economic resources, is perhaps most noteworthy.

Soviet relations with Mozambique since independence have followed a similar course, but Soviet involvement in Mozambique has not been as substantial as in Angola. The USSR, together with China, gave diplomatic support and provided some military assistance to the Front for the Liberation of Mozambique (FRELIMO) before the collapse of the Caetano dictatorship in Portugal in 1974. Unchallenged by rival liberation movements, FRELIMO assumed power without massive assistance from the USSR or Cuba. Yet, in 1977 President Samora Machel announced the establishment of a Marxist–Leninist vanguard party. In 1977, Mozambique signed a twenty-year Treaty of Friendship and Cooperation with the USSR. A divergence in views between Maputo and Moscow, however, developed over the Lancaster House conference on Rhodesian Zimbabwean independence. Machel endorsed the exercise, much to the chagrin of the Soviet leadership.[16] In 1978, Machel's application to join Comecon was refused on the grounds that the Mozambiquean economy was too far below the level of member countries. The USSR's decision to deny entry of Mozambique into Comecon under scores Soviet unwillingness to make a substantial economic commit ment to Mozambique. The lack of Soviet interest in integrating Mozambique into the Soviet bloc led Machel to re-evaluate his relationship with the USSR and in part encouraged him to contem plate restoring contacts with South Africa.[17]

The Friendship Treaty with the USSR provided Mozambique with tanks, armoured vehicles, artillery pieces, surface-to-air missiles and some military aircraft. Approximately 200 Soviet instructors and advisers helped to transform the guerrilla forces into a conventional army. After Zimbabwean independence, South Africa stepped up its support of the National Resistance of Mozambique (MNR), which was waging a campaign of destabilisation in Mozambique. In January 1981, a South African commando team attacked African National Congress (ANC) facilities in Matola on the outskirts of Maputo. The Soviet Ambassador in Mozambique, Valentin Vdovin, subsequently conveyed a message that the USSR would come to the aid of FRELIMO if South African forces ever again crossed Mozambique's borders.[18] To underscore the warning, two Soviet warships visited Maputo harbour in the following months.[19] In 1982, General Alexe Yepishev, the head of the political department of the Soviet Army visited Mozambique to assess the deteriorating security situation brought about by increased MNR activity. However, Soviet suppor did not increase appreciably.

In 1983, Mozambique began negotiations with South Africa which led to the signing of the Nkomati Accord on 16 March 1984. This development certainly could not have come as a complete surprise to the USSR, as Machel had visited Moscow and met with Nikola Tikhonov on 15 February.[20] However, the Soviet Union has criticised the Accord for 'breaking South Africa out of diplomatic isolation on the continent'.[21] The same Soviet observer noted that: 'Strong-arm methods hardly make for durable understandings, especially when the groundwork for them is shaky.' In a communiqué issued in April 1984 at the conclusion of talks between President Chernenko and the Ethiopian leader, Mengistu Haile Mariam, there was indirect criti cism of Mozambique's agreement with South Africa.[22] More re cently, stepped-up military and economic relations between Mozambique and the United States has spurred speculation of a further cooling of relations with Moscow.[23]

In short, Soviet commentators have expressed doubts about the legitimacy and wisdom of the Nkomati Accord. Relations between Mozambique and the Soviet Union have grown more distant and uncertain as a result, and the seventh anniversary of the Treaty of Cooperation, celebrated on 31 March 1984, received scant attention in the Soviet press.[24] Furthermore, in the Soviet statement issued on 25 June, the ninth anniversary of Mozambique independence, there was a warning to 'defend the revolution against the intrigues of internal and foreign enemies'.[25]

In short, in both Mozambique and Angola, the Soviet Union, after reaping the gains of its forceful entry into southern Africa in 1975, are now realising the limits of Soviet power and influence in the region. Yet, current Soviet behaviour would seem to show clear recognition of its disadvantages and limits. The USSR is conscious of the danger of being overextended and the Soviet Union, to date, has avoided open-ended commitments to either regime. The USSR has assisted in the 'tasks of promoting national security' in Mozambique and Angola but has carefully tailored the kinds of military assistance it provides and hedged its own direct role. Contrary to some assertions made in South Africa,[26] there is no evidence of a Brezhnev Doctrine for Angola or Mozambique (direct Soviet military intervention to save a southern African regime faltering internally appears unlikely). For instance, when addressing the question of Angolan defence, 'fraternal assistance' from the USSR is rarely mentioned by Soviet observers as the ultimate guarantor of the MPLA.[27] Indeed, in Veniamin Midtsev's hierarchy, Soviet aid is mentioned fifth, after the 'unbending resolve of the leadership and the people of Angola to uphold the independence of their country', after 'the support from other Frontline States', and after OAU solidarity.[28] By contrast, Soviet assistance to Vietnam and Syria is judged to be of first-order importance.

II

Soviet involvement in southern Africa is not confined to the 'socialist-oriented states' in the region. Indeed, recent initiatives towards other nations and groups in the area deserve consideration.

In Zimbabwe, Soviet influence and involvement has followed a fluctuating pattern. The USSR backed Joshua Nkomo's Zimbabwe People's Revolutionary Army (ZIPRA) forces in the war for national liberation in Rhodesia, while the Chinese preferred aid to Robert Mugabe's Zimbabwe African National Liberation Army (ZANLA) faction. Yet, both Nkomo and Mugabe followed their own interests in the Lancaster House negotiations and excluded the USSR from any indirect role in the transition from white minority to black majority rule. The Soviet expectation of a friendly regime coming to power in Zimbabwe was unfulfilled with the overwhelming electoral triumph of Mugabe in 1980. Mugabe showed a clear preference for Western and Chinese political links and waited for over a year before establishing diplomatic relations with the USSR. More recently, however, relations between Moscow and Harare have improved. There have been several cultural, trade and political agreements signed since 1982,[29] and Soviet representatives applauded Prime Minister Mugabe's attempts to establish closer ties with Eastern Europe.[30] Soviet commentators praised Mugabe for his tour of Hungary, Czechoslovakia and East Germany in May 1983,[31] and have noted recent tensions between the United States and Zimbabwe.[32] For instance, Zimbabwe's abstention in the UN Security Council vote condemning the shooting down of Korean Air Lines flight 007 and its sponsorship of a Security Council resolution critical of US intervention in Grenada were duly noted in the Soviet press. Soviet efforts to rebuild contacts with Mugabe have been relatively successful, and Soviet–Zimbabwean relations have progressed since independence.

The USSR has sought to establish better state-to-state contacts with most of the southern African countries. Cultural, political and trade exchanges with Botswana, Zambia and Lesotho underscore what Albright has described as 'Moscow's new emphasis on government-to-government relations across a broader ideological spectrum' in southern Africa.[33] This suggests that the Soviet Union is desirous of a more continuous, steady involvement in southern African politics. The USSR has traditionally supported liberation struggles in the region, but recent diplomatic moves indicate that the Soviet Union seeks to expand its activities in the post-independence period. However, noting the striking military dimension of Soviet policy coupled with the lack of economic levers in the region, it is difficult to see what form increased Soviet interest might take.

Of course, the USSR's support for Samuel Nujoma's South West Africa People's Organisation (SWAPO) guerrillas struggling against South Africa Defence Forces continues, but recently the USSR has displayed in private discussions and public forums a readiness, if not an eagerness, to participate in the international diplomacy over Namibia's future. During the 1979 Lancaster House negotiations, the USSR counselled the Patriotic Front delegation that true independence could only be achieved through a military victory.[34] Soviet advice went unheeded and the independence process proceeded without Russian participation. The USSR is wary of being discarded as an ally when their role of armourer is no longer needed. Consequently, the Soviet Union follows the twists and turns in the negotiations over Namibia closely and continues to seek an internationally recognised role in the undertaking, commensurate with its position as a superpower having legitimate, though minor, interests in the region.

The Soviet Union's interest, influence and involvement in southern Africa was dramatically and uncharacteristically high in the period from 1975 to 1980. However, in the period since, southern Africa has rescinded in importance to the USSR. The Soviet belief and Western fear that the USSR would establish a zone of Soviet influence across southern Africa has not been realised. Moreover, with challenges in Poland and Afghanistan and domestic difficulties arising from repeated political successions since 1980, the Soviet Union has strong reasons to adopt a lower profile in southern Africa. Yet the USSR maintains an active interest in the region and will continue to do so for the foreseeable future.

III

The establishment of a Soviet naval presence in the Indian Ocean and in the coastal waters of southern Africa also has implications for Soviet policy towards South Africa. In 1968, the USSR deployed a permanent fleet in the Indian Ocean. The number of Soviet ships in the fleet has remained consistent since its introduction, numbering between fifteen and thirty warships and auxiliary craft. In 1970, the Soviet Union deployed a West African patrol as an extension of the USSR's Southern Atlantic fleet. Since the establishment of friendly regimes in Ethiopia, Angola and Mozambique in the 1970s, a host of Soviet cruisers, destroyers, frigates, landing ships and submarines have visited African ports on 'show the flag' exercises. The Soviet naval activity in the Southern Oceans was demonstrated dramatically in 1979 when the aircraft carrier *Kiev* and a flotilla of accompanying ships passed around the Cape of Good Hope. More recently, after the South African military raid in March 1981 on Matola in southern Mozambique, two Soviet warships visited the harbour of Maputo.

The build-up of the Soviet navy in the Indian Ocean has been viewed with some trepidation in the West. Albright has noted that 'Soviet leaders have an interest in impeding Western access to the new raw materials and minerals of Southern Africa and in disrupting Western use of the sea lanes around the southern end of the continent'.[35] Gann and Duignan have raised the issue that Soviet submarines armed with nuclear missiles operating off the African littoral 'would introduce new strategic possibilities', and the West would be better able to counteract this threat 'if they had access to South African harbours and to the excellent naval base at Simonstown'.[36] Furthermore, Vanneman contends that 'Soviet naval activities in Southern Africa suggest a significant escalation of its commitment to employ naval power to protect its interests in the region'. Specifically mentioned was the 'Soviet willingness to employ its forces . . . to support subversion in South Africa'.[37]

There are three quite distinct worries expressed in the preceding statements. The first concerns the fear that Soviet warships might interdict Western shipping passing around, or emanating from, South Africa. The second has to do with the apprehension that the Soviet naval presence in the Indian Ocean favours its strategic position *vis-à-vis* the United States. The third worry is a fear that the USSR, with its demonstrated naval and air transport capabilities, might intervene directly in southern Africa. In the following section, each of these perceived or purported threats will be evaluated in turn. It will be argued that the Soviet naval presence in the Indian Ocean is neither particularly important nor directly relevant for Soviet policy towards South Africa. Moreover, it will be shown that some of the above assumptions are based upon inaccurate or unsubstantiated reasoning. Despite the conventional wisdom that the Soviet navy is preparing to intervene in, or interdict in the seas around, South Africa, logic and experience belie this belief.

The waterways around South Africa are unquestionably important for the transport of oil and other commodities to Western Europe. The number of ships passing around the southern tip of the African continent numbers approximately 27 000 per year. Of these ships, perhaps 8500 are oil tankers. Half of all ships call at South African ports, while the rest circumnavigate the Cape without breaking their voyage. Recent estimates indicate that nearly 70 per cent of Western Europe's oil and 30 per cent of United States' imported oil travels the Cape route. Furthermore, 75 per cent of the strategic raw materials used by the Atlantic Community are transported via the Cape of Good Hope.[38] One commentator noted that:

> Politicians may juggle with figures and pay homage to, or denigrate, countries and ideologies which they like or dislike . . . but they cannot alter geography . . . . The geographical and strategic importance of the South Atlantic, the Indian Ocean and Southern Africa . . . will remain unchanged and the Cape Route will lose none of its importance as an ocean highway.[39]

Since the appearance of Soviet maritime forces in the Indian Ocean, the West has been preoccupied by the threat to the shipping lanes around the Cape. However, there are several factors which are often overlooked when considering the possibility of a Soviet attack on Western shipping. It is difficult to imagine the circumstances leading to a Soviet naval interdiction, let alone the logistical requirements Kremlin planners would face in order to pose such a blockade. Moreover, the likely political and military consequences that would follow an attack should not be underestimated.[40] R. W. Johnson has argued that:

> the whole idea of Russian submarines starving the West into submission by a strategy of protracted interdiction or blockade was . . . absurdly nineteenth century in its conception. The very first ship sinking, after all, would constitute a major act of war and the nuclear bombers and missiles would be in the air only a few minutes later.[41]

In a well reasoned discussion of the potential for a Soviet naval operation in the waters around South Africa, Robert Price asked two pertinent questions: If the USSR wished to interdict Western oil shipments, why would it do so at the Cape? And if the Soviet Union was prepared for a major war with the West, why would it want its navy in South African waters?[42] In answer to the first question, if the USSR wished to stem the flow of oil to Western Europe, it could accomplish this far more efficiently by bombing the oil fields or blockading the Straits of Hormuz.[43] Indeed, Spence has noted that 'if the Soviet Union was bent on a policy of interference with Western shipping . . . there are areas where this would be done more easily than round the Cape'.[44] As for the second question, in the war that would ensue any such provocative Soviet challenge, the USSR would need to have its navy in the North Atlantic and Mediterranean, where it could assist in defending the Soviet homeland, rather than in the distant South Atlantic, sinking Western merchant ships.[45]

What is lacking in the apocalyptic scenarios that can be envisaged for the Indian Ocean has been evidence of a Soviet task force designed to interfere with Western shipping on the sea lanes around South Africa. Consequently, not only is a Soviet interdiction a dubious political proposition, but there are many logistical difficulties associated with such an operation. And finally, a naval blockade in African waters would be strategically untenable given the likely range of military consequences.

The Indian Ocean became relevant to the strategic nuclear balance between the United States and the Soviet Union with the development of missile-bearing submarines. Foltz has observed that 'Southern Africa enters the arcane calculus of the Soviet–American balance of terror principally through the possibility of stationary atomic missile-bearing submarines in the Indian Ocean'.[46] Indeed, the Soviet naval interest in the Indian Ocean was probably spurred by a series of reasonable but incorrect assumptions about United States submarine missile deployment intentions. With the development of the Polaris missile and the Poseidon submarine, the Soviet leadership reasoned that the north-western Indian Ocean would be a likely area of deployment.[47] Thus, in expectation of a US submarine force taking station in the Indian Ocean in the late 1960s or early 1970s, the Soviet Union deployed a fleet in the Indian Ocean from 1968 with sophisticated anti-submarine capabilities.[48] Yet, the projected American deployment in the Indian Ocean did not materialise. Since the primary function of the Soviet navy in the Indian Ocean has remained unfulfilled, because no major US deployment has taken place there, the Soviet fleet has been left to serve Soviet interests in other ways.[49] The significance of the southern Indian Ocean to the overall strategic balance between the superpowers remains limited and South Africa is irrelevant to the nuclear competition between the United States and the Soviet Union.

The USSR's naval presence in the Indian Ocean, however, does have implications for Soviet policy towards South Africa. With the deployment of the *Ivan Rogov*, the first ship of a new class of amphibious assault ship, to the Indian Ocean in 1979, the Soviet Union has gained a capacity to project naval power at great distances.[50] This new ability was given doctrinal justification by the commander-in-chief of the navy, Admiral S. G. Gorshkov. In his book on the sea power of the USSR, Gorshkov listed support for friendly regimes in the Third World and for the national liberation process as important tasks of the Soviet navy.[51] This willingness to use the Soviet navy in Africa has been demonstrated in Ethiopia, where Soviet ships assisted in Mengistu's campaign against the insurgencies in the north and south, and in Angola with the Soviet navy providing logistical and transport support for the MPLA. Yet, Soviet naval activity to date has been modest, and there is little indication that the USSR would intervene directly, on a large scale, in South Africa. Even conservative analysts believe that a major Soviet military operation in South Africa is unlikely. Thompson and Silvers have stated that:

> Several factors make a Soviet invasion of South Africa, in the form of southern and western beachheads and/or a land offensive from the north, a remote contingency . . . and we can discount a massive Russian assault from offshore positions'.[52]

The Soviet Union's naval capability and its association with radical regimes and national liberation movements in southern Africa ensure that the USSR will play a role in future developments in the region. However, South Africa is not central to Soviet strategy or planning and any naval involvement in southern African waters will probably be limited by a host of military and political factors. In addition, Western observers are in general agreement that Soviet military actions in regional disputes can be seen to follow rather than lead local events in the Third World.[53] A dramatic and apocalyptic military intervention into southern Africa is not foreseen as a likely possibility in the immediate future.

IV

Aside from the military dimension of Soviet activity in southern Africa and in the Indian Ocean, the most notable aspect of Soviet policy is apparent in Soviet commentary. Since 1981, Soviet analysts have stressed what Legvold has termed 'the interconnection of United States and South African policies', whereby:

> every measure of economic assistance (the 1982 1.1 billion dollar IMF loan), every step towards military cooperation (easing restrictions on the sale of military–strategic goods) or nuclear cooperation (lifting the ban on exports of nuclear power equipment and plutonium), every US Security Council veto protecting South Africa, and every visit of one country's intelligence or military officials to the other are picked up and trumpeted in Soviet accounts.[54]

In addition, Soviet writers claim that South Africa and the United States are pursuing similar objectives and employing complementary tactics. Accusations of a South Atlantic Treaty Organisation between South Africa and various South American states have also been revived in the Soviet media.[55] The Reagan Administration's policy of 'Constructive Engagement' has been consistently castigated by the USSR, and Soviet propaganda has stressed the significance of Washington's 'unholy alliance' with Pretoria.[56]

Although Western perceptions of Soviet involvement are generally more sophisticated, they are no less negative. The alleged Soviet threat to vital Western shipping lanes and strategic minerals is often cited as the rationale to justify political ties that might otherwise be difficult to defend. The basis of American diplomacy in Southern Africa is to restrict Soviet influence and to deny the USSR an internationally recognised role in any regional diplomacy. Competition, misunderstanding and a lack of communication mark the current state of superpower relations in southern Africa. Henry Kissinger's metaphor that: 'the superpowers often behave like two heavily armed blind men feeling their way around the room, each believing himself in mortal peril from the other, whom he assumes to have perfect vision. Each tends to ascribe to the other a consistency, foresight and coherence that its own experience belies' is particularly apt for the contemporary situation in southern Africa.[57] Soviet activities in Angola and in Ethiopia have contributed to the decline of detente, and a future violent racial clash in South Africa, with each superpower clearly associated with opposing antagonists, could lead to a further breach in relations between the Soviet Union and the United States.

8 Conclusion: Soviet Policy Towards South Africa

There are Cubans and Russians in Angola and Mozambique. Why? What is it they want here? (Interview from Barbara Villet's *Blood River*)

Why are we in Southern Africa? Your question implies that we do not have legitimate interests here; however, we do. (Andrei Y. Urnov, Head of Southern Africa Division, CPSU International Department, 1984)

There are probably as many lists of Soviet objectives in Africa as there are Western analysts studying them. (Dimitri Simes, 1979)

It was stated at the outset that the purpose of this enquiry was to present an historical overview of Soviet policy towards South Africa and to achieve an understanding of the motivations of the USSR on the southern African continent. Towards this end, it will be useful to recall the questions advanced in the introduction concerning the derivation of Soviet foreign policy. These are:

(1) Is any continuity exhibited between Russian and later Soviet policies towards the region?
(2) What factors help or hinder Soviet policy in South Africa?
(3) How have strategic, ideological and commercial factors influenced Soviet activities?
(4) How does the Soviet Union perceive the development of the national liberation struggle in South Africa?
(5) What priority does South Africa hold in the hierarchy of Soviet foreign policy?
(6) What, ultimately, are Soviet interests in Southern Africa?

The following sections seek to answer, in succession, these six questions.

153

I

Is there any continuity expressed in Russian and later Soviet involvement in the region? Many contemporary Western observers, looking at Soviet involvement in South Africa, have tended to operate in a vacuum, neglecting to place Soviet actions within their historical context. The political links which developed between the USSR and various southern African resistance groups in the early 1960s surprised many Western officials and scholars, in part because of the mistaken impression that the Russians were wholly ignorant of Africa and its history. There are, however, several references in recent Soviet publications to the Russian involvement in the Anglo–Boer War.[1] Indeed, what is today a surprisingly extensive body of literature on South Africa began to accumulate at the turn of the century. These early accounts and descriptions of South Africa provide an invaluable source of information for Soviet academics.[2] In addition, the writings of the Russian Marxists from the period of the Anglo–Boer War serve as the foundation for Soviet theoretical research concerning South Africa.[3]

Moreover, in defining political objectives in South Africa and in determining the appropriate means of accomplishing these tasks, there are similarities in policy-making throughout the entire period of Imperial Russian and Soviet involvement in the region. Opposition to Britain's imperial position, the opportunism of the Russian approach, the realisation of the disruptive potential of indigenous nationalist movements, and the utilisation of native South African discontent were all to find their expressions in Soviet policy.[4] In addition, the methods of policy employed by the Soviet regime to gather information and extend its influence resemble those applied during the Czarist period. For instance, there are obvious parallels between Lieutenant Colonel Romeiko-Gurko, sent by the Russian high command to observe the Anglo–Boer War and KGB Major Aleksei Kozlov, who was dispatched to Namibia on a covert operation to determine the strength and effectiveness of SWAPO. Indeed, the use of clandestine agents and 'front organisations' are aspects of Soviet policy which were utilised by Russian statesmen as well. Also, the service of Russian 'volunteers' in Africa is not unique to the Czarist period. The USSR offered to send 'volunteers' to Egypt during the 1956 war with Israel,[5] and Soviet[6] volunteers' and advisers are presently serving in Angola and Mozambique.[6] Furthermore, the provision of military assistance, the supply of medical aid and the high-visibility receptions bestowed upon visiting delegations were notable instruments of Czarist diplomacy practised during the South African conflict. These aspects of Russian foreign policy would find their full expressions under Soviet leadership.

Nevertheless, it must be noted that receiving foreign delegations, providing medical and military aid, sending 'volunteers' and employing clandestine agents are not essential, but rather incidental characteristics of policy used by all states. Indeed, one would expect such instruments of conduct. What is of importance though, is that both Imperial Russia and the Soviet Union have been adversaries of Great Britain in South Africa. (In the post-1945 period the United States joined Great Britain as the one of the primary Western powers in southern Africa). Underlying this long-standing rivalry was a tendency for Russians of both periods to take account of the international dimensions of the situation in southern Africa in the formulation and execution of their respective foreign policies. Russian statesmen understood that a British defeat in South Africa would have potentially dire consequences for Britain's imperial position on northern India. Soviet policy-makers in the mid-1970s perceived a shift in the 'international correlation of forces', owing in part to American failure in the Vietnam War, which reduced the risk of a US response to Soviet initiatives.[7] This condition led to active Soviet participation in the Angolan civil war. In both instances, developments in southern Africa were not viewed in isolation from Moscow.

Although the Czarist government lacked the resources and inclination to make a real commitment for a Russian intervention in the Anglo–Boer War, it was clearly willing to take advantage of conflict and strife in the region. The Soviet Union has no colonial heritage in Africa and the only period of Russian interest in South Africa was during the Anglo–Boer War. Therefore, lacking the resources for a direct Russian military involvement, the only means available for attacking British interests in South Africa was the support of indigenous resistance groups. From the very inception of Soviet power, the USSR has supported the SACP and later the ANC in a sustained quest for influence in South Africa at the expense of the West. This assistance for resistance movements in South Africa is a hallmark of Russian policy in the post-revolutionary period and before.

However, care must be taken not to overstate the continuities in policy between Czarist and Soviet regimes and to acknowledge the contrasts in their respective activities in South Africa. Surely the shift from support for white supremacist Boers to the black (or multiracial) liberation groups is as remarkable as any continuity noted above. In addition, whereas Russian support of the Boers in no discernable way altered the outcome of the Anglo–Boer War, the Soviet Union has influenced political developments in South Africa. Increased military and political capabilities, not the least of these being a strong and influential doctrine of national liberation, have enhanced the Soviet position in southern Africa immeasurably. By virtue of its ties with various resistance groups (ANC, SACP and SWAPO), its prominent position in anti-apartheid forums and in the United Nations, the USSR can influence, to a degree, the flow and tempo of southern African politics. Furthermore, while the Anglo–Russian Entente of 1907 removed a primary motivation for Russian activity in South Africa, the period of 'peaceful coexistence' between East and West in the 1970s did not deter the Soviet Union from involvement in the Angolan civil war. Detente with the West did not prevent the Soviet Union from participation in wars of 'national liberation',[8] and the USSR has stated its intention of continuing support for 'progressive forces' in South Africa.[9]

Finally, the comparison between Imperial Russia and the Soviet Union raises a wider issue concerning the two regimes as powers. The USSR today is a world power and revolutionary power, with real leverage in southern Africa. Indeed, the Soviet Union in the age of national liberation and the Gorshkov navy is in striking contrast to the Russia of Czar Nicholas, or even the USSR of Lenin and Stalin.

With these caveats and qualifications noted, it is probably more accurate to acknowledge that there are not so much continuities as parallels in Russian and Soviet policy towards South Africa. Although there is a remarkable similarity in the tools of statecraft adopted by both regimes in South Africa, the objectives of the USSR and Imperial Russia are manifestly divergent. The Soviet intention to help undermine the old order in South Africa and create in its stead a revolutionary new society represents a dramatic departure from Czarist motivations in the Anglo–Boer War. This dynamic ideological dimension of contemporary Soviet policy is absent from the Czarist approach to South Africa.

II

Second, what factors help or hinder Soviet policy in South Africa? There are several conditions which help to create a favourable environment for Soviet activity towards South Africa. The racial policies of South Africa have drawn wide condemnation from the UN and the OAU, and the Republic is today virtually an international pariah, enjoying close political ties with few states (the United States under the Reagan administration remains an important exception). The Soviet Union has been remarkably successful as the ally of national liberation in Africa in general and South Africa in particular. This derives partially from the fact that the USSR, not being an essential target of African nationalist revolt (again, UNITA's struggle against the MPLA is a notable exception), has supplied the ANC with political support, a degree of ideological inspiration, arms and, most recently, training facilities for guerrilla soldiers.[10] While the Scandinavian countries have been generous with their non-military support to groups struggling against apartheid and the Chinese have provided some assistance, though not continuous or steady, to the PAC, only the Soviet Union has consistently championed the plight of the oppressed population with guns and money. This fact has been duly acknowledged by the UN Unit on Apartheid and other international organisations concerned with South Africa.[11]

However, it is not this low-level assistance to the ANC which is the most significant asset for the Soviet Union, but it is rather the sheer unpopularity of the South African regime on the continent which offers the USSR its greatest scope for activity. For instance, the Soviet-backed Cuban intervention on the side of the MPLA during the Angola civil war would not have been countenanced by the OAU had not South African units crossed Angola's southern frontier. South African involvement in the conflict, as one Soviet scholar noted, 'blessed Soviet activities on behalf of the MPLA'.[12] Furthermore, the political and economic association of Western countries with South Africa, far from acting as an impediment to Soviet encroachment in southern Africa, actually serves to further the influence of the USSR within the national liberation movement in South Africa.[13] Since the Soviet Union has no diplomatic links with South Africa, no stake in the South African economy (apart from a secretive yet lucrative arrangement for the marketing of various minerals) and since the Soviet Union has gained some stature in Black Africa from its opposition to apartheid, the USSR is able to follow a reasonably active line of policy in southern Africa without fear of criticism in international forums.

The general alignment in views between Black Africa and the USSR on the question of apartheid, as evident from nearly forty years of UN debates on the issue, is also notable in that it is one of the few areas relating to Africa where Soviet policy is still important. In every country where a prolonged struggle for independence against a Western colonial power or a white supremacist regime has persisted after 1960, the Soviet Union has played an important role by providing heavy arms supplies to the various national liberation movements.[14] The fight against South Africa's ruling white minority is the last struggle of this kind on the continent. While the Soviet Union has generally played a secondary role to the West and Western-dominated international economic institutions in the process of post-independence economic development in southern Africa, the USSR retains significant influence with the national liberation movement in the on-going struggle against the apartheid regime.

In addition to conditions which favour Soviet policy towards South Africa, there are several corresponding factors that pose difficulties for the derivation and implementation of Soviet foreign policy. First and foremost of these is that South Africa is over 5000 miles away from the Soviet mainland. This great distance alone limits the policy options available to Soviet planners. A further constraint to the formulation of Soviet policy is the lack of first-hand sources of information in South Africa. Since the closure of the Soviet embassy in Pretoria and the cessation of official contacts in 1956, Soviet visitors have been denied the right of entry into South Africa. A.B. Davidson acknowledged that 'it is difficult in Moscow to judge South African reality because the people of our country are deprived of the possibility to see it with their own eyes'.[15] Furthermore, there are no allied Warsaw Pact embassies in the Republic either. The USSR does maintain diplomatic legations in Botswana, Lesotho and Mozambique but these cannot serve as a substitute for an official domicile in Pretoria. Moreover, the lack of economic levers, by comparison with the West, detracts from Soviet influence in southern Africa generally. As a result, there is a notable asymmetry in Soviet activities in the region: the high-profile Soviet military support contrasts markedly with the absence of Soviet economic involvement in southern Africa. Also, the Reagan administration's insistence on excluding the Soviet Union from negotiations and consultations in southern Africa has left the USSR without a direct source of information on the status of the arbitration over Namibian independence.

The distance separating the Soviet Union from South Africa and the difficulty in obtaining first-hand intelligence, means that only a limited choice of policy instruments are available to Soviet leaders.

To date, the USSR has provided qualified diplomatic, military and moral assistance to the ANC, but it has avoided a direct commitment towards the attainment of black majority rule in South Africa. To acquire intelligence from the Republic, the Soviet Union has dispatched and recruited several clandestine agents to South Africa in attempts to gain information concerning the effectiveness of ANC organisation, South Africa's military potential, and the Republic's secretive nuclear programme.

The cultural differences between the Soviet Union and black South Africa are also noteworthy and may pose some obstacles to cooperation. Indeed, it would be hard to imagine two such cultures so completely dissimilar. Black South African history, philosophy, religion and language, with all its many ethnic variations, stands in stark contrast to the Soviet experience. This contrariety should not be disregarded and, although the Soviet Union has rendered generous assistance to the national liberation movement in the struggle for black equality, racism is not unknown in the USSR.[16]

The peculiarities of the Soviet ideological approach to the South African situation, which serves to both help and hinder overall Soviet objectives, will be discussed in greater detail in the next section.

III

Third, how have strategic, ideological and commercial factors influenced Soviet activities? It must be noted at the outset of this discussion that the strategic interests of the USSR in South Africa have generally been exaggerated. As one Soviet analyst noted, 'the USSR is not seeking a zone of exclusive interest in South Africa'.[17] However, there is an objective, East–West dimension to the situation in southern Africa which cannot be ignored. Soviet strategists correctly perceive that the West has clear economic and possibly strategic interests in the preservation of a pro-Western regime in Pretoria, yet they appreciate that southern Africa is not important *per se* to the USSR. Soviet thinking about Africa has advanced far enough to reject a strict 'zero–sum' interpretation of Soviet–American regional competition in southern Africa. Liberation in South Africa need not 'strengthen the military position of the Soviet Union in the world at large', as some Western observers argue.[18] The USSR has witnessed, much to its chagrin, that the strategic advantages from its involvement in southern Africa, to date, have been modest, as both Mozambique and Angola have resisted Soviet requests for bases.[19] Soviet support for national liberation groups and Marxist governments in southern Africa does not prevent these actors from following a foreign policy which is independent of the USSR. Witness that the SWAPO leadership departed from Soviet preference on the Namibia issue by cooperating with the Western contact group of nations, and Mozambique entered into the Nkomati Accord with South Africa against Soviet wishes.

This is not to suggest that Soviet planners would dismiss the opportunity to one day establish naval, air, communications or intelligence facilities in South Africa, but it is doubtful that these distant possibilities serve as the basic motivation for their present-day activities. It is more likely that the fundamental inspiration behind Soviet policy towards South Africa is political rather than military. As Seth Singleton noted: 'Today's strategists are Leninists, not the heirs of Admiral Malan'.[20] Of course, Soviet policy is based on expectations of future developments, yet Soviet specialists on Africa recognise that South Africa 'is a rather solid regime with considerable political, economic and military power' and foresee a white minority regime in power for some time to come.[21] The strategic gains to the Soviet Union from a future black regime in South Africa are by no means guaranteed and many Western observers stress that a military presence in South Africa would ultimately be of little use to the USSR.[22]

The ideological dimension of Soviet policy towards South Africa, on the other hand, is often either dismised or overlooked. However, Soviet literature on South Africa is devoted, in large measure, to Marxist–Leninist interpretations of South African society. South Africa, with the oldest communist party on the continent and a large proletariat, possesses the 'objective conditions' for a socialist revolution. There has always been a strong ideological content in Soviet policy, first towards the SACP, and later towards the ANC. Ideological considerations contributed to Moscow's adoption of numerous controversial positions, including Soviet support for the white labourers in the 1922 Rand Miners strike, the disastrous 'Black Republic' thesis proclaimed at the Sixth Comintern Congress in 1928, the sudden reorientation of Comintern policy following the Soviet entrance into the Second World War, and later the insistence upon multiracial organisation as a criterion for continued Soviet assistance. Soviet ideological orthodoxy has served to alienate some elements of the national liberation movement and only a small Stalinist core of

SACP cadres have embraced all the many twists, turns and reversals in the theory and practice of Soviet policy.

Nevertheless, Soviet theorists hold that Marxism–Leninism is the only belief system which can be used to mobilise the oppressed masses for action in South Africa. This fusion of the instrumental and functional aspects of Marxist–Leninist theory is possibly the most dynamic and effective feature of Soviet ideology. There can be little doubt that Soviet leaders remain faithful Marxist–Leninists and, as such, they hold firmly to the principle that the working class and its political vanguard, the Communist Party, are the only truly consistent and reliable forces in the struggle for socialism. It is from this viewpoint that the USSR approaches South African society, with all its distortions and complexities. Though Soviet observers are cautious and sceptical about South Africa's revolutionary potential, they do not rule out the possibility that future developments might fulfil Marxist–Leninist prophecy. Thus, Soviet ideology influences the perceptions of Soviet theorists and serves to provide an important motivation in the formulation of Soviet foreign policy.

Commercial factors play an uncertain role in the derivation of Soviet policy towards South Africa. Indeed, Soviet support of national liberation has not been at the expense of profitable commercial ties for the marketing of diamonds, gold and platinum. Neither has Soviet advocacy of disinvestment campaigns prevented the KGB from illicitly channelling sophisticated Western technology, ultimately bound for the USSR, through South Africa. However, the clandestine commercial relationship between South Africa and the Soviet Union, while providing an excellent return on mineral sales which benefits both countries, does not appear to affect the overall hostile political relationship. The commercial dimension of the Soviet Union's policy towards South Africa is quite remarkable, yet it is anomalous and the full details of this covert cooperation are known to very few. The USSR's motivations in southern Africa are, largely if not exclusively, political rather than economic.

IV

Fourth, how does the Soviet Union perceive the development of the struggle for national liberation in South Africa? Recent indications suggest that the USSR views the liberation struggle in South Africa as a long process. After a period of heightened expectations in the wake of the Soweto crisis, when one observer stated that 'the era of the South African revolution has come'.[23] Soviet theorists today accede that these assertions were premature. Novel developments, such as the signing of the Nkomati Accord between South Africa and Mozambique, make the tasks of the ANC that much more difficult. One Soviet scholar acknowledged that the agreement will force the ANC to 'broaden its political base in South Africa, and make it more difficult to undertake 'revolution from positions outside the Republic'.[24] Yet, a Soviet official maintained that the Nkomati Accord 'could serve [the ANC] in the long term by hardening their strategy and discipline'.[25] Soviet commentators and policy-makers are in virtual agreement that the white minority regime faces no immediate threat from internal revolution or insurrection.

In the final analysis, Soviet analysts stress that the increasing contradiction between the apartheid system and the growing demands for skilled labour in the South African economy, will ultimately undermine the white minority. The artificial restrictions imposed by the apartheid economy have caused 'a powerful upsurge of the workers' movement', and the ANC led by the vanguard SACP, must continue to build its mass movement in the workplace.[26] While the respective roles of the ANC and SACP in Soviet theory were discussed in a preceding chapter, it should be reiterated that Soviet theorists currently maintain that all strata of South African society, and a wide variety of organisations (including the UDF), are eligible to participate in the national liberation process.

Soviet writers point to several factors which in the Soviet view serve to inhibit the struggle for national liberation. These include: the low level of class and political consciousness of the black African population; the lack of experience and training of the revolutionary forces; the rise of 'black racism' in South African society; the absence of legal leadership of the liberation movement; the spontaneous character of many actions (an obvious reference to the Soweto riots of 1976); and finally, a serious obstacle to the liberation struggle is the 'powerful military–repressive' potential of the white minority state.[27] These taken together will impede, but ultimately will not deter, national liberation.

Despite the difficulties cited above, Soviet analysts dismiss reforms initiated by the ruling Nationalist Party as ineffective attempts to avert the coming revolution. The USSR has historically stated its intention of continuing support for the national liberation movement in southern Africa until the last vestiges of racism and apartheid are swept from Africa.[28] Yet, Soviet scholars note that while Moscow will persist in providing modest assistance for the ANC in 'fulfilment of its internationalist duty', the USSR could not take their place in solving the tasks of national liberation.[29] Thus, Soviet planners envisage a prolonged period of struggle in South Africa in which the USSR, by furnishing military and moral aid to the national liberation movement, will play a supporting role in the process.

V

Fifth, what ranking does South Africa hold in the hierarchy of Soviet foreign policy? Southern Africa, as a whole, ranks behind the Middle East, South Asia, and indeed North Africa, in importance to the USSR.[30] South Africa is a peripheral consideration in the formulation and execution of Soviet foreign policy. Arguments emanating from South Africa and conservative circles in the West that South Africa is the centrepiece of Soviet strategy, are without foundation. Yet, this observation alone is misleading. Angola, too, was peripheral to Soviet interests and was the scene of the most uncharacteristic and dramatic display of Soviet military activism in the Third World to date (excluding Afghanistan). Indeed, the marginal importance of Angola to both superpowers encouraged Soviet and Cuban adventurism in the region.[31] So in this sense, mere geographical rankings are not very helpful.

It should be furthermore noted that the hierarchy of priorities in Soviet foreign policy is not static, but is rather fluid and ever-changing. While South Africa is of relatively low importance to the Kremlin leaders at present, a future race war in the Republic or major conflagration in the region would be likely to pose urgent concerns to the USSR. The peculiar instability of the South African situation has the potential suddenly to create serious and unforseen problems for the international community, and Soviet observers note that South Africa is 'like a sore which does not heal that could flare up to threaten world peace.'[32] This coincides with the observations of many in the West. Robert McNamara has stated that 'South Africa may, and I believe will, become as great a threat to the peace of the world in the 1990s as the Middle East is today'.[33] Thus, it is not unrealistic to speculate that South Africa might one day assume a position of greater prominence in the hierarchy of Soviet foreign policy.

VI

Sixth, what, ultimately are Soviet interests in Southern Africa? It is difficult to find evidence of any 'grand strategy' for a 'total onslaught' against South Africa in Soviet foreign policy. The history of the Soviet state, party and commercial relations with South Africa does not suggest a coherent whole, but rather a collection of disparate policies which do not fit particularly well together. If there is a continuity in Soviet policy, it lies in the fact that developments on the southern African continent are peripheral to Soviet national interests even if these developments are less peripheral today than at earlier periods. Furthermore, domestic considerations, such as the need for hard currency from mineral sales, and international issues, like the quest for Soviet influence in the Third World, which are unrelated to South Africa, have often had an important and sometimes overriding influence upon the shaping of Soviet policy towards South Africa.

Soviet policy cannot be regarded as exclusively offensive or defensive, active or reactive. Although the Soviet Union acts as a revolutionary power in the region seeking to undermine the old order, it has also displayed signs of caution and restraint. Thus, while the USSR generally has a stake in the promotion of instability within South Africa, the Soviet Union also has an interest in preventing external challenges to Mozambique and Angola and halting reversals in the process of nationalist consolidation and socialist transformation in both countries. The Soviet Union now has a stake in the *status quo* in southern Africa even if this will not necessarily provide an overriding consideration, and there are several indications which suggest that the Soviet Union is presently seeking to consolidate its position in southern Africa rather than add to it. The fact that the USSR acts as both a revolutionary and conservative power complicates the search for an adequate definition of its policy objectives.

There are signs that the Soviet Union is ultimately desirous of an internationally recognised role in southern African politics, commensurate with its position as a superpower. Since the attainment of parity with the United States in the mid-1970s, it is evident that Soviet leaders have viewed an equal say on security problems in the Third World as their just due. The clearest enunciation of this view was made by Foreign Ministger Gromyko in 1971 when he declared: 'Today there is no question of any significance which can be decided without the Soviet Union or in opposition to it'.[34] The Soviet hostility towards Western attempts at regional settlements in Zimbabwe and

Namibia derives in part from their exclusion from the process. In a meeting on Soviet and American policy in southern Africa held in Moscow during April 1984, one Soviet participant noted that 'joint efforts to manage relations in regional disputes can have a very positive effect on conflicts and there is room for the US and the USSR both to play a positive role in Southern Africa'.[35] The present situation, where the Soviet Union is denied a legitimate role in international diplomacy over southern Africa, is viewed with particular dissatisfaction.

The primary goal of the Soviet Union currently is to portray, in official statements and theoretical journals, the United States and South Africa as acting in concert in southern Africa. This burgeoning alliance, it is believed, will serve the interests of the USSR by encouraging the polarisation of the region, with South Africa and the United States on one side and the front-line states on the other. In this respect, the signing of the Nkomati Accord between South Africa and Mozambique is undoutedly a significant setback for the USSR. Yet, the Soviet Union remains committed to blocking a settlement in southern Africa along *pax Americana* lines and continues to display doctrinal continuity by stressing that a national liberation struggle in South Africa is inevitable and expected.

Since contemporary Soviet activities are part of an on-going process in southern Africa, it is tempting to speculate about the future of Soviet involvement in the region. It can be cautiously advanced that Soviet foreign policy will continue to be: reactive to developments in the southern African region; opportunistic, in taking account of black South African discontent; cautious, in that Soviet policy-makers are mindful of the risks of international conflagration; and realistic, with the knowledge that the situation on the southern African continent in peripheral to Soviet national interests. Furthermore, there is little doubt that the issue of Soviet policy towards South Africa will grow as a subject of debate and importance in the twilight years of the twentieth century.

Postscript

Since the completion of this manuscript there have been many developments which have relevance for Soviet policy towards South Africa. Indeed, 1985 witnessed increased domestic turmoil and violence in South Africa, the escalation of regional instability in southern Africa as a whole, heightened concern and debate in the United States over the future of apartheid, and the emergence of a forceful and dynamic leader in the USSR.

Following a year of successful domestic and international initiatives undertaken by Pretoria, 1985 saw the government's fleeting gains vanish in the face of black rage and defiance.. The urban townships became ungovernable, and President P. W. Botha declared a state of emergency for many areas of the country and ordered the army into several of the segregated communities. These black uprisings most often occurred spontaneously and not as the result of ANC agitation. The government has arrested and detained scores of United Democratic Front (UDF) and union organisers, but the townships continue to seethe with violence. In general, the ANC leadership in exile was caught off-guard by the suddenness of the internal revolt in South Africa and has had to struggle to keep abreast of the situation.

The ANC managed to step up slightly its guerrilla campaign towards the end of the year, striking against a variety of rather unimportant targets (from a military point of view) and occasionally incurring civilian casualties. Yet, while the ANC has fared poorly when matched against the power of South Africa's security apparatus, the organisation has been generally successful in winning the hearts and minds of many black South Africans and in gaining support from the international community. In June 1985, the ANC held its second consultative conference in Kabwe, Zambia to discuss the present stage of the armed struggle to wrest control from the white minority government. Despite some minor changes in political and revolutionary strategy, the conference resolutions did not include any radical departures from previous policy and reaffirmed the

166

ANC's traditional position as the leading force of black opposition.

The South African government, partially in response to the escalation of domestic unrest, has sponsored a number of efforts to promote regional destabilisation. However, many of the covert military campaigns conducted in the countries to the north have either been clumsy and ineffective or have contradicted recent South African diplomatic initiatives. A joint Zimbabwe–Mozambique military force raided the mountain headquarters of the Renamo rebels and uncovered evidence of continuing South African complicity in the civil war, in strict violation of the Nkomati Accord. Further, a South African commando team was intercepted by the Angolan authorities while on a mission to bomb the oil-producing installations in the Cabinda enclave. The South African Defence Forces also staged a raid on purported ANC offices in Botswana and blockaded the mountainous country of Lesotho during the military coup that ousted Prime Minister Leabua Jonathan. Finally, South Africa has increased its military support for Jonas Savimbi's UNITA movement in its struggle against the ruling MPLA regime in Angola.

In the United States, the South African issue has taken on added significance in government, academic and business circles. The disinvestment campaign continues to pick up steam, particularly on university campuses, and President Reagan initiated limited sanctions against the white minority government. Assistant Secretary of State for African Affairs Chester Crocker's discreet diplomacy to bring independence to Namibia continues but there is no immediate expectation of a comprehensive settlement. The Reagan administration has also taken tentative steps to improve relations with Mozambique and lure President Samora Machel away from his patronage to the USSR. In contrast, there is mounting conservative sentiment in the United States to offer material support to UNITA in the intensifying conflict in Angola. Indeed, Angola is shaping up as a major test for the newly enunciated 'Reagan doctrine' to sponsor anti-Soviet forces in the Third World.

Probably the most important, and possibly an enduring development for Soviet foreign policy in general and Soviet involvement in southern Africa in particular, was the appointment of Mikhail Gorbachev as General Secretary of the CPSU in early 1985. Gorbachev brought a dynamic, forceful style to Kremlin politics and immediately set out to reshape Soviet domestic and foreign policy in his image. During Gorbachev's short tenure in power, Soviet support for the national liberation struggle in South Africa has been reaffirmed but, with so many other pressing issues demanding attention, South Africa has not been a high priority for the Soviet leadership. Nevertheless, while it could be said that current Soviet policies have been inherited from previous leaders, there are clear indications of a continued Soviet interest and involvement in the region under Gorbachev. (The appointment of Eduard Shevardnadze as the new Foreign Minister has at least some significance for southern Africa in that it is one of the few areas which he has demonstrated a command of the subject in meetings with Western diplomats.)

The USSR appears to have drawn the line and staked its prestige on the maintenance of the ruling MPLA regime in Angola. Soviet military support to the Angolan army has increased dramatically since the latter half of 1985, and Russian military advisers serving with Cuban troops were involved in Operation 'Party Congress' directed against Jamba, UNITA's provisional capital in southernmost Angola. With the United States moving ever closer to sponsoring Savimbi's cause and the USSR firm in its commitment to the Angolan government, the stage is now set for an indirect superpower confrontation in southern Africa.

The current strife in South Africa and the surrounding region has spurred unceasing speculation and comment about the Soviet stake in the turmoil. American conservatives have stated that if South Africa falls, 'freedom is not likely to prevail in the rest of the world much longer'. At a recent funeral for slain blacks in South Africa, a Soviet flag was unfurled to the cheers of onlookers and a speaker proclaimed, 'I shall cross to Moscow and I shall return with a bazooka'. Much of this rhetoric has obscured the actual designs of the Soviet Union in South Africa.

Although much has transpired in even the short time between the completion of this book and its final preparation for publication, the recent experience of southern Africa makes the study and understanding of Soviet policy all the more important. The preceding historical background and conclusions will surely remain timely and useful even in the face of continuing political upheaval in southern Africa. It is also hoped that this study will provide further avenues for academic discussion and enquiry, raise important questions for public debate, and perhaps offer some useful insights for Western policymakers confronting the complexities of the current situation in South Africa.

K. M. C.
Harvard University
February 1986

Notes and References

INTRODUCTION

1. Republic of South Africa, *House of Assembly Debates*, 21 March 1980, columns 3317–21.
2. Deon Geldenhuys, 'What Do We Think? A Survey of White Opinion on Foreign Policy Issues', *Occasional Paper*, South African Institute of International Affairs (November 1982) p. 6.
3. Ian Grieg, *The Communist .Challenge to Africa* (London: Foreign Affairs, 1977) p. 29.
4. General G. S. Brown, 'Current Joint Chiefs of Staff Theatre Appraisals: the strategic importance of 7 vital international areas', *Commanders Digest*, vol. 20 (17 March 1977) p. 21.
5. Robert J. Hanks, *The Cape Route* (Cambridge, Massachussetts: Institute for Foreign Policy Analysis, 1981) p. 65. See also John Peel, 'The Growing Threat to Freedom and the North Atlantic Alliance', *South Africa International*, no. 9 (October 1978).
6. William C. J. van Rensburg and D. A. Pretorius, *South Africa's Strategic Minerals: Pieces on a Continental Chess Board* (Johannesburg: Valiant, 1977) p. 126.
7. *The Role of the Soviet Union, Cuba, and East Germany in Fomenting Terrorism and Southern Africa*, Hearings before the Sub-Committee on Security and Terrorism, Committee on the Judiciary, United States Senate, (Washington: Government Printing Office, 1982).
8. Jan du Plessis, *Soviet Strategy towards Southern Africa* (Johannesburg: Foriegn Affairs Association, April 1976) p. 9. This is also a favourite theme of Edward Feit, *Urban Revolt in South Africa* (Illinois: Northwestern University Press, 1971).
9. See for instance Colin Legum, 'The Gorshkov Strategy', *The Observer*, 20 March 1977; Lewis Gann and Peter Duignan, *South Africa: War, Revolution, or Peace* (Stanford: Hoover Institution Press, 1978); and David E. Albright, 'The Communist States and Southern Africa', in Gwendolyn M. Cater (ed.) *International Politics in Southern Africa* (Bloomington: Indiana University Press, 1982).
10. Peter Vanneman and W. Martin James, *Soviet Foreign Policy in Southern Africa* (Pretoria: Africa Institute, 1982) p. 8.
11. W. Scott Thompson and Brett Silvers, 'South Africa in Soviet Strategy', in Bissell and Crocker (eds) *South Africa into the 1980s* (Colorado: Westview, 1979) p. 133.

CHAPTER 1

1. Edward T. Wilson, *Russia and Black Africa Before World War Two* (London: Holmes and Meir, 1974) pp. 78–81.
2. Wilson, *Russia and Black Africa*, pp. 9–78.
3. Nikolai Romanov, 'Nikolai Romanov ob Anglo–Burskoi Voine' ('Nikolai Romanov on the Anglo–Boer War'), *Krasnyi Arkhiv*, no. 3 (1972) pp. 124–7. The author observes that the British will summon reinforcements from India. (English translations of the more obscure Russian titles will be provided in this chapter.)
4. Cited in Elisaveta Kandyba-Foxcroft, *Russia and the Anglo–Boer War, 1899–1902* (Pretoria: CUM Books, 1981) p. 61.
5. Wilson, *Russia and Black Africa*, p. 79.
6. *Diplomatic Note* from Leyds to Reitz, 10 February 1900 (South African Foreign Affairs Archives, Union Buildings).
7. Thomas Pakenham, *The Boer War* (London: Weidenfeld & Nicolson, 1979) p. 388.
8. William Langer, *The Diplomacy of Imperialism, 1890–1902* (New York: Knopf, 1951) p. 652, quoting the British Ambassador in Paris.
9. Osten-Sacken to Muravieff, 30 January 1900, cited in Kandyba-Foxcroft, *Russia and the Anglo–Boer War*, p. 76.
10. Kandyba-Foxcroft, *Russia and the Anglo–Boer War*, pp. 76–7.
11. Langer, *The Diplomacy of Imperialism*, p. 669.
12. Probably a reference to the surrender of Boer General P. C. Cronje to British forces on 27 February 1900.
13. Cited in Kandyba-Foxcroft, *Russia and the Anglo–Boer War*, p. 77.
14. Roy MacNab, *The French Colonel: Villebois-Mareuil and the Boers, 1899–1900* (Cape Town: Oxford University Press, 1975) pp. 170–1.
15. Wilson, *Russia and Black Africa*, p. 23.
16. J. Skvortsoff, *Iz za Zolota i Brilliantov u Burov (On Account of the Boer Gold and Diamonds)* (St Petersburg: 1900) p. 6, Hoover Institution Archives.
17. S. I. Glebov, *Novii Napoleon iz Yuzhnoi Afriki, Voina Transvalia s Angliei (The New Napoleon from South Africa: The Transvaal War with England)* (1901) pp. 6–20 Hoover Institution Archives.
18. V. I. Lenin, *Collectived Works* 4th edition, Volume 4 (*Iskra*: no. 1, December 1900) (London: Lawrence) p. 373.
19. Lenin referred to South Africa and the Boer War in his writings primarily to articulate and explain certain aspects of Marxist–Leninist theory. See for example: Lenin, *Collected Works*, Volume 19, p. 28; Volume 22, pp. 195, 257, 265 and 286; Volume 29, p. 501.
20. Lenin, *Collected Works*, Volume 23 ('Imperialism and the Split in Socialism', *Sbornik Sotsial Demokrata*: no. 2, December 1916) p. 106.
21. Robert C. Tucker (ed.) *The Lenin Anthology* (Norton: New York, 1975) p. 237.
22. Lenin, *Svobodnoye Slovo (Free Word)* (1900) p. 3, Hoover Institution Archives.
23. Skvortsoff, *Iz za Zolota*, pp. 2–3.

24. *Novoye Vremia* (*New Times*) 16 November 1899.
25. Andrzej Walicki (trans. Hilda Andrew-Rusiecka) *A History of Russian Thought*, (Stanford University Press, 1979) p. 309.
26. 'Lev Tolstoy i Zarubezhnyi Mir' ('Tolstoy and the World outside Russia'), *Literaturnoye Nasledstvo*, vol. 69, book 2, p. 163.
27. For further information concerning Russian medical assistance to the Boers note that two of the doctors of the ambulance published detailed reports of its work: A. K. Eberhardt, 'O Kommandirovke na Teatre Voennykh deistvii v Transvaale' ('An Assignment at the Military Front in the Transvaal') *Voenno-meditzinsky zhurnal* (St Petersburg: November 1901) pp. 3145–211; A. O. Sadovsky, 'Vospominania o Transvaale i putevye vpechatlenia' ('Reminiscences of the Transvaal and Travel Impressions') *Voenno-meditzinsky zhurnal* (St Petersburg: May 1902) pp. 1499–534. Precise details of the personnel in the ambulances were given by Colonel E. J. Maximov in *Moskovskie vedomosti*, 3 December 1899. One of the sisters later published a book about her experiences: O. Baumgarten, *Vospominania o Transvaale sestry miloserdia obshchiny St Georgia (Transvaal Reminiscences of a Sister of Mercy of the Community of St George)*(St Petersburg: 1901).
28. Sophia Izedinova (trans. C. Moody) *A Few Months with the Boers*, (Johannesburg: Perskor, 1977) pp. 22–68.
29. Christopher Moody, Professor of Russian Studies, University of Witwatersrand, interview with author, 19 March 1982, South Africa.
30. E. Williams-Foxcroft, 'The Anglo–Boer War in the Dispatches of Russian Military Attaches', *Historia*, vol. 85 no. 1 (1963) pp. 13–44.
31. V. I. Romeiko-Gurko, *Voina Anglii s Uzhno-Afrikanskimi Respublikami, 1899–1901 (England's War with the South African Republics)* (St Petersburg: 1901) pp. 288–322, Hoover Institution Archives.
32. 'Anglo-Burskaia Voina v Donneseniiakh Ruskogo Voennogo Agenta' ('The Boer War in the Dispatches of a Russian Military Agent'), *Krasnyi Arkhiv*, no. 103 (1940) pp. 148–50.
33. Williams-Foxcroft, 'The Anglo–Boer War', pp. 35–44.
34. Wilson, *Russia and Black Africa*, p. 81.
35. D. Zaslavskii, 'Nikolai II – Imperator Kafrov' ('Nicholas II – the Emperor of the Kaffirs') *Krasnyi Arkhiv*, no. 67/70 (1935) pp. 253–5.
36. Zaslavskii, 'Nikolai II', p. 248. Letter received by Lamsdorff from Joubert.
37. Cited in Wilson, *Russia and Black Africa*, p. 89.

CHAPTER 2

1. Resolution of the ECCI to the CPSA, 1930, cited in Sheridan W. Johns, 'Marxism–Leninism in a Multi-Racial Environment: The Origins and Early History of the Communist Party of South Africa, 1914–1932', PhD thesis, Harvard University, 1965, p. 535.
2. V. I. Lenin, *Imperialism: The Highest Stage of Capitalism* (New York: International, 1939) p. 76.

3. Leon Trotsky, *The First Five Years of the Communist International*, Volume I (New York: Pioneer, 1945) p. 24.
4. See Mikhail Pavlovich, *Voprosy Kolonial'noi: Natsional'noi Politiki i IIIi Internatsional* (Moscow: Kommunisticheskogo Internatsionala, 1920) p. 59; and George Padmore, *Negro Workers and the Imperialist War – Intervention in the Soviet Union* (Hamburg: ITUC–NW, 1931).
5. Demetrio Boersner, *The Bolsheviks and the National and Colonial Question: 1917–1928*, pp. 23–4; *K. Marx and F. Engels on Colonialism* (Moscow: Foreign Languages Press) pp. 22–61; and Horace B. Davis, *Nationalism and Socialism: Marxist and Labor Theories of Nationalism to 1917* (New York: Monthly Review) pp. 59–61.
6. Lenin, *Imperialism*, p. 124.
7. Mikhail Pavlovich, 'The World and the Struggle for the Division of the Black Continent', appeared in *Osnovy Imperialisticheskoi Politiki i Mirovaia Voina* (Moscow: 1918).
8. V. I. Lenin, 'Luchshe menshe, da luchshe', *Collected Works*, 4th edition, Volume 33, p. 458.
9. Cited in *International Press Correspondence of the Comintern*, vol. VII, no. 17 (5 February 1927) p. 232.
10. Edward T. Wilson, *Russia and Black Africa Before World War Two* (London: Holmes, 1974) p. 97.
11. N. Bukharin, speech at the Eighth Communist Party Congress, 1919, *Vozmoi S'ezd Kommunisticheskoi Partii: Protokoly* (Moscow: Peoples Press, 1959) p. 47.
12. See Lenin in the English theoretical journal of the Comintern, *The Communist International*, vol. I (London: 1920) p. 1769.
13. Boersner, *The Bolsheviks and the National and Colonial Question*, p. 87.
14. See Sheridan Johns, 'The Birth of the Communist Party of South Africa', *Journal of African Historical Studies*, vol. 9, no. 3 (1976) pp. 371–400.
15. See T. Adler, 'History of Jewish Workers Clubs', paper presented at the African Studies Seminar, University of Witwatersrand, Johannesburg (1977).
16. Sheridan Johns, 'The Comintern, South Africa and the Black Diaspora', *Review of Politics*, vol. 37, no. 2 (1975) pp. 201–10.
17. Wilson, *Russia and Black Africa*, p. 121.
18. E. H. Carr, *The Bolshevik Revolution: 1917–23* (London: Macmillan, 1953) p. 448.
19. Johns, 'The Comintern', *Review of Politics*, pp. 210–11.
20. *Resolution and Decisions, Third World Congress of the Red International of Labor Unions, Held in Moscow, July 1924* (Chicago: no date) pp. 23–4.
21. Sidney P. Bunting, 'The Labour Movement of South Africa' *International Press Correspondence of the Comintern*, vol. II, no. 98 (1922) p. 787.
22. H. J. and R. E. Simons, *Class and Colour in South Africa 1850–1950* (Harmondsworth: Penguin, 1969) p. 282.
23. Sidney P. Bunting, cited in Roger Kanet, 'The Comintern and the "Negro Question"', *The Russian Review*, vol. 12 (1968) pp. 110–15.

24. J. Steklov, 'The Awakening of a Race', *International Press Correspondence of the Comintern*, vol. II, no. 120 (24 November 1922) p. 826.
25. The complete text of the 'Theses on the Negro Question' is contained in the *Bulletin of the IV Congress of the Communist International*, no. 27 (7 December 1922) pp. 8–10; and in Jane Degras, *The Communist International 1919–1943, Documents*, Volume I (Oxford University Press, 1956) pp. 398–401.
26. Johns, 'The Comintern', *Review of Politics*, p. 212.
27. See George Padmore, *Pan-Africanism or Communism? The Coming Struggle for Africa* (London: Dobson, 1955) pp. 348–50. For a detailed history of the ICU see Edward Roux, *Time Longer Than Rope: The Black Man's Struggle for Freedom in South Africa* (University of Wisconsin Press, 1964) pp. 153–97.
28. *The Communist International between the Fifth and Sixth World Congresses, 1924–1928* (London: The Communist Party of Great Britain, 1928) p. 490.
29. Resolution of the ECCI, 'The South African Question', *The Communist International*, vol. VI (1928) p. 55.
30. James Shields, 'Trade Unionism and the Organization of the Native Masses in South Africa', *International Press Correspondence of the Comintern*, vol. VII, no. 41 (1927) pp. 906–7.
31. See Padmore, *Pan-Africanism*, p. 348; Baruch Hirson, interview with author, London, 21 January 1983; and Roux, *Time Longer Than Rope*, pp. 198–254.
32. Padmore, *Pan-Africanism*, p. 348.
33. Wilson, *Russia and Black Africa*, p. 162.
34. See Isaac Deutscher, *Stalin* (New York: Oxford University Press, 1949) pp. 308–12.
35. A comprehensive account of Stalin's role in the formulation of the new negro programme is found in Theodore Draper, *American Communism and Soviet Russia* (New York: Viking Press, 1960) pp. 342–5.
36. 'The South African Question (Resolution of the ECCI)', *The Communist International*, vol. VI, no. 2 (1928) pp. 53–5.
37. Johns, 'The Comintern', *Review of Politics*, p. 204.
38. Padmore, *Pan-Africanism*, p. 306.
39. J. V. Stalin, *Marxism and the National and Colonial Question* (New York: International, 1942) pp. 5–10; and George Padmore, *How Russia Transformed Her Colonial Empire* (London: Dobson, 1946) pp. 85–6.
40. *The Revolutionary Movement in the Colonies: Theses on the Revolutionary Movement in the Colonies and Semi-Colonies*, Sixth Congress of the Comintern, 1928 (London: 1929) cited in Wilson, *Russia and Black Africa*, p. 166.
41. 'The South African Question', *Communist International*, pp. 53–5.
42. Johns, 'The Comintern', *Review of Politics*, pp. 204–5.
43. Edward Roux, *S. P. Bunting: A Political Biography* (Cape Town: Roux, 1944) pp. 89–94.
44. *International Press Correspondence of the Comintern*, vol. VIII, no. 44 (1928) p. 780.
45. Ibid.

46. *International Press Correspondence of the Comintern*, vol. VIII, no. 78 (1928) pp. 1451–3.
47. Johns, 'The Comintern', *Review of Politics*, pp. 226–7.
48. An extensive examination of this aspect of the Comintern programme is given in Baruch Hirson, *Land, Labour, and the Black Republic* (unpublished text, 1983).
49. A summary of the ECCI resolution appeared in *Pravda*, 30 October 1928; and 'The South African Question', *Communist International*, pp. 53–5.
50. These comments were made by Otto Kuusinen, the Head of the Colonial Commission, cited in *International Press Correspondence*, vol. VIII, no. 81 (1928) p. 1528; Bukharin also implied that the South Africans were guilty of racial prejudice, cited in *International Press Correspondence*, vol. VIII, no. 44 (1928) p. 872.
51. Johns, 'The Comintern', *Review of Politics*, pp. 232–4.
52. For a discussion of class and nationalism, see Martin Legassick, *Class and Nationalism in South African Protest: The South African Communist Party and the 'Native Republic', 1928–34* (Syracuse: Eastern African Studies, Syracuse University, 1973).
53. The 'Negro Republic' also failed in the American South for the same reasons. See Wilson Record, *The Negro and the Communist Party* (Chapel Hill: University of North Carolina, 1951) pp. 54–109.
54. Edward Roux, quoted in Edwin S. Munger, *Communist Activity in South Africa*, American Universities Field Staff, Central and Southern Africa Series, ESM–8–58, vol. VI (1958) p. 256.
55. See Max Beloff, *The Foreign Policy of Soviet Russia, 1929–1941*, Volume I (Oxford University Press, 1947) pp. 94–105.
56. Wilson, *Russia and Black Africa*, p. 257.
57. Wilson, *Russia and Black Africa*, pp. 257–8; *VII Congress of the Communist International* (Moscow: Foreign Languages Publishing, 1939) pp. 578–9.
58. See 'For a United Front of the People Against Imperialism', *Umsebenzi*, 26 October 1935, cited in *South African Communists Speak*, Documents from the History of the South African Communist Party (London: Inkululeko, 1981) p. 125.
59. Martin Ebon, *World Communism Today* (New York: Whittlesley House, 1948) pp. 427–8.
60. *International Press Correspondence of the Comintern*, vol. XVIII, no. 25 (1938) p. 617; see also Roger Kanet, The Comintern and the "Negro Question"', *The Russian Review*, p. 117.
61. Padmore, cited in Wilson, *Russia and Black Africa*, p. 261.
62. G. Dimitrov, cited in K. E. McKenzie, *The Comintern and World Revolution* (New York: Columbia University Press, 1963) p. 170.
63. *World News and Views*, vol. XIX, no. 45 (1939) p. 992.
64. *World News and Views*, vol. XIX, no. 56 (1939) p. 1122.
65. *The Negro Worker* (ITUC–NW publication), vol. I, no. 10 (1931) p. 45.
66. Roger Kanet, 'The Comintern and the "Negro Question"', *The Russian Review*, p. 121.
67. Roux, *Time Longer Than Rope*, p. 309.

68. McKenzie, *The Comintern and World Revolution*, p. 182.
69. *Kommunisticheskii Internatsional*, no. 5–6 (1943) pp. 8–10.
70. Terence Africanus (pseud.) 'The First International – 100 Years After', *The African Communist* (London), no. 18 (July–September, 1964) p. 88.
71. Terence Africanus, 'The First International', *The African Communist*, pp. 88–9.
72. A. Lerumo (pseud.) *Fifty Fighting Years* (London: Inkululeko, 1971) pp. 43–62.
73. Alexander Dallin, 'The Soviet Union: Political Activity', Zbigniew Brzezinski (ed.) *Africa and the Communist World* (Stanford University Press, 1963) p. 10.
74. Tom Lodge, Lecturer in Politics, University of Witwatersrand, interview with author, 16 March 1982, Johannesburg, South Africa.
75. *Suid-Afrikaanse Polisie*, 6 September 1949 (South African Ministry of External Affairs).
76. See the statement made by Communist MP Sam Kahn to Parliament, cited in *South African Communists Speak*, p. 214.
77. Munger, *Communist Activity in South Africa*, p. 680.
78. Edward Feit, *Urban Revolt in South Africa: 1960–1964* (Illinois: Northwestern University Press, 1971) p. 292.
79. Roux, *Time Longer Than Rope*, p. 215.
80. Jordan K. Ngubane, *An African Explains Apartheid* (New York, 1963) p. 183.
81. See Document 124: 'The Czechoslovakian Crisis', cited in *South African Communists Speak*, p. 365; and *New Age*, 2 November 1956.
82. Richard Gibson, *African Liberation Movements* (Oxford University Press, 1972) p. 83; and Gail M. Gerhart, *Black Power in South Africa: The Evolution of an Ideology* (London: University of California Press, 1978) pp. 173–81.
83. N. S. Khrushchev, 'Report of the Central Committee to the Twentieth Party Congress', *The Current Digest of the Soviet Press*, vol. 8, no. 4 (7 March 1956) pp. 6–12.
84. See Dan C. Heldman, *The USSR in Africa: Soviet Foreign Policy Under Khrushchev* (London: Praeger, 1981).
85. Thomas Karis and Gail M. Gerhart, *Challenge and Violence*, Volume 3, in Thomas Karis and Gwendolen M. Carter (eds) *From Protest to Challenge* (Stanford: Hoover Institution Press, 1977) pp. 646–7.
86. See *We Accuse: The Trial of Nelson Mandela* (London: The African National Congress) pp. 6–13, Hoover Institution Archives.
87. Gibson, *African Liberation Movements*, p. 57.
88. Tom Lodge, *Black Politics in South Africa Since 1945* (London: Longman, 1983) pp. 295–320.
89. Gibson, *African Liberation Movements*, p. 65.
90. Lodge, *Black Politics in South Africa Since 1945*, p. 298.
91. Anatoly A. Gromyko, Director, Institute of African Studies, interview with author, 19 April 1984, Moscow; see also Kenneth Grundy, *Guerrilla Struggle in Africa* (New York: Grossman, 1971) p. 51.
92. This development received extensive and often sensational coverage in

the West. See *Education of Foreign Revolutionaries in the USSR* (Ankara: Baylan Press, 1973); William Anti-Taylor, *Moscow Diary* (London: Hale, 1967); *African Student Life in Moscow* (Pretoria: ANTICOM, 1968); Andrew Richard Amar, *A Student in Moscow* (London: Quail, 1961); and Seymour M. Rosen, 'Soviet Training Programs for Africa', *Bulletin* (United States Office of Education), no. 9 (1963).

93. Vladilen M. Vasev, Head, Third Africa Department, Soviet Foreign Ministry, interview with author, 21 April 1984, Moscow; B. Ponomarev, 'O gosudarstve natsional'noi demokratii', *Kommunist*, no. 8 (1961) pp. 42–5; and 'On the Directions of the Work in the African Institute', *Vestnik Akademii Nauk SSSR*, no. 5 (May 1965) pp. 16–20.

94. A. B. Davidson, 'A Fascist "Republic" in Africa', *Aziya i Afrika Segodnya*, no. 8 (August 1961) pp. 4–6; M. Kogan, 'The "De Beers" Diamond Monopoly', *Mirovaia Ekonomika i Mezhdunarodnye Otnosheniia*, no. 2 (February 1963) pp. 122–7; 'South African Racists Answer to Sharpeville', *Aziya i Afrika Segodnya*, no. 4 (April 1961); and D. Mukhamedova, 'Race Discrimination Against Indians in the Union of South Africa', *Obshchestvennye Nauki v Uzbekistane*, no. 3 (1961) pp. 57–61.

95. I. Potekhin, 'Pan-Africanism and the Struggle of the Two Ideologies', *Kommunist*, no. 1 (January 1964) pp. 104–13; M. S. Meier, 'The Position of the African Working Class in South Africa', *Narody Azii i Afriki*, no. 6 (1964) pp. 19–31; and V. Gorodnov, 'The South African Working Class and its Role in the Liberation Struggle', *Mirovaia Ekonomika i Mezhdunarodnye Otnosheniia*. no. 3 (1965) pp. 93–9.

96. See James Mayall, *Africa: the Cold War and After* (London: Elek Books, 1971) pp. 165–201.

97. Cited in Gerhart, *Black Power in South Africa*, p. 165.

98. V. P. Gorodnov, 'The South African Republic: Problems of African Nationalism', *Narody Azii i Afriki*, no. 4 (1966) pp. 29–31

99. I. I. Potekhin, *African Problems* (Moscow: Nauka Publishing House, 1969) p. 117.

100. See *Why We Left 'Umkonto We Sizwe'* (ANC in Exile), cited in Gibson, *African Liberation Movements*, p. 71.

101. See *The African Communist*, no. 38 (1969) pp. 1–9.

102. Cited in Gibson, *African Liberation Movements*, p. 75.

103. Lodge, *Black Politics in South Africa Since 1945*, p. 304.

104. Baruch Hirson, *Year of Fire, Year of Ash: The Soweto Revolt* (London: Zed Press, 1979) pp. 277–85. Since 1976, most ANC recruits have been trained in Angola under ANC instructors who have trained either in the Soviet Union or East Germany. In 1978, South African Military Intelligence sources indicated that about 4000 Africans had left after the Soweto uprising and over half of these went into ANC camps.

105. See the remarks of Michael Hough, Director, South African Institute of Strategic Studies in the *Guardian* of 18 May 1983. Comments made by a senior ANC official in London, Govan Mbeki, that the ANC would 'raise the level of the liberation struggle', have not been elaborated upon. See *Summary of World Broadcasts*, Africa series, 1 November 1983.

106. A 1982 CIA study concerning a purported debate within the ANC about the strategy and tactics of armed struggle was leaked to Trans-Africa, a Washington-based lobby group. The report claims that younger ANC activists object to the 'careful' approach of traditional leaders to military operations inside South Africa, *International Herald Tribune*, 5 November 1982.

107. I. A. Ulanovskaia, *South Africa: Racism Doomed* (Moscow: Znanie, 1979) p. 41.

108. A. B. Davidson, 'Southern Africa: Liberation Draws Near', *Pravda*, 28 August 1976.

109. Evgenia A. Tarabrin, Head of International Problems Department, Institute of African Studies, USSR Academy of Sciences, interview with author, 19 April 1984, Moscow.

110. A. B. Davidson, 'Where Is South Africa Going?', *Narody Azii i Afriki*, no. 2 (1978) pp. 17–18; and Y. Shvetsov, 'RSA: The African Working Class Strengthens the Struggle', *Aziya i Afrika Segodnya*, no. 1 (January 1977) p. 11.

111. *The African Communist*, no. 70 (1977) pp. 36–7.

112. Mirza Ibragimov, 'Resolute Support', *Aziya i Afrika Segodnya*, no. 2 (March 1979) p. 22.

113. *The Role of the Soviet Union, Cuba, and East Germany in Fomenting Terrorism in Southern Africa*, Hearings before the Sub-Committee on Security and Terrorism, Committee on the Judiciary, United States Senate (Washington: Government Printing Office, 1982) pp. 2–8.

114. Thomas G. Karis, 'Black Politics in South Africa', *Foreign Affairs* (Winter 1983/84) pp. 394–6.

115. Cited in Karis and Gerhart, *Challenge and Violence*, p. 680.

116. A CIA report compiled in 1976 suggests there were then fewer than 100 SACP members living in exile, *Sunday Times* (London), 26 November 1980.

117. For instance, the ANC has both applauded the Soviet decision to boycott the 1984 Olympics and condemned American missile deployments in Western Europe. See the ANC statement in *Summary of World Broadcasts*, Africa Series, 14 June 1984.

CHAPTER 3

1. *Agreement between the Government of the Union of South Africa and the Government of the Union of Soviet Socialist Republics for the exchange of Consular officers*, Treaty Series No. 2, 21 February (Government Printer: Pretoria, 1942).

2. *Diplomatic Note*, British Governor-General in South Africa to South African Prime Minister, Pretoria; No. 20/1171, December 1921 (South African Government Archives, Union Buildings).

3. Mr Peter Philip, interview with author, 15 April 1982, Cape Town, South Africa.

4. *Diplomatic Note*, South African High Commissioner, London to Secretary of External Affairs, Pretoria; No. 856, 24 October 1941 (South African Ministry of External Affairs).

5. H. Duncan Hall, *North American Supply*, History of the Second World War (London: Longman, 1955) p. 319.
6. Armin Rappaport, *A History of American Diplomacy* (New York: Macmillan, 1975) pp. 362–3.
7. D. J. Payton-Smith, *Oil*, History of the Second World War (London: HMSO, 1971) pp. 456–7.
8. John R. Deane, *The Strange Alliance: Wartime Cooperation with Russia* (New York: Viking, 1947) pp. 108–14.
9. Ibid., p. 93.
10. Eric Rosenthal, *South African Diplomats Abroad* (Pretoria: South African Department of External Affairs, 1979) p. 17.
11. Edwin S. Munger, *The Formulation of South African Foreign Policy* (California: Castle, 1965) p. 28.
12. D. J. Geldenhuys, *South African Foreign Policy*, unpublished thesis, 1982, p. 41.
13. *Diplomatic Note*, British Foreign Office to South African High Commissioner, London; No. 898, 6 November 1941 (South African Ministry of External Affairs).
14. See E. H. Carr, *The Soviet Impact on the Western World* (London: Macmillan, 1946) p. 75.
15. *Diplomatic Note*, British High Commissioner in South Africa to Dominions Office, London; No. 12, 11 February 1942 (British Foreign Office Files, Dominion Affairs).
16. Leif Egeland, *Bridges of Understanding*(Cape Town: Human, 1977) p. 148. Egeland writes that Felipe Pienaar, South African Minister of Lisbon during the war, assiduously studied Russian in the vain hope of being charged with the opening of a South African Mission in the Soviet Union.
17. Rene De Villiers, 'Afrikaner Nationalism', in Monica Wilson and Leonard Thompson (eds) *The Oxford History of South Africa*, Volume II (Oxford University Press, 1975) pp. 390–402.
18. Nicholas Mansergh, *Survey of British Commonwealth Affairs: 1939–1952* (Oxford University Press, 1958) pp. 76–9.
19. Ibid., pp. 158–9.
20. Oswald Pirow, *House of Assembly Debates*, South Africa, 10 February 1942, columns 1780–90.
21. *Diplomatic Note*, British High Commissioner in South Africa to Dominions Office, London; No. 232, 11 February 1942 (British Foreign Office Files, Dominion Affairs).
22. See George Heard, *Stand by the Soviet Union* (Johannesburg: South African Friends of the Soviet Union, 8 September 1941); *Call and Response of the Soviet Jews* (Johannesburg: Jewish Workers Appeal Committee, Medical Aid for Russia, 1942); *The Truth About the Red Army*, People's Pamphlet (Johannesburg: Johannesburg Communist Party, 1939); *What is Behind the Anti-Communist Campaign?*, A Statement to the Central Committee (Cape Town: Communist Party of South Africa); *Civic Week for Medical Aid for Russia*, Souvenir Programme (Johannesburg: Medical Aid for Russia, 2 March 1942).

23. George Heard, *Stand by the Soviet Union*, p. 1.
24. See 'Support the USSR in its fight Against Nazi War! June 22, 1941', *The Communist*, vol. 20 (1941) pp. 579–80.
25. Reverend Douglas Thompson, former President of the South African Friends of the Soviet Union, interview with Tom Lodge (University of Witwatersrand), 27 May 1982, Springs, Transvaal.
26. For an expression of liberal sentiment on the issue, see 'Editorial Opinion', *The Forum*, 22 November 1941, pp. 4–5.
27. *Diplomatic Note*, South African High Commissioner, London to Secretary of External Affairs, Pretoria; No. 543, 18 March 1942 (South African Ministry of External Affairs).
28. Edward L. Crowley (ed.) *The Soviet Diplomatic Corps 1917–1967*, Institute for the Study of the USSR (New Jersey: Scarecrow, 1970) pp. 33–4.
29. *Diplomatic Note*, British Ambassador, Moscow to British Foreign Office, London; No. 9, 2 April 1942 (British Foreign Office Files, Dominion Affairs).
30. *Diplomatic Note*, Presidium of the Supreme Soviet of the USSR (Kalinin and Molotov) to Prime Minister, Pretoria; Protocol No. 319, 30 April 1942 (South African Ministry of External Affairs).
31. *Diplomatic Note*, Kuibyshev to London; No. 432, 2 April 1942 (British Foreign Office, Files, Dominion Affairs) pp. 1–15.
32. Ibid.
33. D. D. Forsyth, former Secretary of External Affairs, interview with author, 17 April 1982, Cape Town.
34. The Decoration of the Soviet Red Cross was awarded to three South Africans in 1947 for assistance rendered during the 'Great Patriotic War'. The recipients were: Dr J. H. Harvey Pirie, National Chairman of the Medical Aid for Russia Fund; Mrs Jessie McPherson, a former Mayor of Johannesburg; and Mr. H. M. Shneir, Secretary of the MAFR Fund. Only eleven such medals had been awarded outside the Soviet Union at that time. *The Outspan* (South Africa), vol. XLI, no. 1024 (14 February 1947) p. 97.
35. A number of German U-boats and disguised surface raiders, including the *Stier*, the *Michel* and the *Thor*, were active in the South Atlantic, often in the waters directly off Cape Town. These raiders accounted for the loss of hundreds of thousands of tons of Allied shipping in transit around the Cape. Captain S. W. Roskill, *The War At Sea, 1939–1945*, Volume II, History of the Second World War (London: HMSO, 1956) pp. 175–219.
36. Philip, interview.
37. Ziabkin was born in Leningrad in 1902 and he attended the Leningrad Polytechnic Institute. The British embassy in Moscow reported that Ziabkin was not 'on any British Black List'. *Diplomatic Note*, Soviet Consulate in Pretoria to Secretary of External Affairs; No. 157, 1 December 1943 (South African Ministry of External Affairs).
38. *Rand Daily Mail* (South Africa), 26 April 1944.
39. *Memorandum*, South African Commissioner of Police to Secretary of

External Affairs; 18 February 1944 (South African Ministry of External Affairs).

40. See Adam Ulam, *Expansion and Coexistence* (London: Secker & Warbourg, 1968) pp. 378–445.

41. *Diplomatic Note*, External Affairs, Cape Town to External Affairs, Pretoria; 6 March 1945 (South African Ministry of External Affairs).

42. *Diplomatic Note*, External Affairs, Pretoria to External Affairs, Cape Town; 8 March 1945 (South African Ministry of External Affairs).

43. J. C. Smuts, jr, *Jan Christian Smuts* (London: Cassell, 1952) p. 122.

44. *Diplomatic Note*, External Affairs, Cape Town to External Affairs, Pretoria; 19 March 1945 (South African Ministry of External Affairs).

45. Paul Samoilovich Atroshenko was born in 1902 in the Smolensk region, and he graduated from the Moscow Power Institute. From 1941 to 1946 he was Senior Assistant to the Chief of the Consular Department of the PCFA. *Diplomatic Note*, Political Secretary, South Africa House to Secretary of External Affairs, Pretoria; 17 June 1946 (South African Ministry of External Affairs).

46. See Amry Vandebosch, *South Africa and the World* (University of Kentucky Press, 1970) pp. 127–35.

47. *House of Assembly Debates*, South Africa, 9 April 1947, column 2385.

48. *House of Assembly Debates*, South Africa, 9 April 1947, column 2395. For further information concerning trade between South Africa and the Soviet Union between 1936–56, consult the *Bureau of Census and Statistics Yearbook*, Union of South Africa.

49. *House of Assembly Debates*, South Africa, 9 April 1947, column 2441.

50. See Daniel Yergin, *Shattered Peace* (Boston: Houghton, 1978) p. 407.

51. See *House of Assembly Debates*, South Africa, 9 April 1947, columns 2378–459.

52. *Diplomatic Note*, First Political Secretary, American Embassy, Pretoria to Secretary for External Affairs, Pretoria; No. 292, 23 July 1948 (South African Ministry of External Affairs). It is probable that this overture was in connection with the 1946 conspiracy trial. During this government inquest, the whole National Executive Committee of the Communist Party was charged with sedition.

53. Gwendolyn M. Carter, *The Politics of Inequality* (London: Thames, 1958) pp. 61–72.

54. Munger, *The Formulation of South African Foreign Policy*, p. 20; and the interview with D. D. Forsyth.

55. See for instance 'South Africa to Break with Russia', *Sunday Express* (South Africa), 18 July 1948.

56. *Memorandum*, Under-secretary of External Affairs; 3 March 1948 (South African Ministry of External Affairs).

57. *Rand Daily Mail*, 4 March 1949.

58. *The Cape Times*, 15 March 1949; and *The Cape Argus*, 14 March 1949.

59. *Rand Daily Mail*, 4 March 1949.

60. *Diplomatic Note*, Secretary of External Affairs to Consul-General, Leopoldville; 14 March 1949 (South African Ministry of External Affairs).

61. *Diplomatic Note*, South African Ambassador in Paris to Secretary of External Affairs; 31 December 1949 (South African Ministry of External Affairs), and the *New York Herald Tribune*, 31 December 1949.
62. *Diplomatic Note*, Consul-General in Leopoldville to Secretary of External Affairs, Pretoria; 9 February 1950 (South African Ministry of External Affairs).
63. *Suid Afrikaanse Polisie*; No. 12/4/1464, 31 August 1949 (South African Ministry of External Affairs).
64. *Soviet Newsviews Digest*, no. 136, 1949, p. 11.
65. See for example Dr Malan's speech at the May 1949 Commonwealth Conference in London.
66. *Diplomatic Note*, Secretary of External Affairs, Pretoria; 2 September 1948 (South African Ministry of External Affairs).
67. *Diplomatic Note*, Secretary of External Affairs, Pretoria to South African High Commissioner, London; July 1950 (South African Ministry of External Affairs).
68. Boris Ivanovich Karavaev was born in the town of Novocherkassk in the Rostov district in 1910. He graduated from the North Caucasian Institute of Water Transport and served from 1939 in the Ministry of Foreign Affairs. Karavaev, easily the most experienced and accomplished diplomat to be nominated to the post of Consul-General in Pretoria, was later appointed chief envoy to Ethiopia in 1955 and subsequently became the Head of the Second African Department in the reorganised Ministry of Foreign Affairs. Karavaev was considered unsuitable by South African authorities because of alleged espionage activities involving British physicists while he was stationed at the Soviet embassy in London. The British Government regarded him as a 'thoroughly unscrupulous and dangerous person' during his tenure in Great Britain. Crowley, *The Soviet Diplomatic Corps*, p. 101; and *Diplomatic Note*, Anthony Hamilton, Political Secretary, South Africa House to Secretary of External Affairs, Pretoria; 17 March 1950 (South African Ministry of External Affairs).
69. Anthony Hamilton, interview with author, 18 April 1982, Cape Town.
70. See the *Rand Daily Mail*, 24 May 1952, and *The Pretoria News*, 10 December 1952.
71. *Suid-Afrikaanse Polisie*; 1 August 1951 (SAMFA), and *Diplomatic Note* Soviet Consul-General, Pretoria to Department of External Affairs, Pretoria; 2 July 1951 (South African Ministry of Foreign Affairs).
72. Nicolai Vasilyevich Ivanov served as the USSR High Commissioner in Austria before being posted to South Africa.
73. As evidence of this, Louw made reference to a recent broadcast of 'Radio Moscow' which urged the non-European population of South Africa to resist the South African government. (Louw mentioned as an addendum that Soviet diplomats had served alcohol to black South Africans, thus violating the Liquor Act.) Eric Louw, *House of Assembly Debates*, South Africa, 1 February 1956, columns 733–4.
74. For further details concerning Louw's decision to expel the Soviet diplomats and the subsequent international reaction to this move, see

The Eric Louw File, Political Archives, The Institute for Contemporary History, The University of the Orange Free State, Bloemfontein.

75. Dan C. Heldman, *The USSR and Africa* (New York: Praeger, 1981) p. 67.
76. *Diplomatic Note*, Secretary of External Affairs, Pretoria; 9 August 1949 (South African Ministry of External Affairs).
77. *Memorandum*, Commissioner of Customs and Excise Department, South Africa; 11 August 1949 (South African Ministry of External Affairs).
78. Roger E. Kanet (ed.) *The Soviet Union and the Developing Countries* (Baltimore: Johns Hopkins, 1974).
79. E. H. Carr, *The Bolshevik Revolution, 1917–1923*, Volume III (London: Macmillan, 1966) pp. 59–108.
80. See Max Beloff, *The Foreign Policy of Soviet Russia, 1929–1941*, Volume I (Oxford University Press, 1947) pp. 94–105.
81. Cherednik's predecessor was Vassily Solodovnikov, former head of the Africa Institute of the USSR Academy of Sciences.

CHAPTER 4

1. Amry Vandebosch, *South Africa and the World* (University of Kentucky Press, 1970) p. 228.
2. For information concerning the UN debate over Namibia see: Solomon Slonim, *South West Africa and the United Nations: An International Mandate in Dispute* (London: Johns Hopkins, 1973); and John Dugard (ed.) *The South West Africa/Namibia Dispute*, Perspectives on Southern Africa, No. 9 (London: University of California, 1973).
3. Richard W. Mansbach, 'The Soviet Union, the United Nations, and the Developing States', in Roger E. Kanet (ed.) *The Soviet Union and the Developing Nations*, (Baltimore: Johns Hopkins, 1974) p. 239.
4. V. Kubalkova and A. A. Cruickshank, *Marxism–Leninism and Theory of International Relations* (London: Routledge & Kegan Paul, 1980) p. 224.
5. Mansbach, 'The Soviet Union, the United Nations, and the Developing States', p. 240.
6. Leland M. Goodrich, *The United Nations* (New York: Crowell, 1959) pp. 23–4.
7. V. I. Lenin, *Polnoe Sobranie Sochinenii* no. 45, 5th edition (Moscow: 1960) p. 241.
8. Alexander Dallin, *The Soviet Union at the United Nations: An Inquiry into Soviet Motives and Objectives* (New York: Praeger, 1962) p. 6. Soviet views of the early period of UN activity can be found in N. N. Unozemtseva, *Organazatsii Ob'edinennykh Natsii: Utogi, Tendentsii, Perspective* (Moscow: 1970) pp. 28–40.
9. For an indication of Soviet thinking on the question of internationalism versus supra-nationalism, see D. B. Levin and G. P. Kaliuzhnaia (eds), *Mezdunarodnoe Pravo* (Moscow: 1964) p. 269.

10. Inis L. Claude, *Swords into Plowshares: The Problems and Progress of International Organizations* (New York: Random House, 1964) p. 130.

11. An early indication of Stalin's scepticism of indigenous nationalist movements in the underdeveloped areas can be found in *Protocoly Tsentral'nogo Komiteta RSDRP (b), Avgust 1918–Fevral 1918* (Moscow: 1958) p. 208.

12. Mansbach, 'The Soviet Union, the United Nations, and the Developing States', p. 241.

13. For instance, see J. V. Stalin, 'Economic Problems of Socialism in the USSR', in L. Grulion (ed.) *Current Soviet Politics* (New York: 1953) pp. 5–8. However, this point is disputed by Paul Marantz, 'Soviet Foreign Policy Factionalism Under Stalin?', *The Soviet Union*, vol. 3, no. 1 (1976) pp. 91–107.

14. N. S. Khrushchev, 'Report of the Central Committee to the Twentieth Party Congress', *The Current Digest of the Soviet Press*, vol. 8, no. 4 (7 March 1956) pp. 6–12.

15. S. I. Viskov (ed.) *Sovietskii Soiuz v Organizatsii Ob'edinenykh Natsii*, Volume II (Moscow: 1965) p. 209; and George A. Brinkley, 'The Soviet Union and the United Nations: the Changing Role of the Developing Countries', *The Review of Politics*, vol. 32, no. 1 (January 1970) p. 97.

16. Edward T. Rowe, 'The Emerging Anti-Colonial Consensus in the United Nations', *Journal of Conflict Resolution*, vol. 8 (1964) pp. 209–16.

17. Thomas Hovet, Jr, *Africa in the United Nations* (Illinois: Northwestern University, 1963) p. 181.

18. Mansbach, 'The Soviet Union, the United Nations, and the Developing States', p. 253.

19. See the discussion concerning Resolution no. 1598 (XV) calling for UN action in South Africa, *Year Book of the United Nations of 1960* (New York: United Nations, 1961) p. 151.

20. See Alvin Z. Rubinstein, *The Soviets in International Organizations, 1953–1963* (Princeton University Press, 1964) pp. 3–40.

21. Brinkley, 'The Soviet Union and the United Nations', p. 102.

22. David T. Cattel, 'The Soviet Union Seeks a Policy for Afro-Asia', in Kurt London, (ed.) *New Nations in a Divided World* (New York: Praeger, 1963) pp. 163–79.

23. Excerpts of Khrushchev's UN address appeared in *Kommunist*, vol. 37, no. 1 (Moscow: 1961) pp. 3–37.

24. The text of Brezhnev's speech appeared in *Pravda*, 4 November 1967, cited in *Current Digest of the Soviet Press*, vol. 19, no. 44 (22 November 1967) pp. 3–20.

25. See the comments of the Soviet representative, Mr Platon D. Morozov, in *Report of the Committee on the Reorganizatii of the Secretariat*, 27 November 1968 (New York: United Nations) pp. 60–1.

26. *International Conference on Sanctions Against South Africa*, UNESCO House, Paris, UN Centre Against Apartheid (New York: United Nations, 1981).

27. A. Leroy Bennet, *International Organizations* (New Jersey: Prentice, 1977) p. 108.

28. Jack Spence, 'South Africa and the Modern World', in Monica Wilson and Leonard Thompson (eds) *The Oxford History of South Africa, 1870–1966* (Oxford: Clarendon Press, 1975) p. 513.
29. James Barber, *South Africa's Foreign Policy 1945–1970* (Oxford University Press, 1973) p. 272.
30. Security Council Resolution No. 181, United Nations, 7 August 1964.
31. Colin Legum, *The United Nations and Southern Africa*, First Series, No. 3 (Brighton: ISIO, 1970) p. 11.
32. *A New Course in South Africa*, Report of the Group of Experts, UN Office of Public Information (1964).
33. Leonard Thompson and Andrew Prior, *South African Politics* (London: Yale University, 1982) pp. 229–31.
34. Ibid.
35. Spence, 'South Africa and the Modern World', p. 515.
36. See the compilation of Khrushchev's United Nations speeches in *Khrushchev in New York* (New York: UN Office of Public Information, 1960).
37. 'Mission of the Special Committee Against Apartheid in Moscow and Kiev', *Unit on Apartheid*, Political and Security Council Affairs, No. 21/75 (1975), p. 6.
38. Bennet, *International Organizations*, p. 111.
39. For the Soviet position on this issue, see V. I. Issraelian, *Sovetskii Soiuz i Organizatsiia ob'edinennykh Natsii, 1961–1965* (Moscow: 1968) pp. 338–54.
40. *Record of the 23rd General Assembly: 1968–1969*, Special Political Committee, cited in Brinkley, 'The Soviet Union and the United Nations', p. 107.
41. *Year Book of the United Nations of 1962*, (New York: United Nations, 1964) pp. 95–6.
42. *Record of the 20th General Assembly: 1965–1966*, Special Political Committee, SP 474, p. 3.
43. *Imperialist Military Collaboration with South Africa* (Helsinki: World Peace Council, 1975).
44. Security Council Resolution, No. 216, United Nations, 12 November 1965.
45. See Ernest W. LeFever, *Crisis in the Congo: A United Nations Force in Action* (Washington: Brookings, 1965); and for a specific reference to the UN turning into an imperialist instrument, consult V. Zhukov, 'Dollar Colonialism in the Congo', *Aziya i Afrika Segodnya*, no. 6 (June 1961), p. 8.
46. Bennet, *International Organizations*, pp. 343–4.
47. James A. Stegenga, 'Peacekeeping: Post Mortems or Previews?', *International Organization*, vol. 27, no. 3 (1973) p. 379.
48. Legum, *The United Nations and Southern Africa*, p. 36. For a discussion about the prospects of a UN force in Namibia, see Anthony Verrier, *International Peacekeeping* (Harmondsworth: Penguin, 1981) pp. 145–55.
49. Lincoln P. Bloomfield, 'The United States, the Soviet Union, and the Prospects for Peacekeeping', *International Organization*, vol. 24, no. 3 (1970) p. 557.
50. Bennet, *International Organizations*, p. 84.

51. Wojciech Morawiecki, 'Institutional and Political Conditions of Partici-pation of Socialist States in International Organizations', *International Organization*, vol. 22, no. 3 (1968) pp. 494–506.
52. For precise costs, see Rosalyn Higgins, *United Nations Peacekeeping: Africa* (Oxford University Press, 1980).
53. Ruth B. Russell, *The General Assembly: Patterns/Problems/Prospects* (New York: Carnegie Endowment, 1970) p. 35.
54. See Amelia C. Leiss (ed.) *Apartheid and UN Collective Measures: An Analysis* (New York: Carnegie Endowment, 1965).
55. 'Text of Basic Principles, May 29, 1972', *Bulletin*, US Department of State, 26 June 1972, p. 899.
56. Stengenga, 'Peacekeeping', p. 384.
57. *United Nations General Assembly*, A/Special Political Committee/SR 652, 1969, p. 50.
58. 'Mission of the Special Committee Against Apartheid to Moscow and Kiev', p. 2.
59. Ibid., p. 3.
60. Toby Trister Gati, 'The Soviet Union and the North–South Dialogue', *Orbis*, vol. 24, no. 2 (Summer 1980) pp. 66–8.
61. Robert S. McNamara, 'The Road Ahead for South Africa', unpublished manuscript, University of Witwatersrand, South Africa, 21 October 1982.
62. David A. Kay, 'The Impact of African States on the United Nations', *International Organization*, vol. 23, no. 1 (1969) pp. 33–47.
63. Richard Walker (New York Correspondent), 'Reds in a Rage over Trade Allegation', *Rand Daily Mail*, 7 December 1978.
64. *Rand Daily Mail*, 7 December 1978.
65. Spence, 'South Africa and the Modern World', p. 518.
66. *Debates of the House of Assembly* (Hansard), Union of South Africa, vol. 95, column 7676 (1958).
67. *Debates of the House of Assembly* (Hansard) Union of South Africa, vol. 107, column 4173, (1961). There is evidence to suggest that 80 per cent of whites in South Africa currently believe their country is beset by a Soviet directed 'total onslaught' in which the United Nations plays a substantial role. Deon Geldenhuys, 'What Do We Think? A Survey of White Opinion on Foreign Policy Issues', *Occasional Paper*, South African Institute of International Affairs (November 1982) p. 6.
68. Brinkley, 'The Soviet Union and the United Nations', pp. 112–13.
69. Jack C. Plano and Robert E. Riggs, *Forging World Order: The Politics of International Organization* (New York: Macmillan, 1967) pp. 154–9.
70. See Edward T. Rowe, 'Changing Patterns in the Voting Success of Member States in the United Nations General Assembly, 1945–1966', *International Organization*, vol. 23, no. 4 (1969) pp. 231–53; and Catherine Senf Manno, 'Majority Decisions and Minority Responses in the UN General Assembly', *Journal of Conflict Resolution*, vol. 10 (1966) pp. 1–20.
71. Stephen P. Gilbert, 'Soviet–American Military Aid Competition in the Third World', *Orbis*, vol. 13 (1970) pp. 117–19.
72. See the remarks of Mendelovich in the plenary meeting, A/PV. 1741, cited in Brinkley, 'The Soviet Union and the United Nations', p. 105.

73. Brinkley, 'The Soviet Union and the United Nations', pp. 105–6.
74. The Third World bloc, at the behest of the African states, successfully manoeuvred their resolution through committee, and the Soviet Union together with the Western powers joined to apply the two-thirds rule to defeat the initiative in plenary session.
75. Mansbach, 'The Soviet Union, the United Nations, and the Developing States', p. 261.
76. Khrushchev's Report to the Party Congress, *The Current Digest of the Soviet Press*, vol. 8, no. 4 (7 March 1956) p. 7.
77. See James Mayall, *Africa: The Cold War and After* (London: Elek Books, 1971).
78. Legum, *The United Nations and Southern Africa*, p. 9.

CHAPTER 5

1. The United States Geological survey has identified twenty-seven minerals as critical to industrial societies.
2. See the remarks of Senator Strom Thurmond, *The Congressional Record*, 5 September 1979 (Washington, DC: Government Printing Office); and 'South Africa: Persian Gulf of Minerals', *Backgrounder*, no. 9/80 (December 1980) South African Embassy in London, p. 1.
3. Dr William Schneider of the Hudson Institute, cited in Alfred E. Eckes, Jr, *The United States and the Global Struggle for Minerals* (Austin: University of Texas, 1977) p. 248.
4. The phrases 'resource supply disruption' and Soviet 'strategy of denial' have gained wide currency in conservative circles. See the various publications from Michael Hough's South African Institute for Strategic Studies.
5. E. H. Carr's term, which refers to two seemingly contradictory policies which are practiced simultaneously. See E. H. Carr, 'The Dual Policy', in *The Bolshevik Revolution, 1917–1923*, Volume III, (London: Macmillan, 1966) pp. 59–108.
6. Timothy Green, *The New World of Gold* (London: Weidenfeld & Nicolson, 1981) p. 61.
7. Michael Kaser, 'Soviet Gold Production', *Soviet Economy in a Time of Change*, Volume II, Joint Economic Committee, Congress of the United States (Washington, DC: Government Printing Office, October 1979), pp. 290–3.
8. V. V. Strishkov, *Mineral Industries of the USSR*, United States Department of the Interior, Bureau of Mines (Washington, DC: Bureau of Mines, 1979); Theodore Shabad, Robert G. Jensen and Arthurt W. Wright (eds) *Soviet Natural Resources in the World Economy* (London: University of Chicago, 1983).
9. In November 1980, Waddell, an executive director of the Anglo-American Corporation of South Africa was spotted at the Bolshoi Theatre in Moscow by BBC correspondent John Osman. When asked what he, a South African, was doing in Moscow, Waddell would only

say that he was just 'passing through'. Michael Cockerell, an investigative reporter for *Panorama*, produced 'South African Gold and Diamonds – the Kremlin Connection' which was aired on 6 April 1981. The reactions of individuals involved in mining ranged from amusement to indignation. The programme was, as one official noted, 'long on entertainment, short on proof'. The controversy raised by public accusations of Soviet–South African complicity caused all parties involved to shut their doors to inquisitors.

10. *The Official Yearbook of the Union of South Africa*, Bureau of Census and Statistics, no. 29, 1954–7, p. 698.
11. Studies of the history of South African diamond mining include: Brian Roberts, *The Diamond Magnates* (London: Hamisch, 1972); Anthony Hocking, *Oppenheimer and Son* (Johannesburg: McGraw-Hill, 1973); and Sir Theodore Gregory, *Ernest Oppenheimer and the Economic Development of South Africa* (Oxford University Press, 1962).
12. Edward Jay Epstein, *The Diamond Invention* (London: Hutchinson, 1982).
13. Epstein, *Diamond Invention*, pp. 163–6.
14. G. Lanning and M. Mueller, *Africa Undermined* (Harmondsworth: Penguin, 1979) p. 58.
15. Epstein, *Diamond Invention*, pp. 163–6.
16. In 1941 an eminent Soviet geologist, Victor Sobolev, argued that the great Siberian 'shield' between the Yenisei and Lena rivers bore a remarkable similarity to the raised plateau of South Africa, where diamond pipes had been discovered. Popugayeva's discovery proved Sobolev's hypothesis correct. A. A. Linari-Linholm, *Occurence, Mining and Recovery of Diamonds* (Johannesburg: 1970) p. 6.
17. John Massey Stewart, 'Siberia: No Longer a Sleeping Land', *Optima*, no. 2 (1976) pp. 85–104.
18. See 'What it is like to live in Siberia during winter', *Smithsonian*, vol. 4, no. 10 (1972) pp. 44–51. Some descriptions of the working conditions can be gleaned from ' "Red" diamonds from Siberia', *The International Diamond Annual* (London: 1970) p. 81.
19. Edward Jay Epstein, 'Have You Ever Tried to Sell a Diamond?', *Atlantic Monthly* (February 1982) p. 26.
20. Timothy Green, *The World of Diamonds* (London: Weidenfeld & Nicolson, 1981) p. 87.
21. Victor Tikhonov cited in *International Diamond Annual* (London: 1971) p. 82.
22. Michael Cockerell, *The Listener*, 9 April 1981, p. 465; Epstein, *Diamond Invention*, p. 103; and 'South Africa and the Soviet Union: Odd Pair in Mineral Markets', *Washington Post*, 4 August 1981.
23. Although there is much speculation concerning the provisions of the agreement, the existence of such a contract is certain. For further sources, see John L. Scherer (ed.) *USSR, Facts and Figures Annual*, Volume VI (Miami: Academic International, 1982) pp. 215–16.
24. Cited in the annual De Beers report for 1963, Epstein, *Diamond Invention*, p. 103.
25. Cited in Epstein, *Diamond Invention*, p. 15; this point was restated by

Nicholas Oppenheimer, Deputy Director of De Beers Corporation, interview with author, 21 March 1984, Johannesburg.

26. Confidential information provided to the author.

27. Neil Behrmann, 'Russian diamond claim strongly rejected', *Rand Daily Mail*, 24 June 1982.

28. Epstein, *Diamond Invention*, p. 16.

29. David Marsh, 'De Beers Blocks UK Statistics on Soviet Diamond Shipments', *Financial Times*, 18 January 1982.

30. Epstein, *Diamond Invention*, pp. 16 and 169.

31. *International Diamond Trade, 1971* (London: 1972) pp. 79–80.

32. Epstein, *Diamond Invention*, p. 16; Harry Oppenheimer, Director of the De Beers Corporation, interview with author, 21 March 1984, Johannesburg.

33. Soviet official cited in Green, *The World of Diamonds*, p. 91; this point was also made by N. Straud, Managing Director, Premier Diamond Mine, interview with author, 27 March 1984, Premier, South Africa.

34. This belief is promoted by: Green, *The World of Diamonds*, pp. 90–3; Doug Hoffe, Chairman of Consolidated Diamond Mines, Namibia, interview with author, 22 April 1982, Windhoek.

35. 'King Solomon's other mines', *The Economist*, 16 May 1981; J. D. F. Jones, 'The Long Shadow Over Gold', *Financial Times*, 23 February 1982.

36. See the chapter entitled 'Monopolies, cartels, embargoes and stockpiles', in W. C. J. van Rensburg and S. Bambrick, *The Economics of the World's Mineral Industries* (Johannesburg: McGraw-Hill, 1978) pp. 210–28.

37. For an account of early gold mining in the Soviet Union see P. F. Lomako (Minister of Non-ferrous Metallurgy of the USSR), 'Non-ferrous metallurgy during the Great Patriotic War', *Tsvetnye metally*, no. 4 (1974) pp. 1–27.

38. S. Mora [K. Zamorski], *Kolyma: Gold and Forced Labour in the USSR*, (Washington, DC: Foundation for Foreign Affairs, 1949) pp. 7–12.

39. Green, *The New World of Gold*, p. 67.

40. Christopher Glynn, *Gold 1979* (London: Privately circulated by Consolidated Gold Fields, 1978) pp. 1–32.

41. The Muruntau complex has been closely investigated in the Gold Fields studies, employing Soviet technical publications, ore samples and satellite photographs. David Potts, *Gold 1980* (London: Privately circulated by Consolidated Gold Fields, 1980).

42. The author was a student at the University of Erevan in Soviet Armenia near the Zod mine on the border with Turkey.

43. J. D. Littlepage and Demaree Bess, *In Search of Soviet Gold*, (New York: Harcourt, 1938).

44. See Alexander Solzhenitsyn, *The Gulag Archipelago*, 3 vols, (London: Fontana, 1973, 1975, 1978); Michael Kaser, *The Soviet Impact on Precious Metals Trading: Gold and Platinum*, paper presented to Centre D'Études en Administration Internationale (October 1981) pp. 2–4.

45. See Central Intelligence Agency, *Handbook, 1979*, p. 69 for estimates of Soviet gold production.

46. Michael Beckett, Executive Director of Consolidated Gold Fields, interview with author, 12 January 1984, London.
47. Rae Westen, *Gold: A World Survey* (London: Croom Helm, 1983) pp. 165–8.
48. P. F. Lomako, 'The non-ferrous metallurgy of the USSR at a new stage', *Tsvetnye metally*, no. 5 (1976) pp. 4–7.
49. Green, *The New World of Gold*, pp. 34–5.
50. Ibid., pp. 66–70.
51. Dr Paul Einzig, 'Gold Policy of the Soviet Government', *Optima*, vol. 9, no. 2 (1959) pp. 60–4; and 'Gold Sales by Soviet Union Push Price Down', *International Herald Tribune*, 7 March 1982, p. 11.
52. David Marsh and Bernard Simon, 'Russia's discreet gold chain', *Financial Times*, 31 March 1981.
53. See *The Nation*, 7 March 1981, p. 263; and 'The Soviet Union: Just Passing Through', *Der Spiegel*, 5 January 1981.
54. David Marsh and Bernard Simon, 'Gold: the game hots up between Russia and South Africa', *Financial Times*, 26 October 1981.
55. Ibid.
56. Marsh and Simon, 'Russia's discreet gold chain'.
57. Confidential information provided to the author.
58. Michael Cockerell, *South African Gold and Diamonds – the Kremlin Connection*, unpublished text, p. 11.
59. G. A. Ariovich, *Soviet Trade Policy and its Implications for South Africa's Mining Sector*, unpublished text (January 1980); this report was later published in an abridged form as G. A. Ariovich and H. F. Kenney, 'The Implications for the South African Economy of Russia's Foreign Trade Policy', *International Affairs Bulletin* (South Africa), vol. 4, no. 2 (1980) pp. 33.
60. Cockerell, *South African Gold and Diamonds*.
61. Bernard Simon, *Financial Times* correspondent, interview with author, 8 April 1982, Johannesburg; this account is supported by certain confidential information provided to the author.
62. This was a sort of Russian homecoming for Consgold. After the successful conclusion of the Bolshevik revolution, Lenin invited Consolidated Gold Fields back into the Soviet Union under the 'new economic policy' of 1921–8 to help run the Lena basin mines they had previously owned. See Kaser, 'Soviet Gold Production', pp. 291–2.
63. These techniques are described in G. Druzhina and Mineyev, 'Recovery of gold from pulps by means of pore carrier extraction', *Tsvetnye metally*, no. 1 (1975) p. 81; G. Druzhina, A. A. Batsuyev and V. A. Khomutnikov, 'Redex sorption of gold and silver from cyanide waste effluents', *Tsvetnye metally*, no. 12 (1976) p. 68. These papers apparently refer to mining technology presently employed at Muruntau.
64. Michael Beckett, Executive Director of Consolidated Gold Fields, interview with author, 12 January 1984, London.
65. Mike Brown, Chief Economist, South African Chamber of Mines, interview with author, 15 March 1982, Johannesburg.
66. For instance, Pyotr Zhmurka, Deputy Minister of Non-ferrous Metallurgy with responsibility for the gold mining industry, was recently fired in the Adropov-initiated anti-corruption campaign because of 'serious

deficiencies in his work', *Economist Foreign Report*, 27 October 1983, p. 6.

67. Bernard Simon, *Financial Times* correspondent, interview with author, 8 April 1982, Johannesburg.

68. The 'platinum group metals' – platinum, palladium, osmium, ruthenium, iridium, and rhodium – usually occur together in nature. Gordon Young, 'Platinum', *National Geographic*, vol. 164, no. 5 (1983) p. 686.

69. Professor Paul Kovaloff, 'The Platinum Market in the Near Future', *South African Mining and Engineering Journal*, 31 July 1926, pp. 6–7.

70. Ibid. See also Kovaloff, *The Platinum Industry in Russia*, government offprint, 1926 (South African Government Archives, Union Buildings); and 'Note of Interview between the Acting Minister of Mines and Professor Kovaloff', MN 385/26, 8 October 1926 (South African Government Archives, Union Buildings).

71. *Financial Times*, 20 February 1982; 8 January 1982; 16 February 1982.

72. The Mining Annual Review, American Bureau of Metal Statistics, the US Bureau of Mines and Metallgesellschaft concur that Soviet platinum production rose between 1975–81.

73. Daniel I. Fine, 'Mineral resource dependency crisis: Soviet Union and United States', in James Arnold Miller, R. Daniel McMichael (eds) *The Resource War in 3-D — Dependency, Diplomacy, Defense*, Pittsburgh. World Affairs Council, 1980) pp. 44.

74. Dniel S. Papp, 'Soviet non-fuel mineral resources: surplus or scarcity', *Resources Policy*, vol. 8 no. 3 (September 1982) pp. 169–70.

75. Louise Du Bolay, Editor of *Gold* Survey for Consolidated Goldfields, interview with author, 2 December 1983, London.

76. Professor William Gutteridge, Head of Politics, University of Aston, Birmingham, interview with author, 5 November 1982, Birmingham; and BBC *Panorama* transcript, 'South African Gold and Diamonds – the Kremlin Connection', 6 April 1981, p. 10.

77. BBC *Panorama* transcript, 'South African Gold and Diamonds – the Kremlin Connection', 6 April 1981, pp. 9–11.

78. Cockerell, *The Kremlin Connection*, unpublished text, p. 7.

79. 'The Moscow Connection: a credible hypothesis', *World Business Weekly*, 6 July 1981, pp. 37–8.

80. Bernard Simon, *Financial Times* correspondent, interview with author, 8 April 1982, Johannesburg.

81. For instance, in 1978 the United States imported from the Soviet Union platinum group metals at a value of only 25 million dollars; Strishkov, *Mineral Industries of the USSR*, pp. 17–18.

82. Fine, 'Mineral resource dependency', *The Resource War*, pp. 42–3.

83. *Financial Times*, 26 October 1981.

84. Y. Von Schutz, Chairman of the Karakul Board of South West Africa, interview with author, 20 April 1982, Windhoek, Namibia.

85. V. I. Lenin, 'The Importance of Gold Now and After the Complete Victory of Socialism', *Collected Works*, Volume 33, August 1921–March 1923 (London: Lawrence & Wishart, 1960–71) p. 113.

86. V. Granov and O. Nakropin, 'Soviet Foreign Policy: Its Class Nature and Humanism', *International Affairs*, no. 11 (December 1965)

pp. 7–13; S. Morkovnikov, 'Soviet Foreign Policy: A Factor for Peace and Progress', *International Affairs*, no. 11 (December 1974) p. 101.

87. Dr Vendulka Kubalkova, University of Queensland, letter to author, 21 June 1982.

88. V. I. Lenin, 'On Compromises', *Collected Works*, Volume 25, June–September 1917 (London: Lawrence & Wishart, 1960–71) p. 305. For a description of Soviet trade doctrine, see B. Vaganov, 'The Leninist Foreign Trade Policy', *International Affairs*, no. 5, (May 1969) pp. 49–53.

89. J. V. Stalin, *Foundations of Leninism* (Moscow: International Publishers, 1939) p. 94; V. Kubalkova and A. A. Cruickshank, *Marxism–Leninism and Theory of International Relations* (London: Routledge & Kegan Paul, 1980) p. 203.

90. See the chapter entitled 'The Dual Policy' in E. H. Carr, *The Bolshevik Revolution, 1917–1923*, Volume III (London: Macmillan, 1966) pp. 59–108.

91. *Isvestiya*, 18 April 1981.

92. Anatoli Gromyko cited in Caryle Murphy, 'South Africa and Soviet Union: Odd Pair on Mineral Markets', *Washington Post*, 4 August 1981; 'How Moscow and Pretoria Carve up the Mineral Market', *Guardian*, 23 August 1981.

93. Vladimir Bykov, cited in BBC *Panorama* transcript, 'South African Gold and Diamonds – the Kremlin Connection', 6 April 1981, pp. 2–10.

94. Ibid.

95. Ibid.

96. Louise Du Bolay, Editor of *Gold* for Consolidated Goldfields, interview with author, 2 December 1983, London; this point is confirmed by confidential information provided to the author.

97. Michael Shafer, 'No Crisis: The Implications of U.S. Dependence on Southern African Strategic Minerals', *Occasional Paper*, South African Institute of International Affairs (November 1983), pp. 2–3; *Commodity Year Book 1981*, (New York: Commodity Research Bureau, 1981) pp. 77, 156, 261–3; *State of South Africa*, Economic, Financial and Statistical Yearbook of the Republic of South Africa (Johannesburg: 1982).

98. See sources in note 97.

99. See sources in note 97.

100. Larry W. Bowman, 'The Strategic Importance of South Africa to the United States', *African Affairs*, vol. 81, no. 323 (April 1982) pp. 183–6.

101. *Sub-Sahara Africa: Its Role in Critical Mineral Needs of the Western World*, a report prepared by the Sub-Committee on Mines and Mining of the Committee on Interior and Insular Affairs of the US House of Representatives (Washington, DC: Government Printing Office, 1980) pp. vii and 19–20; *Congressional Record*, House of Representatives, 5 September 1979.

102. *Congressional Record*, House of Representatives, 5 September 1979.

103. 'USA: Strategic minerals and Africa', *Africa Confidential*, no. 22 (17 June 1981) p. 1.

104. William C. J. van Rensburg and D. A. Pretorious, *South Africa's*

Strategic Minerals, Pieces on a Continental Chess Board (Johannesburg: Valiant, 1977) p. 126.

105. Sandy Feustal, 'African Minerals and American Foreign Policy', *Africa Report*, vol. 23, no. 5 (September 1978) p. 12.

106. Bowman, 'Strategic Importance', *African Affairs*, p. 184.

107. Bruce M. Russett, 'Security and the Resources Scramble', *International Affairs*, vol. 58, no. 1 (Winter 1981–2) pp. 42–58; Michael Tanzer, *The Race for Resources* (London: Monthly Review, 1980).

108. For an excellent study of the role of natural resources in the formulation of foreign policy, see Alfred E. Eckes, *The United States and the Global Struggle for Minerals* (London: University of Texas, 1974) pp. 147–255.

109. Eckes, *Global Struggle*, p. 154.

110. Papp, 'Soviet non-fuel resources', *Resources Policy*, p. 170.

111. Brooks Emeny, *The Strategy of Raw Materials: A Study of America in Peace and War* (New York: Macmillan, 1934) p. 92.

112. Demitri B. Shimkin, *Minerals: A Key to Soviet Power*, (Cambridge, Massachusetts: Harvard University Press, 1953) p. 302.

113. US Central Intelligence Agency, *Soviet Economy: Problems and Prospects* (Washington, DC: Government Printing Office, 1977).

114. James G. Grichar, *The Non-fuel Mineral Outlook for the USSR through 1990*, US Bureau of Mines (Washington, DC: Government Printing Office, 1981); US Central Intelligence Agency, *The Lead and Zinc Industry in the USSR*, ER 80–10072 (March 1980) p. 10.

115. Papp, 'Soviet non-fuel resources', *Resources Policy*, pp. 172–3.

116. Oleg Bogomolov, *Kommunist*, cited in Michael Simmons, 'Moscow tells Comecon to prepare for hard times', *Guardian*, 31 May 1983.

117. Papp, 'Soviet non-fuel resources', *Resources Policy*, pp. 172–4.

118. van Rensburg and Pretorius, *South Africa's Strategic Minerals*, p. 126.

119. Patrick Wall, *The Southern Oceans and the Security of the Free World*, (London: Stacey, 1977) p. 22.

120. James Arnold Miller, *The Strategic Mineral Vulnerability of the West: a Soviet Perspective*, paper presented at the World Balance of Power Conference, Leeds Castle, Kent, Great Britain, 22 July 1983, p. 8.

121. V. Kubalkova and A.A. Cruickshank, *International Inequality* (London: Croom Helm, 1981) p. 162.

122. E. Kridl Valkenier, 'The USSR, the Third World, and the Global Economy', *Problems of Communism* (July/August 1979) p. 17.

123. Christopher Coker,'Adventurism and Pragmatism: The Soviet Union, COMECOM and Relations with African States', *International Affairs*, vol. 57, no. 4 (Autumn 1981) pp. 618–33.

124. Henry Trofimenko, 'America, Russia and the Third World', *Foreign Affairs* (Summer 1981) pp. 1034–6.

125. Seth Singleton, 'The Shared Tactical Goals of South Africa and the Soviet Union', *CSIS Africa Notes*, no. 12 (26 April 1983) p. 2.

126. *Imports of Minerals from South Africa by the United States and the OECD Countries*, prepared for the Sub-committee on African Affairs of the Committee on Foreign Relations, US Senate, by the Congressional Research Service (Washington, DC: Government Printing Office, 1980) p. xi.

127. *South Africa: Time Running Out, The Report of the Study Commission on US Policy Toward Southern Africa* (Berkeley: University of California, 1981) pp. 310–18.
128. Ibid., pp. 450–4; see also Bowman, 'Strategic Importance', *African Affairs*, p. 185.
129. *Imports of Minerals from South Africa*, pp. xv–xvii.
130. Ibid.
131. *South Africa: Time Running Out*, p. 450.
132. 'King Solomon's other Mines', *The Economist*, 16 May 1981.
133. Bowman, 'Strategic Importance', *African Affairs*, p. 184.
134. Robert M. Price, 'Can Africa Afford Not to Sell Minerals', *New York Times*, 18 August 1981.
135. See 'Angola Opens Doors for Cooperation', *Africa*, May 1979; the author has discussed Western investment in Angola in great detail in *Angola, 1983*, International Institute for Strategic Studies, unpublished text, 6 September 1983; Gerald Bender, 'Angola: Left, Right and Wrong', *Foreign Policy*, no. 43 (Summer 1981) p. 66.
136. See 'De Beers Mine in Angola', *Sunday Times*, 16 December 1979; Richard Dowden, 'The dirt on the face of the diamond', *The Times*, 14 October 1983.
137. Robert J. Hanks, *The Cape Route* (Cambridge, Massachusetts: Institute for Foreign Policy Analysis, 1981) p. 64.
138. Alexander L. Taylor, 'A Gem That Lost Its Luster', *Time*, 30 August 1982, p. 66; Bernard Simon, 'Diamond fears drive foreigners from De Beers', *Financial Times*, 21 January 1982.
139. Raymond Vernon, 'Soviet Commodity Power in International Economic Relations', paper presented to Centre D'Etudes en Administration Internationale (October 1981) pp. 1–2. Other studies which challenge the conventional wisdom concerning the potential to establish resource cartels include: Stephen D. Krasner, 'Oil Is The Exception', *Foreign Policy*, no. 14 (Spring 1974) pp. 68–84; D. B. Bobrow and R. T. Kudrle, 'Theory, Policy and Resource Cartels', *Journal of Conflict Resolution*, vol. 20, no. 1 (March 1976) pp. 3–49; Julian L. Simon, 'The Scarcity of Raw Materials', *The Atlantic Monthly*, June 1981, pp. 33–41.
140. William K. Severin, 'Soviet Non-fuel Minerals: Resource War or Business as Usual?' *Materials and Society*, vol. 7, no. 1 (1983) pp. 27–34.

CHAPTER 6

1. John Barron, *KGB: The Secret Work of Soviet Secret Agents* (London: Corgi, 1983); John E. Carlson, 'The KGB', in James Cracraft (ed.) *The Soviet Union Today* (Illinois: University of Chicago, 1983); J. David Dallin, *Soviet Espionage* (New Haven: Yale University Press, 1953); and Jerry Rositze, *KGB: The Eyes of Russia* (Harmondsworth: Penguin, 1983).
2. Ian Grieg, *The Communist Challenge to Africa* (Richmond, Surrey: Foreign Affairs Publishers, 1977) pp. 114–15.

3. Ibid.
4. Barron, *KGB*, pp. 449–51.
5 The author was granted access to the diplomatic file between the Soviet Union and South Africa from the 1942–56 period by the South African Ministry of External Affairs. Refer to the chapter on official relations.
6. *Diplomatic Note*, South African Embassy, London to External Affairs, Pretoria; 20 May 1942 (South African Ministry of External Affairs).
7. Eric Louw, *House of Assembly Debates*, South Africa, 1 February 1956, columns 733–4.
8. *Rand Daily Mail* (South Africa) 29 January 1981; 12 May 1982.
9. Barron, *KGB*, pp. 14, 29.
10. Grieg, *Communist Challenge*, p. 117.
11. Barron, *KGB*, p. 29.
12. Zdenek Cervenka and Barbara Rogers, *The Nuclear Axis* (London: Friedman, 1978).
13. Cervenka and Rogers, *Nuclear Axis*, p. 196; the Chinese publication referred to is *Ta Kung Pao* (Hong Kong: 30 October 1969) which is generally regarded as an outlet for important statements from Beijing. See also Peter Dreyer, *Martyrs and Fanatics* (London: Secker & Warburg, 1981) p. 40.
14. Barbara Carr, *Spy in the Sun* (Cape Town: Timmins, 1969) p. 185.
15. Tass statement, *Guardian* (London) 12 August 1977.
16. *Johannesburg Star* (South Africa) 29 January 1981.
17. Prime Minister P. W. Botha, *House of Assembly Debates*, South Africa, 28 January 1981; and *Sunday Times* (South Africa) 17 August 1982.
18. *Africa Research Bulletin*, Political Social and Cultural Series, vol. 20, no. 12, p. 7076.
19. *The Times* (London) 14 April 1981; *Rand Daily Mail*, 10 October 1981; and *Sunday Tribune* (South Africa) 27 September 1981.
20. Letter to the author from Jacques Moreillon, Member of the Directorate, International Red Cross, 13 July 1982.
21. *Sunday Times* (South Africa) 30 January 1983.
22. Prime Minister P. W. Botha, *House of Assembly Debates*, South Africa, 28 January 1981, columns 230–2.
23. *Sunday Times* (South Africa) 30 January 1983.
24. *The Times*, 28 January 1983, p. 13.
25. *House of Assembly Debates*, South Africa, 30 January 1984, column 64.
26. *Africa Research Bulletin*, Political Social and Cultural Series, vol. 20, no. 12, p. 7075; information provided to the author on a confidential basis.
27. *Sunday Times* (South Africa) 30 January 1983.
28. *Guardian* (London) 30 December 1983; *Daily Telegraph* (London) 30 December 1983.
29. *Time*, 28 January 1983, p. 13.
30. *The Times* (London) 30 December 1983; information provided to the author on a confidential basis.
31. Colonel Kapp, South African Defence Force Information Bureau, interview with author, Pretoria, 22 March 1984.
32. *The Times* (London) 30 December 1983.

33. Professor Robert Schrire, University of Cape Town, interview with author, Cape Town, 28 March 1984.
34. Robert Cabelly, Special Envoy of the Assistant Secretary of State for African Affairs, interview with author, London, 2 November 1983.
35. Curt Kammen, Deputy Chief of Mission, United States Embassy, Moscow, interview with author, Moscow, 20 April 1984.
36. *Johannesburg Star* (South Africa) 22 December 1983.
37. *The Times* (London) 21 November 1983; *Guardian* (London) 21 November 1983.
38. *International Herald Tribune* (London) 21 December 1983; *Daily Telegraph* (London) 21 November 1983.
39. *International Herald Tribune* (London) 19 December 1983.
40. *The Observer* (London) 4 December 1983; *International Herald Tribune* (London) 16 May 1984.
41. Captain John Moore, cited in *Daily Telegraph* (London) 25 November 1983.
42. John Davies, Political Attaché, South African Embassy London, interview with author, 2 February 1984.
43. *Soviet Active Measures*, Hearings before the Permanent Select Committee on Intelligence, House of Representatives (Washington, DC: Government Printing Office, 1982).
44. *Soviet Active Measures*, pp. 4–42.
45. *Soviet Active Measures*, pp. 116–17; 132–3.
46. For instance, Loginov was observed photographing John Forster Square in Johannesburg before his arrest, in strict violation of South African security laws. Commodore Gerhardt also led a lifestyle impossible to maintain merely on the salary of an officer of the South African Navy, a fact which should have aroused suspicion. Admiral Du Plessie, Chief of Staff, South African Military Intelligence, interview with author, Pretoria, 22 March 1984.
47. Gordon Winter, *Inside BOSS* (Harmondsworth; Penguin, 1981) pp. 417–19; and James Barber, 'BOSS in Britain', *African Affairs*, vol. 82, no. 328 (July 1983) pp. 320–8.
48. John Stockwell, *In Search of Enemies* (London: Deutsch, 1978) p. 187.

CHAPTER 7

1. For a clear enunciation of the Soviet approach to the classification of African ideology and development, see the statement by N. Kosukhin, in *Sovetskaya Rossiya*, 16 February 1984.
2. Robert Levgold, 'The Soviet Union's Changing View of Sub-Saharan Africa', in W. Duncan (ed.) *Soviet Policy in the Developing Countries* (London: Ginn–Blaisdell, 1970) p. 74.
3. There are several useful discussions on Soviet involvement in the Angolan Civil War. See for instance: Jiri Valenta, 'Soviet Decision-Making on the Intervention in Angola', in David E. Albright (ed.) *Communism in Africa* (Bloomington: Indiana University Press, 1980)

pp. 87–117, as well as his 'The Soviet–Cuban Intervention in Angola', *Studies in Comparative Communism* (Spring/Summer 1978); Arthur Jay Klinghoffer, *The Angolan War: A Study of Soviet Policy in the Third World* (Boulder: Westview, 1980); Colin Legum, 'Angola and the Horn of Africa', in Stephen S. Kaplan *et al.*, *Mailed Fist, Velvet Glove: Soviet Armed Forces as a Political Instrument* (Washington: The Brookings Institution, 1979); and Peter Vanneman and Martin James, 'The Soviet Intervention in Angola: Intentions and Implications', *Strategic Review* (Summer 1976). But the most balanced and incisive account is Larry C. Napper, 'The African Terrain and US–Soviet Conflict in Angola and Rhodesia', in Alexander L. George (ed.) *Managing US–Soviet Rivalry* (Boulder: Westview, 1983) pp. 155–85.

4. See S. N. MacFarlane, 'Soviet Intervention in Third World Conflict', unpublished paper (Harvard, CFIA, 1983) p. 13; and C. Ebinger, 'External Intervention in Internal War: the Politics and Diplomacy of the Angolan Civil War', *Orbis*, vol. 20, no.3 (1976) pp. 688–690.

5. See *Africa Research Bulletin*, vol. 12, no. 11 (15 December 1985) p. 3820.

6. Jonathan Steele, 'Soviet Relations with Angola and Mozambique', *Chatham House Paper* (London: Royal Institute of International Affairs, 1984) pp. 10–12.

7. See National Foreign Assessment Center, US Central Intelligence Agency, *Communist Aid Activities in Non-Communist Less-Developed Countries, 1979* (October 1980) p. 15.

8. *Pravda*, 13 January 1984.

9. However, South African Defence Forces captured sophisticated SAM–8 and SAM–9 missile systems during operation *Askari* into southern Angola. There have also been reliable reports that the USSR supplied Mig–23 fighter jets, one of the most advanced tactical aircraft now in service, to the Angolan airforce in late 1984. See for instance the statement made by General Viljoen, *Summary of World Broadcasts*, Africa series, 30 January 1984.

10. Tass statement entitled 'South African Aggression Against Angola' in *Pravda*, 5 January 1984.

11. See Dusko Doder, 'Soviet Assails South Africa Over Angola', *International Herald Tribune*, 6 January 1984.

12. J. Marcum, 'Angola', in G. Carter and P. O'Meara (eds) *Southern Africa: The Continuing Crisis* (Bloomington: Indiana University Press, 1979) pp. 193–4.

13. Steele, 'Soviet Relations with Angola and Mozambique', pp. 12–13.

14. Valentin P. Kassatkin, Head of Africa Section, Central Planning Division, Soviet Foreign Ministry, interview with author, 21 April 1984, Moscow.

15. David E. Albright, 'New Trends in Soviet Policy Towards Africa', *CSIS Africa Notes*, no. 27 (29 April 1984) p. 8.

16. See Robert Legvold, 'The Soviet Threat to Southern Africa', paper presented to the South Africa Institute of International Affairs Conference, Natal (January 1984) pp. 15–16.

17. Steele, 'Soviet Relations with Angola and Mozambique', p. 20.

18. See Colin Legum, 'Botha faces Soviet threat', *The Observer*, 1 March 1981.
19. *The Times*, 12 March 1984.
20. *New Times* (Moscow) no. 9 (February 1984) p. 3.
21. Dr Boris Asoyan, Deputy Director, Institute of African Studies, USSR Academy of Sciences, interview with author, 18 April 1984, Moscow.
22. Tass statement, 29 March 1984.
23. See 'US Plans to Aid Mozambique Army', *New York Times*, 17 January 1985.
24. See the 'International Diary' programme presented by Petr Fedorov, *Daily Report*, Foreign Broadcast Information Service, 30 March 1984.
25. *New Times* (Moscow) no. 27 (July 1984) p. 2.
26. For instance, Jan de Plessis, *The Brezhnev Doctrine and South Africa* (Pretoria: Foreign Affairs Association, 1977).
27. Legvold, 'The Soviet Threat to Southern Africa', p. 27.
28. Veniamin Midtsev, 'Explosive Situation', *New Times*, no. 34 (August 1982) pp. 9–10.
29. Albright, 'New Trends in Soviet Policy Towards Africa', pp. 3–8.
30. Vladilen M. Vasev, Head, Third Africa Department, Soviet Foreign Ministry, interview with author, 23 April 1984, Moscow.
31. *Pravda*, 24 May 1983.
32. For a discussion about relations between the United States and Zimbabwe, see Carol Lancaster, 'US Aid to Africa: Who Gets What, When and How', *CSIS Africa Notes*, no. 25 (31 March 1984) pp. 2–4.
33. Albright, 'New Trends in Soviet Policy Toward Africa', p. 10.
34. Seth Singleton, 'The Shared Tactical Goals of South Africa and the Soviet Union', *CSIS Africa Notes*, no. 12 (26 April 1983) p. 4.
35. David E. Albright, 'The Communist States and Southern Africa', in Gwendolyn M. Carter and Patrick O'Meara (eds) *International Politics in Southern Africa* (Bloomington: Indiana University Press, 1982) p. 15.
36. Lewis Gann and Peter Duignan, *South Africa: War, Revolution or Peace* (Stanford: Hoover Institution Press, 1978) p. 59.
37. Peter Vanneman, *Soviet Foreign Policy in Southern Africa* (Pretoria: Africa Institute, 1982) pp. 43–5; and W. Scott Thompson and Brett Silvers, 'South Africa in Soviet Strategy', in Richard E. Bissell and Chester A. Crocker (eds) *South Africa into the 1980s* (Boulder: Westview, 1979) pp. 142–4.
38. Robert J. Hanks, *The Cape Route* (Cambridge, Mass.: Institute for Foreign Policy Analysis, 1981) pp. 3–45.
39. Stewart Menaul, 'The Indian Ocean in the Next Decade', *South Africa International*, vol. 5, no. 4 (April 1975) p. 178; see also Dieter Braun, *The Indian Ocean* (London: Hurst, 1983) pp. 8–11.
40. Larry W. Bowman, 'The Strategic Importance of South Africa to the United States', *African Affairs*, vol. 82, no. 323 (April 1982) p. 177.
41. R. W. Johnson, *How Long Will South Africa Survive?* (Oxford Univesity Press, 1977) p. 213.
42. Robert M. Price, *United States Foreign Policy in Sub-Saharan Africa: National Interest and Global Strategy* (Berkeley: Institute of International Studies, 1978) pp. 10–14.

43. Bowman, 'The Strategic Importance of South Africa', p. 178.
44. J. E. Spence, *The Strategic Significance of Southern Africa* (London: Royal United Service Institution, 1970) p. 46.
45. Price, *United States Foreign Policy in Sub-Saharan Africa*, pp. 12–14; and Bowman, 'The Strategic Importance of South Africa', p. 178.
46. William J. Foltz, 'United States Policy Toward South Africa: Economic and Strategic Constraints', *Political Science Quarterly*, vol. 92 (Spring 1977) p. 57.
47. For a detailed discussion of this point see G. Jukes, 'The Indian Ocean in Soviet Naval Policy', *Adelphi Paper*, no. 87, (London: International Institute for Strategic Studies, 1972).
48. For a discussion of anti-submarine warfare in Soviet naval doctrine, see R. W. Herrick, *Soviet Naval Strategy* (Annapolis: US Naval Institute, 1967).
49. G. Jukes, 'Soviet Naval Policy in the Indian Ocean', in Larry W. Bowman and Ian Clark (eds), *The Indian Ocean in Global Politics* (Boulder: Westview, 1981) p. 176.
50. Jukes, 'Soviet Naval Policy in the Indian Ocean', p. 185.
51. S. G. Gorshkov, *Morskaya Moshch' Gosudarstva* (Moscow: Voyennoye Izdatelstvo Ministerstva Oborony SSSR, 1976) pp. 4–55; see also Bradford Dismukes and James McConnell (eds), *Soviet Naval Diplomacy* (New York: Pergamon, 1979) pp. 62–120.
52. Scott Thompson and Silvers, 'South Africa in Soviet Strategy', p. 145.
53. See D. Price, 'Moscow and the Persian Gulf', *Problems of Communism*, vol. 28, no. 2 (1979) p. 13.
54. Legvold, 'The Soviet Threat to Southern Africa', p. 29; see also Y. Tarabrin, 'US Expansionist Policy in Africa', *International Affairs* (Moscow), no. 10 (October 1983) pp. 41–9.
55. An early statement of this can be found in Dmitry Volsky, 'Southern Version of NATO', *New Times* (Moscow) no. 36 (September 1976) pp. 8–9.
56. Y. Tarabrin, 'Afrika v Globalnoi Strategii Imperializma', *Mirovaya Ekonomika i Mezhdunarodnye Otnosheniya*, no. 2 (February 1982) pp. 25–37; and A. Urnov, 'Alyans Vashington–Pretoriya i Afrika', *Mirovaya Ekonomika i Mezhdunarodnye Otnosheniya*, no. 3 (March 1982) pp. 56–66.
57. Cited in Philip Geyelin, 'Superpower Metaphor: Blind Misreading the Blind', *International Herald Tribune*, 7 October 1983.

CHAPTER 8

1. See for example A. B. Davidson, 'Where is South Africa Going?', *Narody Azii i Afriki*, no. 2, (1978) p. 16. The author discusses the impressions of the last group to travel 'unhindered' and to any degree in South Africa: the Russian volunteers who went to the Transvaal at the time of the Anglo–Boer War.

2. For publications referring specifically to the Russian involvement in the Anglo–Boer War, see: *Bibliografiia Afriki* (Moscow: Institute Afriki, 1964) pp. 176–9; A. I. Shifman, 'Lev Tolstoy i Anglo-byrskaya voina' ('Leo Tolstoy and the Anglo–Boer War'), *Narody Azii i Afriki*, no. 2, (1969) pp. 75–86; and A. I. Nikitina, *Zakhvat burskikh respublic Angliei 1899–1902 (England's Seizure of the South African Republics)* (Moscow: 1970).

3. L. A. Dyomkina, 'Scientific and Theoretical Conference on the 60th Anniversary of the South African Communist Party', *Africa in Soviet Studies 1983* (Moscow: USSR Academy of Sciences, Africa Institute, 1983) p. 236.

4. Edward T. Wilson, *Russia and Black Africa Before World War Two* (London: Holmes and Meir 1974) p. 88.

5. Alvin Z. Rubinstein (ed.) *The Foreign Policy of the Soviet Union* (New York: Random House, 1960) p. 387.

6. Yevgeny A. Tarabrin, Head of International Problems Department, Institute of African Studies, USSR Academy of Sciences, interview with author, Moscow, 16 April 1984.

7. Stephen T. Hosmer and Thomas W. Wolfe, *Soviet Policy and Practice toward Third World Conflict* (Lexington, Massachusetts: Lexington Books, 1982) pp. 4–22.

8. M. A. Suslov, 'The Communist Movement in the Vanguard of the Struggle for Peace and Social and International Liberation', *Kommunist*, (11 September 1975), pp. 3–9.

9. Vladilen M. Vasev, Head of Third Africa Department, Soviet Ministry of Foreign Affairs, interview with author, Moscow, 23 April 1984.

10. Mirza Ibragimov, 'Resolute Support', *Asia and Africa Today*, no. 2 (1979) p. 3.

11. 'Mission of the Special Committee Against Apartheid in Moscow and Kiev', *Unit on Apartheid*, Political and Security Council Affairs, no. 21/75 (1975) p. 6.

12. Vladimir Kokorev, Scientific Fellow, Institute of African Studies, USSR Academy of Sciences, interview with author, Moscow, 17 April 1984.

13. This point was made repeatedly at a recent conference of the African–American Institute in Harare, Zimbabwe, reported in the *International Herald Tribune*, 19 January 1983.

14. This includes aid to the FLN in Algeria, the MPLA in Angola, the PAIGC in Guinea-Bissau, FRELIMO in Mozambique, ZAPU in Zimbabwe/Rhodesia, SWAPO in Namibia, and the ANC in South Africa.

15. A. B. Davidson, 'Where is South Africa Going?', *Narody Azii i Afriki*, p. 6.

16. See Andrew Amar, *A Student in Moscow* (London: Fischer, 1961) pp. 34–5; Aderogba Ajao, *On the Tiger's Back* (New York: Cleveland Press, 1962) p. 24; and Roger E. Kanet, 'African Youth: The Target of Soviet African Policy', *Russian Review*, no. 27 (1968) pp. 161–75.

17. Valentin P. Kassatkin, Head of Africa section, Central Planning Divi-

sion, Soviet Foreign Ministry, interview with author, 21 April 1984.

18. L. H. Gann and Peter Duignan, *South Africa: War, Revolution or Peace?* (Stanford: Hoover Institution Press, 1979) p. 18.
19. J. Marcum, 'Angola', in G. Carter and P. O'Meara (eds) *Southern Africa: The Continuing Crisis* (Bloomington: Indiana University Press, 1979) pp. 193–4.
20. Seth Singleton, 'The Shared Tactical Goals of South Africa and the Soviet Union', *CSIS Africa Notes*, no. 12 (26 April 1983) p. 2.
21. Andrei Y. Urnov, Head of Southern Africa Division, CPSU International Department, interview with author, 21 April 1984; see also the remarks of A. A. Gromyko, *Komsomolskaya Pravda*, 20 July 1982.
22. See for instance, R. W. Johnson, *How Long Will South Africa Survive?* (New York: Oxford University Press, 1977) p. 213; and Robert M. Price, *US Foreign Policy in Sub-Saharan Africa: National Interest and Global Strategy* (Berkeley: Institute of International Studies, 1978) pp. 11–14.
23. A. B. Davidson, 'Southern Africa: Liberation is Near', *Pravda*, 28 August 1976.
24. Andrei Pritvozov, Scientific Fellow, Institute of African Studies, USSR Academy of Sciences, interview with author, Moscow, 17 April 1984.
25. Alexander N. Gogitidze, Chief of South Africa Section, Third Africa Department, Soviet Foreign Ministry, interview with author, Moscow, 23 April 1984.
26. I. A. Ulanovskaya, 'RSA: Two Sides of the Colour Barrier', *Aziya i Afrika Segodnya*, no. 12 (December 1977) p. 19.
27. I. A. Ulanovskaya, *South Africa: Racism Doomed* (Moscow: Znanie, 1978) p. 41.
28. Mirza Ibragimov, 'Resolute Support', *Asia and Africa Today*, no. 2 (1979) pp. 2–8.
29. See for example, 'The Supreme Internationalist Duty of a Socialist Country', *Pravda*, 27 October 1965.
30. See Roger E. Kanet (ed.) *The Soviet Union and the Developing Countries* (London: Johns Hopkins, 1974).
31. S. Bialer, *Stalin's Successors* (Cambridge University Press, 1980) p. 229.
32. Georgi A. Arbatov, Director, Institute for USA and Canada Studies, USSR Academy of Sciences, interview with author, Moscow, 23 April 1984.
33. This comment is from the text of a lecture delivered at the University of Witwatersrand, South Africa, *The Times*, 22 October 1982.
34. Cited in V. Aspaturion, 'Soviet Global Power and the Correlation of Forces', *Problems of Communism*, vol. XXIX, no. 3 (1980) p. 1.
35. Anatoly A. Gromyko, Director, Institute of African Studies, USSR Academy of Sciences, interview with author, Moscow, 21 April 1984.

Selected Bibliography

This bibliography lists the primary and secondary sources consulted in the writing of this book. It does not include every work examined but only those that were found relevant. The entries are arranged in alphabetical order, with the bibliography classified in the following manner:

I PRIMARY SOURCES

1 Archives and Private Collections
2 Official Documents and Parliamentary Debates
3 Reference Works and Collections of Documents
4 Publications of the Comintern and Its Affiliates
5 United Nations Publications
6 United States Government Publications and Congressional Reports
7 Interviews and Correspondence
8 Daily and Weekly Press

II SECONDARY SOURCES

1 Western Books and Articles
2 Soviet Books and Articles (the standard form of transliteration from Cyrillic to Roman script has been used)

I PRIMARY SOURCES

1 Archives and Private Collections

Africana Library, Institute of Africa Studies (early Soviet literature on South Africa) USSR Academy of Sciences, Moscow, Soviet Union.

Document Collection, Institute for the Study of Marxism (South African Communist Party publications, 1950–65) University of Stellenbosch, Stellenbosch, South Africa.

The Eric Louw File (material relating to the closure of the Soviet Embassy in

Pretoria, 1954–7) Political Archives, Institute for Contemporary History, University of the Orange Free State, Bloemfontein, South Africa.

Government Archives, Republic of South Africa (documents and papers, 1906–30) Union Buildings, Pretoria, South Africa.

Hoover Institution Library (collection of Communist Party of South Africa pamphlets, 1922–73) Hoover Institution of War and Peace, Stanford University, Palo Alto, California, United States.

Johannesburg Public Library (publications of the South African Friends of the Soviet Union) Johannesburg, South Africa.

Kandyba-Foxcraft Library (private collection of letters from the Anglo–Boer War period) Pretoria, South Africa.

Krasnyi Arkhiv (Russian writings on South Africa, 1900–5) State Historical Collection, Moscow, USSR.

State Archives of the Cultural History Museum (material from the period of the Anglo–Boer War) Pretoria, South Africa.

Transvaal Archival Depot (early photos from the Anglo–Boer War) Pretoria, South Africa.

2 Official Documents and Parliamentary Debates

Great Britain. Diplomatic Correspondence between Great Britain and the Union of South Africa, 1940–5 (Public Record Office, British Foreign Office Files, Dominion Affairs).

Republic of South Africa. *Debates of the House of Assembly* (after 31 May 1961) (Pretoria: Government Printer)

Republic of South Africa. *Official Yearbook*. Department of Foreign Affairs and Information, years 1980–4 (Johannesburg: van Rensburg Publications).

Union of South Africa. *Debates of the House of Assembly* (Pretoria: Government Printer)

Union of South Africa. Diplomatic Correspondence between the Union of South Africa and the Union of Soviet Socialist Republics, 1941–53 (Pretoria, Union Buildings, South African Ministry of External Affairs).

Union of South Africa. *Economic Yearbook*. Bureau of Census and Statistics, years 1950–8

Union of South Africa. Official documents and papers, 1900–22 (Pretoria, Union Buildings, South African Government Archives).

Union of South Africa. *Treaty Series Number 2* (1942). Agreement between the Union of South Africa and the Union of Soviet Socialist Republics about the exchange of Consular officers, 21 February 1942, London.

3 Reference Works and Collections of Documents

Degras, Jane (ed.) *The Communist International, 1919–1943: Documents*, 3 volumes (Oxford University Press, 1956–65).

Hammond, T. T. (ed.) *Soviet Foreign Relations and World Communism* (Princeton University Press, 1965).

Kalley, Jacqueline, *South Africa's Foreign Relations, 1980–1984* (Johannesburg: South African Institute of International Affairs, 1984).

Kun, Bela (ed.) *Kommunisticheskii Internatsional v Dokumentakh, 1919–1932* (Moscow: partiinoe, 1933).

Rogaly, Gail Lynda, *South Africa's Foreign Relations: 1961–1979* (Johannesburg: South African Institute of International Affairs, 1980).

Scherer, John L. (ed.) *USSR, Facts and Figures Annual*, Volume 6 (Miami: Academic International, 1982).

Schoeman, Elna, *South Africa and the United Nations* (Johannesburg: South African Institute of International Affairs, 1981).

South African Communists Speak, Documents from the history of the South African Communist Party (London: Inkululeko, 1981).

Sworakowski, W. S. *The Comintern and Its Front Organizations – A Research Guide* (Stanford: Hoover Institution Press, 1965).

4 Publications of the Comintern and its Affiliates

The Comintern between the Fifth and Sixth World Congresses, 1924–8 (London: CPGB, 1928).

The Communist International, bi-monthly theoretical journal of the ECCI, 1920–37.

Ford, James, *The Communists and the Struggle for Negro Liberation* (New York: CPUSA, 1936).

International Press Correspondence of the Comintern, published bi-weekly from the Comintern headquarters, 1920–37.

ITUC–NW. A Report of the Proceedings and Decisions of the First International Conference of Negro Workers (Hamburg: ITUC–NW, 1930).

Jones, D. Ivon, *Communism in South Africa* (Johannesburg: 1921).

The Negro Worker, Official Organ of the ITUC–NW, published monthly, 1928–37.

Padmore, George, *Negro Workers and the Imperialist War – Intervention in the Soviet Union* (Hamburg: ITUC–NW, 1931).

Piatyi Vsemirnyi Kongress Kommunisticheskogo Internatsionala: Stenograficheskii Otchet, 2 volumes (Moscow: Gos, 1925).

RILU. Report of the Fourth Congress of the RILU (London: 1928).

RILU. The Tasks of the International Trade Union Movement. Resolutions and Decisions of the Third World Congress of the RILU (London: 1924).

Stenograficheskii Otchet VI Kongressa Kominterna. Volumes III–IV (Moscow: Gos, 1929).

Stenograficheskii Otchet XI Plenum IKKI (Moscow: Gos, 1931).

World News and Views Comintern journal published weekly, 1938–43.

5 United Nations Publications

United Nations, *International Conference on Sanctions Against South Africa*, UNESCO House, Paris, UN Centre Against Apartheid (New York: 1981).

United Nations, *Khrushchev in New York*, UN Office of Public Information (New York: 1960).

United Nations, 'Mission of the Special Committee Against Apartheid in Moscow and Kiev', *Unit on Apartheid*, Political and Security Council Affairs, No. 21/75 (New York: 1975).

United Nations, *A New Course in South Africa*, Report of the Group of Experts, UN Office of Public Information (New York: 1960).

United Nations, *Report of the Committee on the Reorganization of the Secretariat*, 27 November 1968 (New York).

United Nations, *Year Book of the United Nations*, years 1946–8, 1952–7, 1960–8, 1976–80, 1983 (New York).

6 United States Government Publications and Congressional Reports

The Congressional Record (Washington, DC: Government Printing Office).

Imports of Minerals from South Africa by the United States and the OECD Countries, Sub-Committee on African Affairs, Committee on Foreign Relations, United States Senate (Washington DC: Government Printing Office, 1980).

The Lead and Zinc Industry in the USSR, Central Intelligence Agency, ER 80–10072 (Washington DC: Government Printing Office, 1980).

Mineral Industries of the USSR, compiled by V. V. Strishkov, United States Department of the Interior, Bureau of Mines (Washington, DC: Bureau of Mines).

The Non-fuel Mineral Outlook for the USSR through 1990, compiled by James S. Grichar, United States Bureau of Mines (Washington DC: Government Printing Office, 1981).

Soviet Active Measures, Hearings before the Permanent Select Committee on Intelligence, United States House of Representatives (Washington DC: Government Printing Office, 1982).

Soviet Economy in a Time of Change, Volume II, Joint Economic Committee, Congress of the United States (Washington, DC: Government Printing Office, 1979).

Soviet Economy: Problems and Prospects, Central Intelligence Agency (Washington DC: Government Printing Office, 1977).

Sub-Sahara Africa: Its Role in Critical Mineral Needs of the Western World, Sub-Committee on Mines and Mining of the Committee on the Interior and Insular Affairs, United States House of Representatives (Washington DC: Government Printing Office, 1982).

7 Interviews

Arbatov, Georgi. Director, Institute for the Study of the USA and Canada, USSR Academy of Sciences, Full Member of the Soviet Central Committee, 21 April 1984, Moscow.

Asoyan, Boris R. Deputy Director, Institute of African Studies, USSR Academy of Sciences, 16 April 1984, Moscow.

Barratt, John. Director of the South African Institute of International Affairs, 1 April 1982, Jan Smuts House, Johannesburg.

Brown, Mike. Chief Economist, South African Chamber of Mines, 15 March 1982, Johannesburg.

Cabelly, Robert. Special Envoy for Chester Crocker, Assistant Secretary of State for African Affairs, 2 November 1983, London.

Coatan, R. H. Retired South African Diplomat, former Ambassador, 15 April 1982, Cape Town.

Cockerell, Michael. Investigative reporter, BBC *Panorama* programme, 24 February 1982, London.

Du Bolay, Louise. Editor of the *Gold* survey, Consolidated Goldfields of Great Britain, 2 December 1983, London.

Du Plessie, Admiral. Chief of Staff, South African Military Intelligence, 22 March 1984, Pretoria.

Du Toit, General. Professor of National Strategy, Rand Afrikaans University, former Director of South African Military Intelligence, 21 March 1984, Johannesburg.

Egeland, Leif. Retired South African Diplomat, former High Commissioner, 22 April 1984, Johannesburg.

Fendrick, Reed, Political Officer, American Embassy, South Africa, 25 March 1982, Pretoria.

Forsyth, D. D. Former Minister of External Affairs, South African Government, 17 April 1982, Cape Town.

Fraseur, Robert. Political Officer, American Embassy, Great Britain, 31 October 1983, London.

Gromyko, Anatoly A. Director, Institute of African Studies, USSR Academy of Sciences, 19 April 1984, Moscow.

Gogitdze, Alexander. Chief of South African Section, Third Africa Department, Soviet Foreign Ministry, 23 April 1984, Moscow.

Hamilton, Anthony. Retired South African Diplomat, former Ambassador, 16 April 1984, Pretoria.

Hirson, Baruch. Exiled South African political writer, author of *Soweto: Year of Fire, Year of Ash*, 21 January 1983.

Johnson, R. W. Politics Tutor, Magdalen College, Oxford University, author of *How Long Will South Africa Survive?*, 8 June 1982, Oxford.

Kapp, Colonel. Public Relations Officer, South African Defence Forces, 22 March 1984, Pretoria.

Kaser, Michael. Reader in Economics, Professorial Fellow, St Antony's College, Oxford University, 27 October 1981, Oxford.

Kassatkin, Valentin P. Ambassador, Soviet Diplomatic Corps, Head of

Africa Section, Central Planning Division, Soviet Foreign Ministry, 23 April 1984, Moscow.

Kokorev, Vladimir. Scientific Fellow, Institute of African Studies, USSR Academy of Sciences, 17 April 1984, Moscow.

Kravtcova, Tanya. Scientific Fellow, Institute of African Studies, USSR Academy of Sciences, 17 April 1984, Moscow.

Kremenuk, Victor A. Head of Division on US Relations with the Third World, Institute for the Study of the USA and Canada, USSR Academy of Sciences, 21 April 1984, Moscow.

Loushkova, Tamara. Scientific Fellow, Institute of African Studies, USSR Academy of Sciences, 19 April 1984, Moscow.

Low, Stephen. American Foreign Service Officer, former Ambassador to Zambia, US Delegate to Lancaster House Negotiations, 22 April 1984, Moscow.

MacFarlane, Neil. Professor of Soviet Studies, University of Virginia, former Tutor of International Politics, Balliol College, Oxford University, 21 June 1984, Oxford.

McHenry, Donald. Senior Fellow, Georgetown University, former Ambassador to the United Nations, 22 April 1984, Moscow.

Moody, Christopher. Professor of Russian Studies, University of Witwatersrand, 19 March 1982, Johannesburg.

Nel, Philip. Acting Director, Institute for the Study of Marxism, University of Stellenbosch, 29 March 1984, Stellenbosch.

O'Connor, M. De Beers Executive, Charter Consolidated, 28 March 1983, London.

Oppenheimer, Harry. Director, De Beers Corporation, 21 March 1984, Johannesburg.

Oppenheimer, Nicholas. Assistant Director, De Beers Corporation, 21 March 1984, Johannesburg.

Philip, Peter. Retired South African Diplomat, Protocol Officer in Pretoria between 1946–9, 15 April 1982, Cape Town.

Pritvorov, Andrei. Scientific Fellow, Institute of African Studies, USSR Academy of Sciences, 17 April 1984, Moscow.

Schrire, Robert. Professor of Political Science, University of Cape Town, 28 March 1984, Cape Town.

Simon, Bernard. *Financial Times* Correspondent, South Africa, 8 April 1982, Johannesburg.

Sinitsin, Sergei Y. Chief of Namibia Section, Third Africa Department, Soviet Foreign Ministry, 23 April 1984, Moscow.

Smets, L. L. C. De Beers Executive, Charter Consolidated, 28 March 1983, London.

Straud, N. Managing Director, Premier Diamond Mine, 26 March 1984, Premier.

Tarabrin, Yevgenia A. Head of International Problems Department, Institute of African Studies, USSR Academy of Sciences, 16 April 1984, Moscow.

Thompson, Douglas. Reverend, Executive Director, South African Friends of the Soviet Union between 1939–48, 27 May 1982, Springs, Transvaal.

Tichomirov, Vladimir. Scientific Fellow, Institute of African Studies, USSR Academy of Sciences, 17 April 1984, Moscow.

Urnov, Andrei Y. Head of Southern Africa Division, CPSU International Department, 21 April 1984, Moscow.

Vale, Peter. Director of Studies, South African Institute of International Affairs, Jan Smuts House, 19 March 1984, Johannesburg.

Vanneman, Peter. Chairman, Department of Political Science, University of Arkansas, 9 April 1982, Pretoria.

Vasev, Vladilen M. Head, Third Africa Department, Soviet Foreign Ministry, 21 April 1984, Moscow.

Von Schutz, Y. Chairman of the Karakul Board of South West Africa/Namibia, 20 April 1982, Windhoek, Namibia.

White, David. Head of Research Division, South Africa Department, British Foreign and Commonwealth Office, 7 November 1983, London.

Correspondence

Kubalkova, Vendulka. Department of Government, University of Queensland, St Lucia, Queensland, Australia, 21 June 1982.

Moreillon, Jacques. Member of the Directorate, Comité International De La Croix-Rouge, Geneva, Switzerland, 13 July 1982.

Murphy, Caryle. Southern Africa Bureau, *The Washington Post*, Johannesburg, South Africa, 23 November 1981

8 Daily and Weekly Press

Western Publications

Africa Business
Africa Confidential
Current Digest of the Soviet Press
Daily Telegraph
Der Spiegel
The Economist
Economist Foreign Report
Financial Times
Foreign Broadcast Information Service
Guardian
International Herald Tribune
Johannesburg Star (South Africa)
The Listener
New African
Newsweek
New York Times

The Observer
Rand Daily Mail (South Africa)
Summary of World Broadcasts (BBC)
Sunday Express (South Africa)
Sunday Times (South Africa)
Sunday Tribune (South Africa)
Time
The Times
Washington Post
World Business Week

Soviet Publications

Isvestiya
Krasnaya Zvezda
New Times
Pravda
Sovetskaya Rossiya

II SECONDARY SOURCES

1 Western Books and Articles

Ajao, Aderogba, *On the Tiger's Back* (New York: Cleveland Press, 1962).
Albright, David L., 'The Communist States and Southern Africa' in Gwendolyn M. Carter (ed.) *International Politics in Southern Africa* (Bloomington: Indiana University Press, 1982).
Ariovich, G. A., *Soviet Trade Policy and its Implications for South Africa's Mining Sector* (unpublished text, January 1980).
Ariovich, G. A. and Kenney, H. F., 'The Implications for the South African Economy of Russia's Foreign Trade Policy', *International Affairs Bulletin* (South Africa) vol. 4, no. 2 (1980).
Aspaturian, V., 'Soviet Global Power and the Correlation of Forces', *Problems of Communism*, vol. 29, no. 3 (1980).
Barber, James, *South Africa's Foreign Policy 1945–1970* (Oxford University Press, 1973).
Barber, James, *The Uneasy Relationship: Britain and South Africa* (London: Heinemann, 1983).
Barron, John, *KGB: The Secret Work of Soviet Secret Agents* (London: Corgi, 1983).
Bebe, Lucius, *Soviet Strategy Towards South Africa* (Potchefstroom, South Africa: Institute for the Advancement of Calvinism, 1971).
Beloff, Max, *The Foreign Policy of Soviet Russia 1929–1941*, Volume I (Oxford University Press, 1947).

Bender, Gerald, 'Angola: Left, Right and Wrong', *Foreign Policy*, no. 43 (Summer 1981).

Bennet, A. Leroy, *International Organizations* (New Jersey: Prentice, 1977).

Bialer, S., *Stalin's Successors* (Cambridge University Press, 1980).

Bissell, Richard E. and Crocker, Chester A. (eds) *South Africa into the 1980s* (Boulder: Westview, 1979).

Bloomfield, Lincoln P., 'The United States, the Soviet Union and the Prospects for Peacekeeping', *International Organization*, vol. 24, no. 3 (1970).

Boërsner, Dimitri, *The Bolsheviks and the National and Colonial Question* (Geneva: Librarie Droz, 1957).

Bowman, Larry W., 'The Strategic Importance of South Africa to the United States', *African Affairs*, vol. 81, no. 323 (April 1980).

Bowman, Larry W. and Clark, Ian (eds) *The Indian Ocean in Global Politics* (Boulder: Westview, 1981).

Braun, Dieter, *The Indian Ocean* (London: Hurst, 1983).

Brayton, Abbott A., 'Soviet Involvement in Africa', *Journal of Modern African Studies*, vol. 17, no. 2 (June 1979).

Brinkley, George A., 'The Soviet Union and the United Nations: The Changing Role of the Developing Countries', *The Review of Politics*, vol. 32, no. 1 (January 1970).

Brzezinski, Zbigniew (ed) *Africa and the Communist World* (Stanford University Press, 1963).

Carlson, John E., 'The KGB' in James Cracraft (ed.) *The Soviet Union Today* (Illinois: University of Chicago, 1983).

Carr, Barbara, *Spy in the Sun* (Cape Town: Timmins, 1969).

Carr, E. H., *The Soviet Impact on the Western World* (London: Macmillan, 1946).

Carr, E. H., *The Bolshevik Revolution 1917–1923*, Volume III (London: Macmillan, 1966).

Carter, Gwendolyn M., *The Politics of Inequality* (London: Thames, 1958).

Cervenka, Zdenek and Rogers, Barbara, *The Nuclear Axis* (London: Friedmann, 1978).

Chatterjee, Debi, 'Soviet Union and Apartheid', *IDSA Journal* (October 1978).

Claude, Inis L., *Swords into Plowshares: The Problems and Progress of International Organization* (New York: Random House, 1964).

Cockerell, Michael, *South African Gold and Diamonds – The Kremlin Connection* (unpublished text, 1981).

Coker, Christopher, 'Adventurism and Pragmatism: The Soviet Union, COMECON and Relations with African States', *International Affairs*, vol. 57. no. 4 (Autumn 1981).

Cooper, Jr, Bert H., *Soviet Penetration of Black Africa: An Historical Analysis of Soviet Relations with Africa South of the Sahara*, unpublished thesis, George Washington University, 1961.

Crowley, Edward L. (ed.) *The Soviet Diplomatic Corps 1917–1967*, Institute for the Study of the USSR (New Jersey: Scarecrow, 1970).

Dallin, Alexander, *The Soviet Union at the United Nations: An Inquiry into Soviet Motives and Objectives* (New York: Praeger, 1962).

Dallin, J. David, *Soviet Espionage* (New Haven: Yale University Press, 1953).

Davis, H. B., *Nationalism and Socialism: Marxist and Labour Theories of Nationalism to 1917* (New York: Monthly Review, 1967).

Deane, Jonh R., *The Strange Alliance: Wartime Cooperation with Russia* (New York: Viking Press, 1947).

Deutscher, Isaac, *Stalin: A Political Biography* (New York: Random House, 1960).

Draper, Theodore, *American Communism and Soviet Russia* (New York: Viking Press, 1960).

Dreyer, Peter, *Martyrs and Fanatics* (London: Secker & Warburg, 1981).

Ebon, Martin, *World Communism Today* (New York: Whittlesley House, 1948).

Eckes, Alfred E., *The United States and the Global Struggle for Minerals* (London: University of Texas, 1974).

Egeland, Leif, *Bridges of Understanding* (Cape Town: Human, 1977).

Epstein, Edward Jay, 'Have You Ever Tried to Sell a Diamond?' *The Atlantic Monthly* (February 1982).

Epstein, Edward Jay, *The Diamond Invention* (London: Hutchinson, 1982).

Feit, Edward, *South Africa: The Dynamics of the African National Congress and African Opposition in South Africa* (Stanford: Hoover Institute Press, 1968).

Feit, Edward, *The Dynamics of the African National Congresss* (London: Institute of Race Relations/Oxford University Press, 1962).

Feit, Edward, 'Urban Revolt in South Africa', *Journal of Modern African Studies*, vol. 8, no. 1 (April 1970).

Gann, L. H. and Duignan, Peter, *South Africa: War, Revolution or Peace* (Stanford: Hoover Institute Press, 1979).

Gati, Toby Trister, 'The Soviet Union and the North–South Dialogue', *Orbis*, vol. 24, no. 2 (Summer 1980).

Geldenhuys, D. J., *South African Foreign Policy* (unpublished thesis, 1982).

George, Alexander L. (ed.) *Managing US–Soviet Rivalry* (Boulder: Westview, 1983).

Gerhart, Gail M., *Black Power in South Africa: The Evolution of an Ideology* (London: University of California Press, 1978).

Gibson, Richard, *African Liberation Movements* (Oxford University Press, 1972).

Gilbert, Stephen P., 'Soviet–American Military Aid Competition in the Third World', *Orbis*, vol. 13 (1970).

Goodrich, Leland M., *The United Nations* (New York: Crowell, 1959).

Green, Timothy, *The New World of Gold* (London: Weidenfeld & Nicolson, 1981).

Green, Timothy, *The World of Diamonds* (London: Weidenfeld & Nicolson, 1981).

Gregory, Sir Theodore, *Ernest Oppenheimer and the Economic Development of South Africa* (Oxford University Press, 1962).

Grieg, Ian, *The Communist Challenge to Africa* (London: Foreign Affairs Publishers, 1977).

Grundy, Kenneth, *Guerrilla Struggle in Africa* (New York: Grossman, 1971).

Hall, H. Duncan, *North American Supply*, History of the Second World War (London: Longman, 1955).

Hanks, Robert J., *The Cape Route* (Cambridge, Massachusetts Institute for Foreign Policy Analysis, 1981).

Heldman, Dan C., *The USSR and Africa* (New York: Praeger, 1981).

Higgins, Rosalyn, *United Nations Peacekeeping: Africa* (Oxford University Press, 1980).

Hocking, Anthony, *Oppenheimer and Son* (Johannesburg: McGraw-Hill, 1973).

Holdsworth, Mary, 'Soviet Writings on Africa', *Contact* (Summer 1961).

Hooker, J. R., *Black Revolutionary: George Padmore's Path from Communism to Pan-Africanism* (New York: Praeger, 1967).

Hosmer, Stephen T. and Wolfe, Thomas W., *Soviet Policy and Practice toward Third World Conflict* (Lexington, Massachusetts: Lexington Books, 1982).

Hovet, Jr, Thomas, *Africa in the United Nations* (Illinois: Northwestern University, 1963).

Johns, Sheridan, 'Comintern, South Africa and the Black Diaspora', *Review of Politics*, vol. 37, no. 2 (1975).

Johns, Sheridan, 'The Birth of the Communist Party of South Africa', *International Journal of African Historical Studies*, vol. 9, no. 2 (1976).

Johnson, R. W., *How Long Will South Africa Survive?* (New York: Oxford University Press, 1977).

Kandyba-Foxcroft, E., *Russia and the Anglo–Boer War 1899–1902* (Pretoria: CUM Books, 1981).

Kanet, Roger E., 'African Youth: The Target of Soviet African Policy', *Russian Review*, no. 27 (1968).

Kanet, Roger E. (ed.) *The Soviet Union and the Developing Countries* (London: Johns Hopkins, 1974).

Kanet, Roger E. (ed.) *Soviet Foreign Policy in the Eighties* (New York: Praeger, 1982).

Karis, Thomas and Carter, Gwendolen M. (eds) *From Protest to Challenge: A Documentary History of African Politics in South Africa 1882–1964*. 4 volumes (Stanford: Hoover Institute Press, 1972–77).

Karis, Thomas, 'Black Politics in South Africa', *Foreign Affairs* (Winter 1983/84).

Kaser, Michael, 'Soviet Gold Production', *Soviet Economy in a Time of Change*, Volume II, Joint Economic Committee, Congress of the United States (Washington, DC: Government Printing Office, 10 October 1979).

Kaser, Michael, *The Soviet Impact on Precious Metals Trading: Gold and Platinum*, Paper Presented to Centre d'Études en Administration Internationale (October 1981).

Kay, David A., 'The Impact of African States on the United Nations', *International Organization*, vol. 23, no. 1 (1969).

Krasner, Stephen D., 'Oil is the Exception', *Foreign Policy*, no. 14 (Spring 1974).

Kubalkova, V. and Cruickshank, A. A., *Marxism–Leninism and the Theory of International Relations* (London: Routledge & Kegan Paul, 1980).

Kubalkova, V. and Cruickshank, A. A., *International Inequality* (London: Croom Helm, 1981).

Langer, William, *The Diplomacy of Imperialism 1890–1902* (New York: Knopf, 1951).

Lanning, G. and Mueller, M., *Africa Undermined* (Harmondsworth: Penguin, 1979).

Lodge, Tom, *Black Politics in South Africa since 1945* (London: Longman, 1983).

LeFever, Ernest W., *Crisis in the Congo: A United Nations Force in Action* (Washington, DC: Brookings, 1965).

Legum, Colin, *The United Nations and Southern Africa* (Brighton: University of Sussex, Institute for the Study of International Organisation, 1970).

Legum, Colin, 'The Soviet Union, China and the West in Southern Africa', *Foreign Affairs*, vol. 54 (July 1976).

Legvold, Robert, *Soviet Policy in West Africa* (Cambridge, Massachusetts: Harvard University Press, 1970).

Leiss, Amelia C. (ed.) *Apartheid and UN Collective Measures: An Analysis* (New York: Carnegie Endowment, 1965).

Lerumo, A., *Fifty Fighting Years* (London: Inkululeko, 1971).

Littlepage, J. D. and Bess, Demaree, *In Search of Soviet Gold* (New York: Harcourt, 1938).

MacNab, Roy, *The French Colonel: Villebois-Mareuil and the Boers 1899–1902* (Cape Town: Oxford University Press, 1975).

Manno, Catherine Senf, 'Majority Decisions and Minority Responses in the UN General Assembly', *Journal of Conflict Resolution*, vol. 10 (1966).

Mansergh, Nicholas, *Survey of British Commonwealth Affairs 1939–1952* (Oxford University Press, 1958).

Marcum, J., 'Angola' in G. Carter, and P. O'Meara, (eds) *Southern Africa: The Continuing Crisis* (Bloomington: Indiana University Press, 1979).

Marks, S., *Reluctant Rebellion* (Oxford University Press, 1970).

Mayall, James, *Africa, the Cold War and After* (London: Elek, 1971).

McEwan, Christopher B., *The Soviet Union and the Conventional Threat to South Africa: A Strategic Analysis* (Johannesburg: South African Institute of International Affairs, 1976).

McKenzie, Kermit E., *Comintern and World Revolution 1928–1943* (London: Columbia, 1964).

McLane, Charles B., *Soviet–African Relations*, Volume 3 (New York: Columbia University Press, 1974).

Morison, David, *The USSR and Africa* (Oxford University Press, 1964).

Munger, Edwin, S., *Communist Activity in South Africa*. American Universities Field Staff, Central and Southern Africa Series. ESM–8–58, Vol. VI (1958).

Murawiecki, Wojcieck, 'Institutional and Political Conditions of Participation of Socialist States in International Organizations', *International Organization*, vol. 22, no. 3 (1968).

Ogunbadejo, Oye, 'Soviet Policies in Africa', *African Affairs*, vol. 79, no. 316 (July 1980).

Padmore, George, *Pan-Africanism or Communism? The Coming Struggle for Africa* (London: Dobson, 1955).

Pakenham, Thomas, *The Boer War* (London: Weidenfeld & Nicholson, 1979).

Papp, Daniel S., 'Soviet Non-fuel Mineral Resources: Surplus or Scarcity', *Resources Policy*, vol. 8, no. 3 (September 1982).

Payne, Richard J., 'The Soviet/Cuban Factor in the New United States Policy Towards Southern Africa', *Africa Today* (June 1978).

Payton-Smith D. J., *Oil*, History of the Second World War (London: HMSO, 1971).

Plano, Jack. C. and Riggs, Robert E., *Forging World Order: The Politics of International Organization* (New York: Macmillan, 1967).

du Plessis, Jan, *Soviet Strategy towards Southern Africa* (Johannesburg: Foreign Affairs Association Study Report, April 1976).

Price, Robert M., *US Foreign Policy in Sub-Saharan Africa: National Interest and Global Strategy* (Berkeley: Institute of International Studies, 1978).

Rappaport, Armin, *A History of American Diplomacy* (New York: Macmillan, 1975).

Record, Wilson, *The Negro and the Communist Party* (Chapel Hill: University of North Carolina Press, 1951).

van Rensburg, W. C. J., 'South Africa's Role as Supplier of Raw Materials to the World', *South African Journal of African Affairs*, vol. 4, no. 2 (1974).

van Rensburg, W. C. J. and Pretorius, D. A., *South Africa's Strategic Minerals: Pieces on a Continental Chess Board* (Johannesburg: Valiant, 1977).

van Rensburg, W. C. J. and Bambrick, S., 'Monopolies, Cartels, Embargoes and Stockpiles', *The Economics of the World's Mineral Industries* (Johannesburg: McGraw-Hill, 1978).

Roberts, Brian, *The Diamond Magnates* (London: Hamisch, 1972).

Rosenthal, Eric, *South African Diplomats Abroad* (Pretoria: South African Department of External Affairs, 1979).

Rositze, Jerry, *KGB: The Eyes of Russia* (Harmondsworth: Penguin, 1983).

Roskill, *The War at Sea 1939–1945*, Volume II, History of the Second World War (London: HMSO, 1956).

Roux, Edward, *Time Longer than Rope: The Black Man's Struggle for Freedom in South Africa* (University of Wisconsin Press, 1964).

Rowe, Edward T., 'The Emerging Anti-Colonial Consensus in the United Nations', *Journal of Conflict Resolution*, vol. 8 (1964).

Rowe, Edward T., 'Changing Patterns in the Voting Success of Member States in United Nations General Assembly 1945–1966', *International Organization*, vol. 23, no. 4 (1969).

Rubinstein, Alvin Z. (ed.) *The Foreign Policy of the Soviet Union* (New York: Random House, 1960).

Rubinstein, Alvin Z., *The Soviets in International Organizations, 1953–1963* (Princeton University Press, 1964).

Rubinstein, Alvin Z., *Soviet and Chinese Influence in the Third World* (New York: Praeger, 1975).

Rubinstein, Alvin Z., 'Soviet Policy in the Third World in Perspective', *Military Review* (July 1978).

Russell, Ruth B., *The General Assembly: Patterns/Problems/Prospects* (New York: Carnegie Endowment, 1970).

Schatten, Fritz, *Communism in Africa* (New York, Praeger, 1966).

Schneider, William, *Southern Africa and the Politics of Raw Materials* (Croton-on-Hudson: Hudson Institute, 1978).

Severin, William K., 'Soviet Non-Fuel Minerals: Resource War or Business as Usual?' *Materials and Society*, vol. 7, no. 1 (1983).

Shabad, Theodore, Jensen, Robert G. and Wright A. W. (eds) *Soviet Natural Resources in the World Economy* (London: University of Chicago, 1983).

Shafer, Michael, 'No Crisis: The Implications of US Dependence on Southern African Strategic Minerals', *Occasional Paper*, South African Institute of International Affairs (November 1983).

Shimkin, Demitri, *Minerals: A Key to Soviet Power* (Cambridge, Massachusetts: Harvard University Press, 1953).

Simons, H. J. and R. E., *Class and Colour in South Africa 1850–1950* Harmondsworth: Penguin, 1969).

Singleton, Seth, 'The Shared Tactical Goals of South Africa and the Soviet Union', *CSIS Africa Notes*, no. 12 (26 April 1983).

Smuts, Jr, J. C. *Jan Christian Smuts* (London: Cassell, 1952).

South Africa: Time Running Out, Report of the Study Commission on United States Policy Towards Southern Africa (Berkeley: University of California, 1981).

Spence, Jack, 'South Africa and the Modern World' in Monica Wilson and Leonard Thompson (eds) *The Oxford History of South Africa 1870–1966* (Oxford University Press, 1975).

Stegenga, James A., 'Peacekeeping: Post Mortems or Previews?' *International Organization*, vol. 27, no. 3 (1973).

Stockwell, John, *In Search of Enemies* (London: Deutsch, 1978).

Tanzer, Michael, *The Race for Resources* (London: Monthly Review, 1980).

Thompson, Leonard and Prior, Andrew, 'South Africa in Soviet Strategy' in Richard E. Bissell and Chester Crocker (eds) *South Africa into the 1980s* (Boulder: Westview 1979).

Tucker, Robert C., (ed.) *The Lenin Anthology* (New York: Norton, 1975).

Ulam, Adam, *Expansion and Coexistence* (London: Secker & Warburg, 1968).

Vandebosch, Amry, *South Africa and the World* (University of Kentucky Press, 1970).

Vernon, Raymond, 'Soviet Commodity Power in International Economic Relations', Paper presented to Centre D'Études en Administration Internationale (October, 1981).

Verrier, Anthony, *International Peacekeeping* (Harmondsworth: Penguin, 1981).

Villet, Barbara, *Blood River* (New York: Everest House, 1982).

De Villers, Rene, 'Afrikaner Nationalism' in Monica Wilson and Leonard Thompson (eds) *The Oxford History of South Africa*, Volume II (Oxford University Press, 1975).

Walicki, Andrzej (trans. Hilda Andrews-Rusiecka) *A History of Russian Thought* (Stanford: University Press, 1979).

Walshe, A. P., *The Rise of African Nationalism in South Africa* (New York: Hurst, 1970).

Westen, Rae, *Gold: A World Survey* (London: Croom Helm, 1983).

Williams-Foxcroft, E., 'The Anglo-Boer War in the Dispatches of Russian Military Attachés', *Historia*, vol. 85, no. 1 (1963).

Wilson, Edward T., *Russia and Black Africa Before World War II* (London: Holmes and Meir, 1974).

Winter, Gordon, *Inside BOSS* (Harmondsworth: Penguin, 1981).

Yergin, Daniel, *Shattered Peace* (Boston: Houghton, 1978).

2 Soviet Books and Articles

Some Western Communist sources are included.

The African Communist no. 70, Third Quarter (1977).

Africanas, Terence (pseud.) 'The First International – 100 Years After', *African Communist* (July 1964).

Baryshnikov, I. V. 'Raw Material Resources of Africa', *International Affairs* (Moscow) no. 12 (December 1974).

Borisoglebskii, Yu. 'Liquidation of the Strongholds of Colonialism and Racism – Demand of the Times', *Mezhdunarodnaya Zhizn*, no. 7 (July 1979).

Butlitsky, A. 'RSA: Crisis of the Racist Regime', *Aziya i Afrika Segodnya*, no. 9 (September 1977).

Dadoo, Yusuf. 'Crisis in the Citadel of Racism and Apartheid', *World Marxist Review*, no. 4 (April 1977).

Dadoo, Yusuf, 'South Africa: Revolution on the Upgrade', *World Marxist Review*, no. 7 (July 1978).

Davidson, A. B., 'Where is South Africa Going?', *Narody Azii i Afriki*, no. 2 (1978).

Dolgopolov, Colonel Y., *Contemporary National Liberation Wars* (Moscow: Military Publishing House, 1977).

Dyomkina, L. A., 'Scientific and Theoretical Conference on the 60th Anniversary of the South African Communist Party' *Africa in Soviet Studies*, 1983 (Moscow: USSR Academy of Sciences, Africa Institute, 1983).

Gorodnov, V. P., 'The South African Working Class and its Role in the Liberation Struggle', *Mirovaya Ekonomika i Mezhdunarodnye Otnosheniya*, no. 3 (1965).

Gorodnov, V. P., 'Soweto – grief and anger of South Africa', *Aziya i Afrika Segodnya*, no. 6 (June 1977).

Gorodnov, V. P., 'The Phenomenon of Soweto', *Narody Azii i Afriki*, no. 2 (April 1978).

Gorshkov, Admiral S. G. *The Sea Power and the State* (Maryland: Naval Institute Press, 1979).

Granov, V. and Nakropin, O., 'Soviet Foreign Policy: Its Class Nature and Humanism', *International Affairs* (Moscow), no. 11 (December 1965).

Gromyko, A. A., 'The Leninist Peace Theory: Uniting Theory with Practice', *Kommunist*, no. 14 (October 1976).

Gromyko, A. A., 'Neo-Colonialism's Manoeuvres in Southern Africa', *International Affairs* (Moscow), no. 12 (December 1977).

Gromyko, A. A., 'African Realities and the Conflict Strategy Myth', *New Times*, no. 51 (December 1978).

Gromyko, A. A., *Afrika: Progress, Trudnosti i Perspektivy* (Moscow: International, 1981).

Ibragimov, M., 'Resolute Support', *Aziya i Afrika Segodnya*, no. 2 (March/April 1979).

Issraelian, V. I., *Sovetskii Soyuz i Organizatsiya ob 'edinennykh Natsii 1961–1965* (Moscow: 1968).

Kislov, A., Vasilkov, V., 'The Current Stage of US Policy in Africa', *Aziya i Afrika Segodnya*, no. 9 (September 1978).

Krasnopevtseva, T. 'RSA: Military and Economic Potential', *Aziya i Afrika Segodnya*, no. 2 (February 1979).

Kudriavtsevtsev, V. 'Africa Fights for its Future', *International Affairs*, no. 5 (May, 1978).

Lenin, V. I. *Imperialism: The Highest Stage of Capitalism* (New York: International, 1939).

Lenin, V. I. *Collected Works* (London: Lawrence & Wishart, 1960–1971).

Levin, D. B. and Kalyuzhnayn , G. P. (eds) *Mezhdunarodnoe Pravo* (Moscow: International, 1964).

Lomako, P. F. 'Non-ferrous metallurgy during the Great Patriotic War', *Tsvetnye Metally*, no. 4 (1974).

Lomako, P. F. 'The non-ferrous metallurgy of the USSR at a new stage', *Tsvetnye Metally*, no. 5 (1976).

Marx, K. and Engels, F. *Selected Works in One Volume* (London: Lawrence & Wishart, 1968).

Medtsev, Veniamin, 'RSA: Explosive Situation', *New Times*, no. 34 (August 1982).

Nzo, Alfred, 'Powerless to stop the Storm', *World Marxist Review*, no. 6 (June 1979).

Ponomarev, B., 'The World Significance of the Great October Revolution', *Kommunist*, no. 17 (November 1977).

Potekhin, I. I., 'Pan-Africanism and the Struggle of the Two Ideologies', *Kommunist*, no. 1 (January 1964).

Potekhin, I. I., *African Problems* (Moscow: Nauka, 1969).

Runov, A., 'South Africa: Citadel of Racism and Reaction', *International Affairs* (Moscow), no. 11 (November 1976).

Sharinova, V. M., 'The Economic Situation in the RSA in the Second Half of the Seventies', *Narody Azii i Afriki*, no. 2 (March/April, 1978).

Shvetsov, Yu, 'RSA: The African Working Class Strengthens the Struggle', *Aziya i Afrika Segodnya*, no. 1 (January 1977).

Solodovnikov, V., 'A New Phase of Struggle in Africa', *International Affairs*, no. 5 (May 1976).

Stalin, J. V., *Foundations of Leninism* (Moscow: International, 1939).

Stalin, J. V., *Marxism and the National Question*, (Moscow: International, 1942).

Suslov, M. A., 'The Communist Movement in the Vanguard of the Struggle for Peace and Social and International Liberation', *Kommunist* (11 September 1975).

Tarabrin, Y., 'Africa in a New Turn of the Liberation Struggle', *Mirovaya Ekonomika i Mezhdunarodnye Otnosheniya*, no. 2 (February 1979).

Tarabrin, Y., 'Afrika v globalnoi strategii imperializma', *Mirovaya Ekonomika i Mezhdunarodnye Otnosheniya*, no. 2 (February 1982).

Turkatenko, N. D., 'Washington's Calculations and Miscalculations in Southern Africa' *USA: Economics, Politics and Ideology*, no. 2 (1977).

Tyunkov, Yuri, 'Battle for Human Dignity', *New Times*, no. 27 (July 1976).

Ulanovskaya, I. A., 'Trade Unions in the RSA', *The Working Class and the Contemporary World*, no. 3 (May/June, 1976).

Ulanovskaya, I. A., 'Bantustans in the RSA – Production of Racism', *The Working Class and the Contemporary World*, no. 3 (June 1977).

Ulanovskaya, I. A., 'RSA: Two Sides of the Colour Barrier', *Aziya i Afrika Segodnya*, no. 12 (December 1977).

Ulanovskaya, I. A., 'The Labour Movement in the RSA', *Narody Azii i Afriki*, no. 2 (March/April 1978).

Ulanovskaya, I. A., *South Africa: Racism Doomed* (Moscow: Znanie, 1978).

Uralov, K., 'The Acute Problem of Southern Africa', *International Relations* (Moscow) no. 5 (May 1977).

Urnov, A., 'Alyans Vashington-Pretoriya i Afrika', *Mirovaya Ekonomika i Mezhdunarodnye Otnosheniya*, no. 3 (March 1982).

Vaganov, B., 'The Leninist Foreign Trade Policy', *International Relations* (Moscow) no. 5 (May 1969).

Vashnevskii, M. A., 'Washington's African Manoeuvres', *USA: Economics, Politics and Ideology*, no. 8 (August 1977).

Viskov, I. (ed.) *Sovietskii Soyuz v Organizatsii Ob'edinennykh Natsii*, Volume II (Moscow, 1965).

Volsky, Dmitri, 'Southern Version of NATO', *New Times*, no. 36 (September 1976).

Yastrebova, I., 'New Aspects of South African Reality', *Aziya i Afrika Segodnya*, no. 6 (June 1978).

Zhukov, V., 'Dollar Colonialism in the Congo', *Aziya i Afrika Segodnya*, no. 6 (June 1961).

Index

218